# Intentional Interviewing and Counseling

Allen E. Ivey

University of Massachusetts

Brooks/Cole Publishing Company
Monterey, California

*To*

*Robert Marx and Susan Kennedy-Marx*
*Joseph and Marie Litterer*

*who listened*

Brooks/Cole Publishing Company
A Division of Wadsworth, Inc.

Printed in the United States of America
10 9 8 7 6 5

**Library of Congress Cataloging in Publication Data**

Ivey, Allen E.
    Intentional interviewing and counseling.

    Bibliography: p.
    Includes index.
    1. Interviewing.     2. Counseling.     I. Title.
BF637.I5I93     1983         158'.3          82–14689
ISBN 0–534–01331–7

Subject Editor: *Claire Verduin*
Manuscript Editor: *Susan Weisberg*
Production Editor: *Richard Mason*
Interior Design: *Katherine Minerva*
Cover Design: *David Aguero*
Illustrations: *Tim Keenan*
Cartoons: *Zig Kapelis*
Typesetting: *Graphic Typesetting Service, Los Angeles, California*

# BEFORE YOU START

## HOW CAN YOU USE THIS BOOK MOST EFFECTIVELY?

My first courses in counseling were fascinating. I enjoyed the theoretical ideas and the information about testing and vocations, but what I enjoyed most was the course on theories of counseling. To me, this was what the whole process was about.

*But* then came the second semester and my first real opportunity to work with clients. I found myself overwhelmed by the amount of information brought to me by troubled and concerned people. The theories in the books on interviewing didn't apply easily and directly to the immediate problems of the interview. How was I to survive and help people? Somehow I did, but to this day I am not sure if some of those early clients benefited much from my work with them.

This book is about clarifying the interviewing process so you can enter the interview with specific skills, competencies, and concepts that give you a place to start. If you can take the ideas you learn from this book and use them in your interviewing practice with specific effects, the book will have provided you with a base on which to build your own natural style of helping.

Before you begin, let's review together the central concepts and structure of this book.

## NATURAL STYLE

I used to think there was a "right way" to help another person. I no longer believe that. I have found again and again that my natural approach and style works for me, though not always for someone else. This has led me to encourage beginning counselors and interviewers to look to themselves and their natural style and strengths. "Natural style" may be described as your original and "natural" way of helping people *before* you undertake formal training in interviewing and counseling. The ideas in this book can enlarge your competence and possibilities for effective interviewing, but you should select those ideas that appeal most to *you*.

At the same time, you will eventually find out that your natural style doesn't work with everyone you talk to. If you wish to reach more people, you may want to try an alternative approach to supplement your own approach. But again, add only what fits naturally.

## AUDIOTAPE, VIDEO RECORDING, AND PRACTICE

This book is oriented toward a *practical* approach to counseling and interviewing. Each concept and communication skill must be practiced if it is to be truly useful.

My first recommendation is that you purchase an inexpensive audio-tape recorder. This is one of the necessary tools of the trade. You'll need frequent practice and feedback from audiotape if you are to master the skills at the highest level and become an effective interviewer.

Videotape is an even better tool. It is increasingly available in many colleges, schools, and community settings. Try to see yourself as others see you at least once during the time you work with this book.

Each chapter includes a variety of practice exercises. To really learn something from this book, you should practice these concepts in small groups and use them in your daily life.

## MASTERING THE CONCEPTS OF BASIC INTENTIONAL INTERVIEWING

The practice exercises in each chapter are identified as *Mastery-Level Exercises*. They provide specific ways you can master the concepts of the chapter, use them in the interview, and, finally, teach them to others.

Four levels of mastery are identified in each chapter, and you'll have to decide the level of competence you want to reach with each skill or concept.

▲ *Level 1* (identification) The most elementary mastery of the skills requires the ability to identify and classify interviewing behavior. Most often this will be by observing others' behavior in a practice session.

▲ *Level 2* (basic mastery) This involves being able to perform the skills in an interview—for example, demonstrating that you can use both open and closed questioning even though you may not use the skills at a high level.

▲ *Level 3* (active mastery) Intentional interviewing demands that you have a variety of skills that you can use for specific purposes. For example, attending behavior skills should increase client talk-time in the interview, while the lack of them usually reduces client talk. Active mastery means that you can produce specific client results from your interviewing leads and behavior.

▲ *Level 4* (teaching mastery) One way to achieve deeper mastery of a skill is to teach that skill to someone else. Other people who wish to learn about the interview can profit from your teaching them specific skills. In addition, many clients can gain from being taught skills of interviewing, which are simply effective communication skills.

As you move through this book, assess your level of mastery of the concepts. Mastery occurs when you can recognize the skills, use them in the interview with specific client impact, and also teach them to others.

## STRUCTURE OF THE BOOK

Each chapter is focused on one specific skill or skill area of the interview. Chapter 1 presents the basic concepts of the book. Chapters 2 through 8 develop a solid foundation of listening skills. Each of these chapters is organized as follows:

| | |
|---|---|
| *Introduction.* | The skill is introduced and defined briefly. An exercise designed to make the skill personally meaningful to you is presented. |
| *Transcript.* | An example interview demonstrates the skill in action. |
| *Instructional reading.* | The single skill or skill area is elaborated with more applications and details. |
| *Key points of the chapter.* | The major points of the chapter are summarized. Included here are the functions of the skill in the interview, what the skill is, how it may be used effectively, and with whom. |
| *Practice exercises and self-assessment.* | The all-important practice follows that will enable you to identify, use, and teach the skill. |

1. *Individual practice.* Can you identify the presence or absence of the skill? A short series of practice and observation exercises will provide the opportunity to test your ability to understand the central aspects of behavior.

2. *Systematic group practice.* Practice by yourself is a good beginning, but you will need to work with someone else in a role-played interview if you are to obtain precise feedback on your use of attending. (If no group is available, adapt the systematic practice exercise for practice with a friend or family member.)

3. *Self-assessment and follow-up.* At the conclusion of the chapter you'll find a self-assessment form where you can evaluate your performance on this skill and assess its value to you.

| | |
|---|---|
| *Feedback form.* | Each chapter includes a form you can use to observe the behavior of others (or yourself) in the interview. |

Chapter 9 presents several influencing skills of the interview, and Chapters 10 and 11 illustrate how to integrate attending and influencing skills into an interview. Finally, Chapter 12 presents specific suggestions illustrating how you can teach interviewing skills to others.

## A FINAL WORD

This book discusses many concepts and specifics of effective interviewing derived from years of research and actual experience. The ideas presented here "work" and can make a difference to your impact on the client.

Your special challenge is to maintain a focus on yourself and your practice in the interview. Read the book from your own point of view. Study each idea and determine whether it feels comfortable to you, appears correct, and sounds as if it will be helpful to you and your clients. Only those concepts and skills that fit with your experience should be added to your natural style. If the concept doesn't feel right at first, still try it on and see if it fits, as you would try on a new jacket. What seems awkward at first may be a favored method later in your interviewing practice.

In Chapter 1 I suggest you audiorecord an interview *before* you study further. This will provide you with a baseline for examining your natural or present style before you become deeply involved with interview training and analysis. An early recording will help you note your changes and additions as you move through the book. I hope the book aids in identifying and facilitating your definition of how you want to help others.

Note to the Instructor: An Instructor's Manual with test questions and additional classroom exercises is available from Brooks/Cole Publishing Company. Masters for making overhead transparencies are also available from the publisher.

*Allen E. Ivey*

# ACKNOWLEDGMENTS

Robert Marx has contributed to this book through constant support, challenge, and encouragement. Many of the new concepts and ideas contained here were developed or sharpened in conversations we had while jogging through the streets of Amherst or in animated office discussions. Joe Litterer and I joined forces in 1979 and explored the commonalities of counseling and business interviews. The precision of his thinking forced my conceptions of the interview to a new level. This book would not have been possible without these two men.

Conversations with Victor Frankl and Otto Payton led me to include the new skill of reflection of meaning in the original manuscript. The feedback skill was developed with Joe Litterer and the logical consequences skill with Mary Bradford Ivey. At a time when the manuscript was nearing completion and still lacked integration, Bill Matthews and Ken Blanchard were key voices. Bill Matthews challenged me to emphasize more the function of each skill in the microtraining framework, and together we developed the five-stage model of the interview. Discussion with Ken Blanchard led to the client developmental level and interviewer style concepts.

Robert Marx, Mary Bradford Ivey, and I are jointly responsible for developing the audiotapes and transcripts presented in several chapters. These interviews are role-plays, much like those we expect students to engage in for practice. (All interviews have been edited slightly to clarify points, but are essentially close to the originals.)

The final review and testing of this book took place at Flinders University, Adelaide, Australia, where I served as Distinguished Visitor in Psychology and Senior Fulbright Scholar. Through co-teaching with Mary Bradford Ivey, several clarifications in and extensions of this book were developed. Particularly, I thank Mary and Lia and Zig Kapelis, who helped give final form to this book. Appreciation is extended to

Kevin Heath, Leon Mann, Norman Feather of Flinders University, and to Bob Manthei of the University of Canterbury, New Zealand. Carol McNally, Kay Guest, and the M. Psych. and diploma students were a wonderful support group.

Reviewers who offered suggestions for improvement and criticisms of the manuscript were: Margaret P. Korb, Santa Fe Community College, Marianne H. Mitchell, Indiana University, Florence L. Phillips, Texas Tech University, Kathleen Ritter, California State College, Bakersfield, James C. Schmidt, Oakland University, and Gerald L. Stone, University of Iowa.

The skills and concepts in this book rely on the work of many different individuals and researchers over the past eighteen years, notably that of Bruce Oldershaw, Norman Gluckstern, Wes Morrill, Gene Oetting, Dean Miller, Cheryl Normington, Dick Haase, John Moreland, Jerry Authier, David Evans, Margaret Hearn, Max Uhlemann, Lynn Simek-Downing, Susan Kennedy-Marx, Dwight Allen, Paul Pedersen, Lanette Shizuru, Derald Sue, and Steve Rollin. I acknowledge and thank them as well.

Finally, it has been joyful to work with the group at Brooks/Cole, notably with Claire Verduin, Sue Ewing, Richard Mason, Katherine Minerva, and David Aguero. I thank them all.

# CONTENTS

## 8   Focusing: Tuning in with Clients and Directing Conversational Flow   152

## 9   The Influencing Skills and the Combination Skill of Confrontation   169

## 10   Achieving Specific Goals in the Interview: Selecting and Structuring Skills   208

# 11 Skill Integration: Putting It All Together 262

# 12 Teaching Interviewing Skills 301

CHAPTER **1**

# Toward Intentional
# Interviewing and Counseling

You can make a difference in the lives of others in your work as an interviewer or counselor. This difference can be for the better . . . or for the worse. The interaction of the individual interview can enrich others or hinder their growth.

You have undoubtedly experienced an interview where you weren't heard and your point of view wasn't seen, and which perhaps left you feeling less in touch with yourself. And you have likely encountered

helping relationships that brightened your outlook, provided an experience of warmth and good feeling, and brought forward ideas that enabled you to attack issues in your life more confidently. In the effective interview you probably felt listened to and heard.

This book is about effective *intentional interviewing*. It is about developing specific skills that will enable you to help others. Through step-by-step study and practice, you will encounter and master specific interviewing skills that will:

▲ Enable you to define what you and others are doing in the interview to achieve specific results.
▲ Expand your skill repertoire so you will be able to generate an almost infinite number of responses to any client statement with a predicted result in client behavior.
▲ Illustrate how interviewing skills may be adapted for use in a variety of settings ranging from interviewing and counseling to nursing, business management, social work, and other fields.

## COUNSELING AND INTERVIEWING

The terms *counseling* and *interviewing* are often used interchangeably in this book. Though the overlap is considerable, interviewing may be con-

sidered the more basic process used for information gathering, problem solving, and information or advice giving. Interviewers may be guidance and counseling staff, medical personnel, business people, or members of any of a wide variety of helping professions. Counseling is a more intensive and personal process. It is generally concerned with helping normal people cope with normal problems and opportunities. Though many people who interview may also counsel, the concept of counseling is most often associated with the professional fields of social work, guidance, psychology, pastoral counseling, and, to a limited extent, psychiatry.

We can clarify this difference with some examples. The personnel manager may interview an employee for a new job but in the next hour counsel an employee deciding whether or not to take a new post in a distant town. The guidance counselor may interview each child in the class during the term for ten minutes to check on course selection but also may counsel some of them when problems arise. The psychologist may interview a person to obtain research data and the next hour be found counseling a client concerned over an impending divorce. Even in the process of a single contact, a social worker may interview a client to obtain financial data and then move to counseling on personal relationships.

Many people who interview at some time find themselves doing counseling. Most counselors at some time find themselves doing some interviewing. Both interviewing and counseling may be distinguished from psychotherapy, which is a more intense process concerned with working with deeply seated personality or behavioral difficulties. Most therapists at some time find themselves functioning as interviewers and counselors.

## INTENTIONALITY AS A GOAL FOR INTERVIEWING AND COUNSELING

Imagine that you are a helper working with a client. What would you say in response to the following?

*Client:* (Talking about a conflict on the job) I just don't know what to do about Bob. It seems he's always on me, blaming me even when I think I do a good job. He's new on the job, I know. Perhaps he doesn't have much experience as a supervisor. But he's got me all jumpy. I'm so nervous I can't sleep at night, and yesterday I even lost my lunch. My family isn't doing well, either. Sandy doesn't seem to understand what's going on and is upset. Even the kids aren't doing well in school. What do you suggest I do?

How would you respond? Write it below:

I would say: "_____

_____

_____

_____

_____

_____."

What you say and how you formulate the central issues of the presented problem may say as much about you and your style as they say about the client or interviewee. One of the goals of this book is to help you look at yourself and your typical response style. Your present way of conceptualizing the world of the other person is a valuable natural tool. At the same time, if you compare what you wrote with others, you'll find that they probably responded differently. A key question is, *Who had the correct response in this case?*

The answer to "correctness," of course, is that there are many possible, useful responses in an interviewing situation. At one time, an open question ("Could you tell me more?") may be most facilitative. Another time, it may be more useful to reflect feelings ("Looks like you feel terribly anxious and upset over the situation with Bob.") Again, there are times when self-disclosure and direct advice may be what is needed ("My experience with Bob is . . . and I suggest you try . . .").

Beginning interviewers are often eager to find the "right" answer for the client. In fact, they are often so eager that they give quick patch-up advice that is often inappropriate. How ideal it would be to find the "perfect empathic response" that would unlock the door to the client's world and free the individual for more creative being. However, the tendency to search for the single "right" response and move too quickly can be damaging.

*Intentional interviewing is concerned not with which single response is correct, but with how many potential responses may be helpful.* Intentionality is a core goal of effective interviewing. We can define it as follows:

Intentionality is acting with a sense of capability and deciding from a range of alternative actions. The intentional individual has more than one action, thought, or behavior to choose from in responding to changing life situations. The intentional individual can generate alternatives in a given situation and approach a problem from different vantage points, using a variety of skills and personal qualities, adapting styles to suit different cultural groups.

The intentional interviewer remembers a basic rule of helping: if something you try doesn't work, don't try more of the same . . . try something different!

Lack of intentionality shows in the interview when the helper persists in using only one skill, one definition of the problem, and one theory of interviewing, even when the theory isn't working. Intentionality demands the ability to be flexible at the moment and try new approaches.

This book is about generating an increased array of alternatives to help others through both interviewing and counseling. This goal will be achieved through the careful delineation and mapping of *microskill* units of the interview.

## THE MICROSKILLS APPROACH

Microskills are communication skill units of the interview that will help you develop a more intentional and rounded ability to interact with a client. They will provide specific alternatives for you to use with different types of clients. Microskills form the foundation of intentional interviewing.

The microskills hierarchy (see Figure 1-1) summarizes the successive steps of intentional interviewing. The skills of the interview rest on a foundation of culturally appropriate *attending behavior*, which includes patterns of eye contact, body language, vocal qualities, and verbal tracking. Attending behavior is the first microskill unit of this program. In your study and practice sessions you will have the opportunity to define this skill further, see attending demonstrated in an interview, read about further implications of this skill, and, finally, practice attending yourself.

Once you have mastered attending behavior, you will move up the microskills hierarchy to learn client observation, questioning, paraphrasing, and other basic listening skills. It is important to remember that the foundation for effective interviewing and eventual skill integration is the ability to listen to and understand the client. Attending and observational skills enable you to understand a client problem as the client sees, feels, and hears it *before* you begin with action. You'll find that these foundation skills are sometimes all that is needed for effective interviewing.

Microskills of focusing and interpersonal influence stand next in the hierarchy. In the section of the book that deals with these skills, you'll have the opportunity to study and master skills such as directives (telling a client to engage in specific actions), interpretation (providing the client with an alternative frame of reference for viewing a concern), and others such as feedback, logical consequences, and confrontation. Confrontation, near the peak of the microskills hierarchy, is concerned with

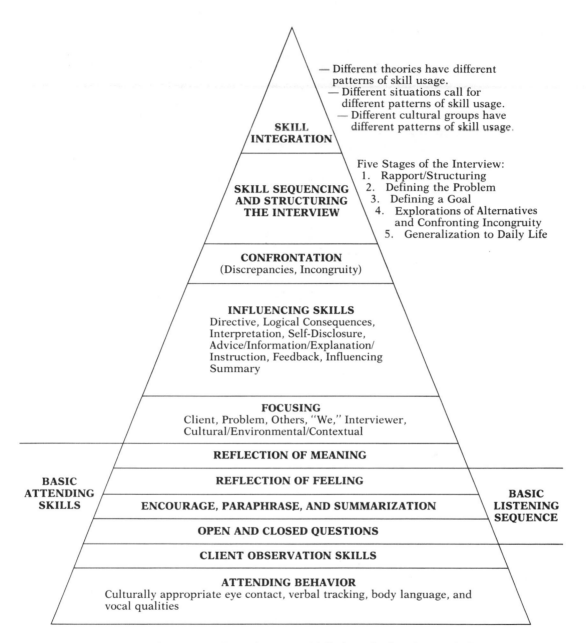

The pyramid from bottom to top:

**ATTENDING BEHAVIOR**
Culturally appropriate eye contact, verbal tracking, body language, and vocal qualities

**CLIENT OBSERVATION SKILLS**

**OPEN AND CLOSED QUESTIONS**

**ENCOURAGE, PARAPHRASE, AND SUMMARIZATION**

**REFLECTION OF FEELING**

**REFLECTION OF MEANING**

**FOCUSING**
Client, Problem, Others, "We," Interviewer, Cultural/Environmental/Contextual

**INFLUENCING SKILLS**
Directive, Logical Consequences, Interpretation, Self-Disclosure, Advice/Information/Explanation/ Instruction, Feedback, Influencing Summary

**CONFRONTATION**
(Discrepancies, Incongruity)

**SKILL SEQUENCING AND STRUCTURING THE INTERVIEW**

**SKILL INTEGRATION**

Left side: **BASIC ATTENDING SKILLS**

Right side: **BASIC LISTENING SEQUENCE**

Right of Skill Integration:
— Different theories have different patterns of skill usage.
— Different situations call for different patterns of skill usage.
— Different cultural groups have different patterns of skill usage.

Right of Skill Sequencing:
Five Stages of the Interview:
1. Rapport/Structuring
2. Defining the Problem
3. Defining a Goal
4. Explorations of Alternatives and Confronting Incongruity
5. Generalization to Daily Life

1. Attending behavior and client observation skills form the foundation of effective communication, but are not always the appropriate place to begin training.
2. The basic listening sequence of attending skills (open and closed questions, encouraging, paraphrasing, reflection of feeling, and summarization) is often found in effective interviewing, management, social work, physician diagnostic sessions, and many other settings.

**FIGURE 1–1** The microskills hierarchy. Copyright 1982 Allen E. Ivey, Box 641, N. Amherst, Mass. 01059

identifying discrepant and incongruent client behavior and facilitating client examination of conflict.

With mastery of attending, focusing, influencing, and confrontation skills, you are prepared to learn skill sequencing and structuring the interview. You will find that microskills may be organized into patterns that produce specific reactions for client benefit. Once you have mastered the various microskills, you will have reached the top of the hierarchy, skill integration. Integrating your skills can be a springboard to generating your own conception of the interview and its purposes.

As one route toward your own integration of skills, examine Figure 1-2, which presents examples of microskill usage in different types of theoretical orientations to counseling and in different situations, such as vocational planning, medical diagnostic interviewing, and business problem solving. This chart reveals that many differing theories and fields all use the basic microskills of communication.

Once you have mastered the microskills hierarchy, you are ready to use these skills and concepts in many alternative settings and will find you can master complex theories of counseling more easily. For example, the business problem-solving interview involves the same microskills in roughly the same proportion as might be found in a group working on vocational planning. The context and content of the interviews might be very different, but the skills are similar. On the other hand, the microskill usage of a psychodynamic therapist differs quite markedly from a modern Rogerian counselor. Although the microskills are basic to communication in many different settings and styles, individual and group usage of skills varies widely.

## ALTERNATIVE SETTINGS AND MICROSKILLS

Microskills training began with an emphasis on human-services settings, such as school counseling and community mental-health clinics. Very shortly, however, it was discovered that the basic skills of interviewing were equally valid in the business setting. The basic listening skill sequence is an example.

In defining the nature of a client's problem in a mental-health clinic, the interviewer often begins the session with an open question—for

instance, "Could you tell me what's on your mind today?" This question is coupled with appropriate attending behavior, encouraging, and effective nonverbal communication. Later the interviewer may paraphrase the client's ideas to ensure clarity of understanding: "Let me see if I have heard you correctly. You've been saying so far that your problem is . . . Am I hearing your views accurately?" Then the counselor likely will reflect feelings—"You seem to be feeling angry/

**FIGURE 1–2.** Examples of microskill leads used by interviewers of differing theoretical orientations

| | MICROSKILL LEAD | Nondirective | Modern Rogerian encounter | Behavioral | Psychodynamic | Gestalt | Trait and factor | Tavistock group | Vocational group (such as life planning) | Business problem solving | Medical diagnostic interview | Correctional interrogation | Traditional teaching | Student-centered teaching | Eclectic |
|---|---|---|---|---|---|---|---|---|---|---|---|---|---|---|---|
| **ATTENDING SKILLS** | Open question | ○ | ○ | ◐ | ◐ | ● | ● | ○ | ◐ | ◐ | ◐ | ● | ◐ | ● | ◐ |
| | Closed question | ○ | ○ | ● | ○ | ◐ | ◐ | ○ | ◐ | ◐ | ◐ | ● | ● | ◐ | ◐ |
| | Encourage | ◐ | ◐ | ◐ | ○ | ◐ | ◐ | ○ | ◐ | ◐ | ◐ | ◐ | ○ | ◐ | ◐ |
| | Paraphrase | ● | ● | ◐ | ◐ | ○ | ◐ | ○ | ◐ | ◐ | ◐ | ◐ | ○ | ◐ | ◐ |
| | Reflection of feeling | ● | ● | ○ | ◐ | ○ | ◐ | ○ | ◐ | ◐ | ◐ | ◐ | ○ | ● | ◐ |
| | Reflection of meaning | ◐ | ● | ○ | ◐ | ○ | ○ | ◐ | ○ | ○ | ○ | ○ | ○ | ◐ | ◐ |
| | Summarization | ◐ | ◐ | ◐ | ○ | ○ | ◐ | ○ | ◐ | ◐ | ◐ | ◐ | ○ | ◐ | ◐ |
| **INFLUENCING SKILLS** | Feedback | ○ | ● | ○ | ○ | ◐ | ○ | ○ | ◐ | ◐ | ○ | ○ | ◐ | ● | ◐ |
| | Advice/information/ and others | ○ | ○ | ◐ | ○ | ○ | ● | ○ | ● | ● | ◐ | ◐ | ● | ● | ◐ |
| | Self-disclosure | ○ | ◐ | ○ | ○ | ○ | ○ | ○ | ◐ | ◐ | ○ | ○ | ○ | ◐ | ◐ |
| | Interpretation | ○ | ○ | ○ | ● | ● | ○ | ● | ◐ | ◐ | ◐ | ◐ | ○ | ◐ | ◐ |
| | Logical consequences | ○ | ○ | ◐ | ○ | ○ | ◐ | ○ | ◐ | ● | ◐ | ● | ● | ◐ | ◐ |
| | Directive | ○ | ○ | ● | ○ | ● | ◐ | ○ | ◐ | ● | ◐ | ◐ | ● | ◐ | ◐ |
| | Influ. summary | ○ | ○ | ◐ | ○ | ○ | ◐ | ○ | ● | ● | ◐ | ○ | ◐ | ◐ | ◐ |
| | **CONFRONTATION** (Combined Skill) | ◐ | ◐ | ◐ | ◐ | ● | ◐ | ● | ◐ | ◐ | ◐ | ● | ◐ | ◐ | ◐ |
| **FOCUS** | Client | ● | ● | ● | ● | ● | ● | ○ | ◐ | ◐ | ◐ | ● | ◐ | ● | ◐ |
| | Counselor, interviewer | ○ | ◐ | ○ | ○ | ○ | ○ | ○ | ○ | ◐ | ◐ | ○ | ○ | ◐ | ◐ |
| | Mutual/group/"We" | ○ | ◐ | ○ | ○ | ○ | ○ | ● | ○ | ◐ | ○ | ○ | ○ | ◐ | ◐ |
| | Other people | ○ | ○ | ◐ | ◐ | ◐ | ◐ | ○ | ◐ | ○ | ○ | ◐ | ○ | ● | ◐ |
| | Topic or problem | ○ | ○ | ◐ | ◐ | ○ | ● | ○ | ● | ● | ● | ● | ● | ● | ◐ |
| | Cultural/ environmental context | ○ | ○ | ◐ | ○ | ○ | ◐ | ○ | ◐ | ◐ | ○ | ○ | ○ | ◐ | ◐ |
| | **ISSUE OF MEANING** (Topics, key words likely to be attended to and reinforced) | Feelings | Relationship | Behavior problem solving | Unconscious motivation | Here and now behavior | Problem solving | Authority, responsibility | Future plans | Problem solving | Diagnosis of illness | Information about crime | Information/ facts | Student ideas/ info./facts | Varies |
| | **AMOUNT OF INTERVIEWER TALK-TIME** | Low | Medium | High | Low | High | High | Low | High | High | High | Medium | High | Medium | Varies |

Legend

● Frequent use of skill
◐ Common use of skill
○ May use skill occasionally

happy/discouraged over the situation"—and may ask some closed questions "Did you try . . . ? Who did what?" to check on and define the client's problem. Finally, at the close of the problem definition phase of the interview, the counselor often summarizes the problem as the client has described it: "In other words, the problem seems to be that. . . ."

*The situations of counseling and management are different, but the patterning of skill usage is almost identical.* A manager whose subordinate has a problem on the production line uses a similar sequence of skills. "Could you tell me what is the general issue with the production line?" may be coupled with appropriate attending and nonverbal behavior and encouraging, followed by closed questions to diagnose the issue. The effective manager paraphrases in a form quite similar to the counselor to check on the accuracy of listening. Reflection of feeling as a skill does not figure as prominently in management, but it does often show itself briefly—for instance, "You feel pretty uptight about the production snag." Finally, before moving to problem resolution and action via influencing skills, the manager often summarizes the problem to ensure clarity.

In a similar fashion, the physician or nurse diagnosing a headache works through the basic listening sequence to ensure accurate diagnosis. The social worker concerned with a welfare case often uses the same skill sequence, as does the police officer obtaining information by interviewing the victim about a crime. Helping professionals and nonprofessionals in many settings use similar basic communication skills.

## CROSS-CULTURAL IMPLICATIONS OF MICROSKILLS

One of the critical issues in microskills work is the fact that different skills may have different effects among peoples of differing cultural backgrounds. Intentional interviewing demands awareness of the fact that different cultural groups have differing patterns of communication and microskill usage. Eye contact patterns differ, for example. In our culture middle-class patterns call for rather direct eye contact, but in some cultural groups direct eye contact is considered rude and intrusive. Some groups find the rapid-fire questioning techniques of many North Americans offensive. Many Spanish-speaking groups have more varying vocal tone and sometimes a more rapid speech rate than English-speaking people.

Thus, it is incorrect to assume that the communication patterns emphasized in this book work with everyone, regardless of cultural background. However, the microskill map can provide a clue as to why your interviewing techniques may not be working. If, for example, you find that questions are ineffective, don't use more of the same thing. Perhaps you need to slow down, or try another skill, such as self-disclosure or even advice giving.

Clients from varying cultural backgrounds may have differing expectations of the interview. Less advantaged socioeconomic groups, for example, often expect advice and suggestion rather than drawn-out talk and analysis of the problem.

Another interesting finding from recent examination of interviewing is that men and women may at times differ in their interviewing styles. Women tend to use the reflective listening techniques (such as paraphrasing and reflection of feeling), whereas men may use more questioning and interpretive statements.

While cultural and individual differences clearly exist in microskill patterns, the fact remains that people talk and people listen. Attending and influencing skills appear to be used in some form by all cultures. Thus, a mastery of microskill concepts, although in varying patterns and situations, should provide a useful tool for analyzing and understanding cultural differences in communication. The microtraining framework will provide you with a set of skills to facilitate communication across traditional cultural barriers if you are willing to flex and use them intentionally. Many resources are available on cultural differences in communication; perhaps most beneficial will be Hall's *The Silent Language* (1959). A recent videotape illustrates specific cultural differences in counseling (Ivey and Shizuru, 1981). Also Ivey (1981) considers cross-cultural counseling issues.

## TEACHING MODEL FOR LEARNING MICROSKILLS

Teaching workshops and courses on communication skills and interviewing is an increasingly important role of professionals in the helping fields. Microskills are well adapted for teaching beginning interviewers, whether they are in community volunteer groups, police departments, management, teaching, or any of a myriad of settings.

The final chapter of this book stresses teaching interviewing skills to others and provides suggestions for you to generate your own teaching plan. The models suggested in Chapter 12, based on years of research and clinical experience with microskills, follow a consistent and simple plan: (1) warm-up and introduction to the skill; (2) example of the skill in action; (3) reading; (4) practice— *in microtraining, practice is the most important dimension of the program;* (5) self-assessment and generalization.

These five steps provide a working model by which you can learn the skills yourself and pass them on to others. The chapters of this book follow this same basic organization. You will find as you teach other people these skills that you develop increased understanding of them and an even higher mastery level than you had attained before.

## RESEARCH VALIDATION OF THE MICROSKILLS APPROACH

Over 150 data-based studies have been completed on the microtraining model (Kasdorf & Gustafson, 1978). To these studies should be added more than 17 years of clinical testing of the model with trainees in counseling, business, and many other settings. The basic finding of the research data is the classic "more research is needed." However, the following practical points may be made with some assurance:

1. The skills of the microskills hierarchy have been shown again and again to be clear and teachable and show consistent construct validity.
2. Students who are trained via the model used in this book are able to recognize and classify interviewing skills with accuracy.
3. Students are able to demonstrate their mastery of these skills on audiotape or videotape following completion of training.
4. Students who practice the skills do improve and change their pattern of microskill usage as a result of this training. Personal involvement makes the difference in whether or not learning "takes."
5. The complete training package of introductory exercises, video or audio model, reading, and experiential practice appears to be most effective. Practice with the single skills to *mastery* levels appears to be particularly important to the development of competence.
6. Not only does the training seem to affect trainees, their clients also seem to change behavior. Clients of students who have gone through microskills training appear to change their verbal patterns and to have more complex patterns of thinking.
7. Different counseling theories do indeed appear to have differing patterns of microskill usage. The microtraining framework may be used to teach complex interviewing behavior according to alternative theoretical perspectives on the interview.

For those who are interested, Kasdorf and Gustafson's (1978) review of microtraining research is strongly recommended. The microtraining framework's feasibility and effectiveness have now been established over a considerable time, and thousands of students have experienced the framework in one form or another. Examine the framework and determine what it has to offer *you* for improving your understanding and skills in the interview.

## YOU AND THE MICROTRAINING PROCESS:
## A SUGGESTED EXERCISE

When the concept of intentionality was introduced early in this chapter, you were asked to give your own answer to an interviewee suffering from a conflict on the job. Microtraining seeks to give you additional alternatives for intentional responding to the client. However, these responses must be genuinely *you*. If you adopt a response simply because it is recommended, it is likely to be ineffective for you and your client. Not all parts of the microtraining framework are appropriate for everyone. You have a natural style of communicating, and it is that natural style we would like to add to—not change.

You are about to engage in a systematic study of the interviewing process. By the end of the book you will have been given many ideas for analyzing your interviewing style. Along the way, you will find it helpful to have nearby a record of where you were *before* you started this training. Your present natural style is a baseline you will likely want to keep and honor. Identifying who you are and what you do before beginning systematic training can be invaluable.

As such, it would be useful for you to now audiorecord yourself in a natural interview. Without further training and analysis, find someone who is willing to role play a client with a concern, problem, opportunity, or issue. Interview that client for at least 15 minutes using your own natural communication style.

Since you are going to audiorecord that interview, be sure to ask the role-played client the critical closed question "May I record this interview?" Also inform the client that, if he or she wishes, the tape recorder may be turned off at any time. Common sense demands ethical practice and respect for the client.

You can select almost any topic for the interview. If you work in a business setting, a friend discussing a business problem may be appropriate. If you are in human services, perhaps a colleague can role play a client he or she had in the past, and you can test your natural skills. A useful topic is interpersonal conflict, for example concerns over family or decisions about a new job opportunity.

Save the audiotape until a later time. At that point you will want to listen to it again, perhaps even make a transcript of what you and your client say, and analyze your behavior, noting its impact on your client. After completion of this book, you may want to record another interview noting the similarities and differences in your style. Comparing your behavior at the beginning and after you have had some training will help you evaluate the microskills training. After all, it is *you* who will ultimately determine the worth of this program.

## Box 1-1  Key points

KEY POINT                DISCUSSION

*Intentionality*         Intentionality is the major goal of this book. It is a major
                         goal for the interviewing process itself. Intentionality is
     acting with a sense of capability and deciding from a
                         range of alternative actions. The intentional individual
                         has more than one action, thought, or behavior to choose
                         from in responding to life situations. The intentional
                         individual can generate alternatives from different
                         vantage points, using a variety of skills and personal
                         qualities within a culturally appropriate framework.

*Microskills*            Single communication skill units (for example, questions,
                         interpretation) of the interview. Microskills are taught
                         one at a time to ensure mastery of basic interviewing
                         competencies.

*Microskills*            The organization of microskills into a systematic
*hierarchy*              framework for eventual integration of skills into the
                         interview in a natural fashion. The microskills rest on a
                         foundation of attending (listening) skills followed by
                         focusing and influencing skills, confrontation, and
                         eventual skill integration.

*Use of skills with*     Different counseling and interviewing theories have
*different*              varying patterns of skill usage; however, they all use the
*situations and*         communication skill units. Basic skills of interviewing
*theories*               and counseling appear in many situations such as
                         medicine, management, and social work, although the
                         content of the interview may vary.

*Basic listening*        A sequence of attending skills (question, encourage,
*sequence*               paraphrase, reflection of feeling, summary) is basic to
                         problem definition and is used in many different settings.
                         Discussed in detail in Chapter 10, the basic listening
                         sequence may be the most important concept of this
                         book.

*Cultural*               While different cultural groups use the microskills,
*differences*            different patterns of use with different meanings may be
                         expected. Do not expect the framework here to be
                         relevant to all cultures without some adaptation.

**Box 1-1 continued**

| KEY POINT | DISCUSSION |
|---|---|
| *Teaching model* | The microskill teaching model includes: (1) warm-up and introduction to the skill; (2) example of the skill in operation; (3) reading; (4) practice; and (5) self-assessment and generalization. Most of the chapters of this book follow the same model. |
| *Research validation* | The microskill model has been validated by over 150 data-based studies and 17 years of clinical practice. The skills can be learned, and they do have an impact on clients, but they must be constantly practiced or they may disappear. |
| *You and microskills and the interview* | Microskills are only useful if they relate to your own natural style in the interview. Before you move further in this book, audiorecord an interview with a friend or classmate, make a transcript of this interview, and later—as you learn more about interview analysis—analyze your behavior in that interview. You'll want to compare it with your behavior at the conclusion of this book. |

## REFERENCES AND RECOMMENDED SUPPLEMENTARY READING

Advanced Development Division. *Tuning in: Intentional attending.* Trainer's manual. Ottawa: Occupational and Career Analysis and Development Branch, Employment and Immigration Canada, 1980. This manual describes the use of basic attending skills in the work of the Canadian Employment Service.

Evans, D., Hearn, M., Uhlemann, M., and Ivey, A. *Essential interviewing: A programmed approach to effective communication* (2nd ed.). Monterey, Calif.: Brooks/Cole, 1983. A programmed text covering most of the basic microskills discussed in this book.

Hall, E. *The Silent Language.* New York: Fawcett, 1959. Despite its age, this slim paperback volume still provides one of the best summaries of issues in cross-cultural communication.

Ivey, A. *Microcounseling: Innovations in interviewing training.* Springfield, Ill.: Charles C Thomas, 1971. The original microcounseling text, which first outlined the microtraining paradigm in depth.

Ivey, A. Counseling and psychotherapy: Toward a new perspective. In T. Marsella and P. Pedersen (Eds.), *Cross-cultural counseling and psychotherapy.* New York: Pergamon, 1981. Cross-cultural implications of counseling and therapy are considered in some detail. A new theoretical perspective on microskills is presented.

Ivey, A., and Authier, J. *Microcounseling: Innovations in interviewing, counseling, psychotherapy, and psychoeducation.* Springfield, Ill.: Charles C Thomas, 1978. An updated version of the 1971 text, approximately doubled in size. Research data, instruments for evaluation of the interview, new theoretical material, and transcripts are included.

Ivey, A., and Gluckstern, N. *Basic attending skills and basic influencing skills.* Training manual and videotapes. North Amherst, Mass.: Microtraining, 1974, 1976. Original editions on which this book is based.

Ivey, A., and Litterer, J. *Face to face: Communication skills in business.* Training manual and videotapes. North Amherst, Mass.: Amherst Consulting Group, 1979. A business version for management training utilizing concepts of microtraining. Available in German, Swedish, and Australian adaptations.

Ivey, A., Normington, C., Miller, C., Morrill, W., and Haase, R. Microcounseling and attending behavior: An approach to pre-practicum counselor training. *Journal of Counseling Psychology*, 1968, *15*, Part II (Separate Monograph), 1–12. The original publication on microcounseling, outlining three basic research studies on the efficacy of the model.

Ivey, A., and Shizuru, L. Issues in cross-cultural counseling. North Amherst, Mass.: Microtraining, 1981. Videotape and workbook illustrating cultural differences in microskills.

Ivey, A., with Simek-Downing, L. *Counseling and psychotherapy: Skills, theories, and practice.* Englewood Cliffs, N.J.: Prentice-Hall, 1980. An introductory text in counseling and psychotherapy that illustrates how the microskills may be used in alternative theoretical orientations. A summary of the theoretical orientation of the 1981 Ivey paper on theory is included.

Jessop, A. *Nurse-patient communication: A skills approach.* Training manual and videotapes. No. Amherst, Mass.: Microtraining, 1979. Microskills applied to the nursing context.

Kasdorf, J., and Gustafson, K. Research related to microtraining. In A. Ivey and J. Authier, *Microcounseling: Innovations in interviewing, counseling, psychotherapy, and psychoeducation.* Springfield, Ill.: Charles C Thomas, 1978. Detailed analysis of the 150 data-based studies on microtraining completed as of that date.

# CHAPTER 2

# Attending Behavior: Basic to Communication

**How can attending behavior be used to help you and your clients?**

*Major Function*

Attending encourages client talk. You will want to use attending behavior to help a client talk more freely and openly, and to reduce interviewer talk.

Conversely, the lack of attending behavior can also serve a useful function. Through inattention, you can help other people talk less about topics that are destructive or nonproductive.

*Secondary Functions*

Knowledge and skill in attending results in:

▲ Communicating to the client that you are interested in what is being said.
▲ Increasing your awareness of the client's patterns of attending.
▲ Modifying your patterns of attending to establish rapport with each individual. Different people and different cultural groups often have different patterns of attending.
▲ Having some recourse when you are lost or confused in the interview. Even the most advanced professional doesn't always know what is happening. When you don't know what to do, attend!

## INTRODUCTION

Foremost in any interview or counseling situation is the ability to make contact with another human being. We make this contact both through listening and talking and by nonverbal means. *Listening* to other people is most critical as it enables them to continue to talk and explore. Effective attending behavior may be considered the foundation skill of this program.

How can we define effective listening more precisely? A simple warm-up exercise may help in this process. It will help if you work with someone else, but you can do it in your imagination, especially if you recall parallel experiences in your own life.

One of the best ways to understand quality listening is to experience the opposite—*poor listening.* Find a partner for a role-played interview and together think of incorrect things that an ineffective listener or interviewer does. If no partner is available, think back on some bad interviews you have gone through. Spend about three minutes role playing the poor interview (or recalling the many aspects of the ineffective session). The emphasis here is on what is wrong; you should feel free to exaggerate in order to underline the many things that can cause a session to go poorly.

List below the many behaviors, traits, and qualities that are characteristic of the ineffective interviewer or counselor who fails to listen.

_____

_____

_____

_____

_____

_____

This exercise is often humorous. We recall with laughter the bored interviewer, the uninterested counselor, or the ineffective therapist. Yet, as you recall your own experience of not being heard, your strongest memory may be a feeling of emptiness when you needed help. Or perhaps you recall anger at the insensitivity of the interviewer. Lists of ineffective interviewing behaviors sometimes run to thirty items or more. If you are to be effective and competent, the obvious choice is to do the opposite of the ineffective counselor. The first transcript below gives a negative example you can begin to work from.

Obviously you can't learn all the qualities and skills immediately. Rather it is best to learn them step-by-step. The foundation skill of attending behavior consists of four dimensions and is critical to all other skills. To communicate that you are indeed listening or attending to someone else, you need:

1. *Eye contact.* If you are going to talk to people, look at them.
2. *Attentive body language.* Clients know you are interested if you face them squarely and have a slight forward trunk lean, have an expressive face, and use facilitative, encouraging gestures.
3. *Vocal qualities.* Your vocal tone and speech rate also indicate clearly how you feel about another person. Think of how many ways you can say "I am really interested in what you say" just by altering vocal tone and speech rate.
4. *Verbal tracking.* The client has come to you with a topic of interest; don't change the subject. Keep the topic to that indicated by the client.

The four attending behaviors all have one goal in common: to reduce interviewer talk-time and provide the client with an opportunity to talk and examine issues concretely and in more detail. You can't learn about the client if you are doing the talking!

## EXAMPLE INTERVIEWS

The first interview presented, part of a job interview, is deliberately designed to be a particularly ineffective session. This will help provide contrast with the second interview. Note how patterns of eye contact, body language, vocal tone, and failure to maintain verbal tracking can disrupt a session.

### NEGATIVE EXAMPLE

*Al:* The next thing on my questionnaire is your past job history. Tell me a little bit about it, will ya? (The vocal tone is casual, almost uninterested. Eye contact is on the form, not on the client.)

*Hank:* Well, I guess the job that, uh . . .

*Al:* Hold it! That's the doorbell. I'll be back in a minute. (Long pause) Uh, okay, okay, where were we? (Impatiently)

*Hank:* The job that really comes to mind is my work as a camp counselor during my senior year of high school . . .

*Al:* (Interrupts) Oh, yeah, I did a camp counselor job myself. I did it at Camp Eagle in Minnesota. Geez, I had a really good time doing that. I'm glad to hear that. Yeah, that was really great fun. What else have you been doing?

*Hank:* Ah . . . well, I . . . ah . . . wanted to tell you a little bit more about this counseling job, I . . .

*Al:* (Interrupts) I got that down, so tell me about something else. Did you ever work on a farm?

*Hank:* Ah . . . no, I didn't. (Looks puzzled and confused.)

*Al:* I liked working on a farm a lot.

*Hank:* I lived in St. Louis, it was . . .

*Al:* (Interrupts) I don't like that town much.

*Hank:* I was miles from the closest farm. I mean I don't see how I could have worked on a farm (Defensive vocal tone). I did work at my dad's grocery store when I was in grade school and high school. I would come down Saturday morning and . . . (Note that Al has taken control of the topic from Hank, and Hank is talking about what Al wants to talk about rather than determining his own direction. Attending behavior demands that we listen to the client and go the way he or she wishes. This interview may seem far-fetched, but in fact many interviews are not as different from this as we would wish.)

*Al:* Yeah, that sounds like something I ought to write down. (Pauses and looks at his form for a period of time) . . . What did you do for him?

*Hank:* Well, uh, it was a grocery store and I sold . . .

*Al:* (Interrupts) Do you like to eat?

*Hank:* Yeah . . . ah . . . (Looks confused) . . . I like to cook too.

*Al:* You? Interested in cooking? (Scornful look)

*Hank:* (Angrily) Yes, I'm good at it too! What . . .

*Al:* That's a weird thing to do!

Comment: This interview is extreme, but it does illustrate the many different ineffective responses the insensitive interviewer can direct to a client. Almost every time Al spoke, he changed the topic. His body language was slouched, the gestures were uninterested or scornful, and his vocal qualities were harsh.

*POSITIVE EXAMPLE*

*Al:* Well, Hank, the next thing on this form, uh, is something about your job . . . jobs you've had in the past. Could you tell me a little bit about some of the jobs you've had? (Al uses the client's name and structures this part of the interview briefly. He then asks an open question to obtain information from Hank's perspective. He sits squarely facing the client, leans slightly forward, maintains good eye contact, and his vocal tone and facial expression indicate interest.)

*Hank:* Sure. The job that comes to mind really, is the one I had in my senior year in high school and during my college years as a camp counselor for the YMCA. (Hank's vocal tone is confident and relaxed. He seems eager to explore this new area.)

*Al:* Yeah? Tell me more?

*Hank:* Well, I was . . . it was at a point where I was really looking for a profession to engage in when I got older, and I realized while I was working at this camp with these kids, taking responsibility for them and helping them learn things, that I have always really wanted to work with people. And, uh . . .

*Al:* Uh-huh. (Lets Hank know he is listening.)

*Hank:* . . . I think I began to realize that psychology was a major that I was interested in.

*Al:* I see. So working in a camp with people was one of the things that you liked. Could you give me an example of one of the things that happened in that camp that you particularly liked? (Helps Hank be specific and concrete.)

*Hank:* Well, I seemed to be able to get the kids in the group to work well together. It was an overnight camp, and there were kids from lots of different racial groups, from different socioeconomic classes, and I seemed to be able to organize them in a way that really built on the strengths of everybody. And we resolved a lot of their conflicts. I think I made them feel . . . helped them feel pretty good about themselves.

*Al:* So, you resolved a lot of conflicts, and you helped them feel pretty good. How did that make you feel?

*Hank:* Oh, I was delighted. I felt like my cabin was the most cohesive group in the camp sometimes. I felt real increased self-esteem because I had helped, you know, us become a pretty good unit together, and we also had lots of fun, you know, I learned to play the ukelele and we had some singing sessions. I really couldn't believe I was getting paid to be up in that beautiful country up in northern Michigan every summer, and be with these kids, and I thought, "Gee, you know, this could be a profession for me, that would be great. If I can just do something like this all year round."

*Al:* So, this leads you to think that you might like to continue this type of work where you could work with people and do it, like you say, all year round.

*Hank:* Right.

*Al:* What are some things along that line that you've thought of that you might want to do?

*Hank:* Well, as I was saying, I thought I might . . . at that time I thought I might become a therapist to help people who, you know, had real personal problems. I thought I even might become a camp director at some point. That was another possibility. I knew that I really wanted to work with people rather than with things, and I knew that I really had an attachment to the outdoors. I wanted to live someplace where I could experience being away from some of the hustle and bustle and noise of the city. So, that particular job was one, I think, that had the greatest impression on me.

*Al:* So, of all the jobs you've had, that really makes the deepest impression—the chance to work with people and be with them and so forth.

Just by way of contrast, could you share, maybe, a job where you didn't have those feelings, maybe that you disliked? (Clarifies interests via contrasts.)

*Hank:* Oh, I had a job as a paper route . . . as a paper boy, and I found that to be rather tedious. I went around, you know, every day delivering these papers, and it was in Chicago and there were a lot of tenement buildings in this area where I grew up . . .

*Al:* Uh-huh.

*Hank:* Sometimes the papers were so thick, I couldn't throw them up to the upper floors, and I had to walk them all the way up. It was bitter cold in the winter, and the pay wasn't very good. But I was determined not to quit, you know, I didn't want to be seen as a quitter . . .

*Al:* Ah-hah.

*Hank:* And some of my friends had the same kind of job.

*Al:* You said you were determined not to quit . . .

*Hank:* Right.

*Al:* Could you go a little further with that?

*Hank:* Well, I had a couple of friends who would deliver these papers and they delivered from, you know, August to October, and as soon as it got cold out, they'd quit and just live off their allowance that their parents gave them. I decided that I was going to tough it out through the winter, and the guy who was the boss down there, he told me in May when I finally quit 'cause school was out, he said, "Hank, you're a good kid, you know, you stuck through the winter." Somehow, that meant a lot to me.

*Al:* So, to sort of wind up here at this particular part, because you sort of talked about a job you liked and a job you didn't, can you put anything together about what that guy told you? Your sticking through the winter, that may even tie in with some of the stuff you talked about at first . . . the job in the camp. And, it seems to me, you can put those two together in terms of a pattern. (Al invites Hank to take an active part and put his own interpretations forward to help understand the patterns.)

*Hank:* Well, I guess . . . in the job I didn't like so much, the paper route, because it was so tedious and repetitive, I did appreciate getting that reward in the end, that I wasn't a quitter. But it didn't really help me learn that much about myself, except that one thing that I could really tough it out if I had to. In the other job, really, I felt a lot of challenge. I felt like I could use some of my natural talents. I could learn to, you know, help people get along with one another. I could teach them in a way that didn't scare them, and I began to feel a lot better about myself as a person. I was a little insecure as a teenager, and all of a sudden I was watching myself do something really well. And I think that just had much more of an impression on my life.

*Al:* So, Hank, one thing that seems to be in common in the two jobs is that you like to feel good about yourself, it's important to do a good job. Is that correct?

*Hank:* That's right. I never thought of that.

Comment: Throughout this interview, Al maintains culturally appropriate eye contact, body language, verbal tracking, and vocal qualities. Hank, in turn, responds with the same. There are very few, if any, topic jumps on Al's part. His task appears to be bringing out Hank's ideas and opinions. Where there are possible topic jumps, Al has related something from earlier in the interview to what is being discussed. Through this process of simple attending, Hank comes to a new understanding of one of his major constructs underlying vocational choice—that is, wanting to feel good about himself through a job well done. Here we note the relationship of personal issues to the world of work.

The particular technique Al used in the positive example may be called *contrast interviewing.* A positive experience is identified and discussed in some depth. Then a negative experience is similarly identified and discussed. As the two are contrasted and compared, clients often reveal much of themselves and what is important to them in life and work. The identification of positive experience is particularly important in interviewing and counseling. Many clients will grow faster with emphasis on strengths rather than on weaknesses and problems.

## INSTRUCTIONAL READING

 Nonverbal dimensions of attending demonstrate to clients that they are truly heard. They lead to that central goal of attending—giving the client talk-time—and provide you with useful behaviors to help others talk more freely. The following points represent some critical refinements on eye contact, body language, vocal tone, and verbal tracking.

*EYE CONTACT*

When an issue is interesting to clients, you will find that their pupils tend to dilate. On the other hand, when the topic is uncomfortable or boring, pupils may contract. If you have a chance to observe your face carefully on videotape, you'll note that you as a counselor or interviewer indicate to your clients your degree of interest in the same fashion.

You'll also want to notice breaks in eye contact. Clients often tend to look away when discussing issues that particularly depress them. You may find yourself avoiding eye contact on certain topics. There are counselors who say their clients seem to talk about "nothing but sex" and counselors who say their clients never bring up the topic. I suspect that, between pupil dilation and eye contact breaks, both types of counselors indicate to their clients what topics are appropriate.

Cultural differences in eye contact abound. Direct eye contact is considered a sign of interest in White middle-class culture. However, even there a person often gives you more eye contact while listening and somewhat less while talking. Research indicates, moreover, that some Blacks in the United States may have reverse patterns; that is, they may look more when talking and slightly less when listening. Among some Hispanic groups, eye contact by the young is a sign of disrespect. Imagine the problems this may cause the teacher or counselor who tells a youth "Look at me!" when this directly contradicts basic cultural values. Some other cultural groups (for instance, certain native American, Eskimo, or Aboriginal Australian groups) generally avoid eye contact, especially when talking about serious subjects.

## BODY LANGUAGE

The anthropologist Edward Hall once examined film clips of Southwest Indians and Whites and found over 20 different behaviors in the way they walked. Just as cultural differences exist in eye contact, body language patterns differ.

A comfortable space for North Americans is slightly more than arm's length, and the British may prefer even larger distances. South American Spanish-speaking people often prefer half that distance, and those from the Middle East may talk literally eyeball to eyeball. As a result, the slight forward trunk lean we recommended with attending behavior is obviously not going to be appropriate all the time. A natural, relaxed body style that is your own is likely to be most effective.

Just as shifts in eye contact tell us about potentially uncomfortable issues for clients, so do changes in body language. A person may move forward when interested and away when bored or frightened. As you talk, notice people's movement in relation to you. How do you affect them? Note yourself in the interview. When do you change body posture markedly? Are there patterns you need to be aware of?

## VOCAL QUALITIES

Your voice is an instrument that communicates much of the feeling you have toward another person or situation. Changes in pitch, volume, and speech rate say things similar to changes in eye contact and body language.

Keep in mind that different people are likely to respond to your voice differently. Try this exercise with a group of three or more people.[1]

---

[1]This exercise was developed by Robert Marx, Western Washington University.

Ask the group to close their eyes while you talk to them. Talk in your normal tone of voice on any subject of interest to you. As you talk to the group, ask them to notice your vocal qualities. How do they react to your tone, your volume, your speech rate, perhaps even your regional or ethnic accent? Continue talking for two to three minutes. Then ask them to give you feedback on your voice. Summarize what you learn below.

_____

_____

_____

_____

This exercise often reveals a point that is central to the entire concept of attending. *People differ in their reactions to the same stimulus.* Some people find one voice interesting, whereas others find that same voice boring, and still others may consider it warm and caring. This exercise and others like it reveal again and again that people differ, and what works with one person or client may not work with another.

*Verbal underlining* is another useful concept. As you examine your own behavior, you will find yourself giving louder volume and increased vocal emphasis to certain words or short phrases. Clients, of course, do the same. The key words a person underlines via volume and emphasis are often concepts of particular importance to them.

Awareness of your voice and the changes in others' vocal qualities will enhance your skills in attending. Again, note the timing of vocal changes as they may indicate comfort or discomfort, depending on the cultural group of the client. Speech hesitations and breaks often indicate confusion or stress.

The three nonverbal components of attending behavior are supplemented by verbal tracking, staying on the topic of the client. Verbal tracking is one of the most powerful tools in the counselor's skill repertoire.

## VERBAL TRACKING

Staying with the client's topic is critical in verbal tracking. Just as they shift nonverbal dimensions, people change and shift topics when they aren't comfortable. And cultural differences appear even on a basic dimension such as verbal tracking. In middle-class U.S. communication direct verbal tracking is most appropriate, but in some more subtle Asian cultures the direct verbal following we use may be considered rude and intrusive.

*Selective attention* is a special type of verbal tracking that counselors and interviewers need to be especially aware of. We tend to listen to some things and ignore others. Over time, we have developed patterns of listening that enable us to hear some topics more clearly than others. For example, take the following statement, in which the client presents several issues.

*Client:* I'm so fouled up right now. I just got notice that the plant is closing and I'll lose my job. I don't even know whether or not I'm eligible for unemployment. On the way home someone hit my car. I forgot to get their license number. And finally, when I got home, the kids had left the apartment in a mess, and there was a letter from my parents that really upset me.

There are obviously several different directions the interview could go. List those several directions below. To which one(s) would you selectively attend?

_____

_____

_____

_____

There are no correct answers. In such a situation different interviewers would place varying emphasis on different issues. Some interviewers consistently listen attentively to only a few key topics while ignoring other possibilities. Be alert to your own potential patterning of responses. It is important that no issue get lost, and it is equally important not to attack all at once as confusion will result.

The concept of verbal tracking may be most helpful to the beginning interviewer or to the experienced interviewer who is lost or puzzled about what to say next in response to a client. *Relax*, take whatever the client has said in the immediate or near past and direct attention to that through a question or a brief comment. You don't need to introduce a new topic. Build on the client's topics, and you will know the client very well over time.

## THE VALUE OF NONATTENTION

There are times when it is inappropriate to attend to client statements. For example, a client may talk insistently about the same topic over and over again. A depressed client may want to give the most complete description of how and why the world is wrong. Many clients only want to talk about negative things. In such cases, intentional nonattending may be useful. Through failure to maintain eye contact, subtle shifts in body posture and vocal tone, and deliberate topic jumps to more positive topics, you can facilitate interview progress.

The most skilled counselors and interviewers use attending skills to open and close client talk, thus facilitating effective use of the limited time in the interview.

## SUMMARY

There is no need to talk about yourself or give long answers when you attend to someone else. Give the client ownership of "air-time." Your main responsibility as a helper is to assist others in finding their own answers. You'll be surprised how able they are to do this if you are willing to attend.

Respect yourself and the other person. Ask questions and make comments on things that interest you and seem relevant to you. If you are truly interested in what is being said, attending behavior follows automatically. But keep in mind that, as you become more interested, you may be tempted to overinvolve yourself. The goal of attending is to listen to the other person. Your patterns of eye contact, body language, vocal qualities, and verbal tracking are the skills that enable you to help another person express him- or herself. Read Box 2-1 for a summary of this chapter's major ideas, then start on the practice exercises on page 27 and following.

---

## Box 2-1  Key points

*Why?*

The four attending behaviors all have one goal in common: to reduce interviewer talk-time while providing the client with an opportunity to talk and examine issues. You can't learn about the other person or the problem while you are doing the talking! Lack of attending may also be used to stop needless client talk, at any time during the interview.

*What?*

Attending behavior consists of four simple, but critical, dimensions:

1. *Eye contact.* If you are going to talk to people, look at them.
2. *Attentive body language.* In general, clients know you are interested in them if you face them squarely and

**Box 2-1 continued**

have a slight forward trunk lean, have an expressive face, and use facilitative, encouraging gestures.

3. *Vocal qualities.* Your vocal tone and speech rate indicate much of how you feel about another person. Think of how many ways you can say "I am really interested in what you say" just by your vocal tone and speech rate.

4. *Verbal tracking.* The client has come to you with a topic of interest; don't change the subject. Keep to the topic initiated by the client. If you change the topic, be aware that you did and realize the purpose of your change.

*How?*

Attending is easiest if you focus your attention on the client rather than on yourself. Note what the client is talking about, ask questions, and make comments that relate to client topics. For example:

*Client:* I am so confused. I can't decide between a major in chemistry, psychology, or language.

*Interviewer:* (Nonattending) Tell me about your hobbies. What do you like to do? *or* What are your grades?

*Interviewer:* (Attending) Tell me more. *or* You feel confused? *or* Could you tell me a little bit about how each subject interests you? *or* Opportunities in chemistry are promising now. Could you explore that field a bit more? *or* How would you like to go about your decision?

Note that all attending responses follow the client's verbal statement. Each might lead the client in a very different direction. Interviewers need to be aware of their patterns of *selective attention* and how they may unconsciously direct the interview. Finally, nonattending responses may be helpful in certain contexts.

*With whom?*

Attending is vital in all human interactions, be they counseling, a medical interview, or a business decision meeting. It is important to note that different cultural groups may have different patterns of attending. Some may maintain distinctly different patterns of eye contact, for example, and consider the direct gaze rude and intrusive. The attending interviewer is constantly aware of group, cultural, and individual differences in attending patterns.

**Box 2-1 continued**

*And?*        A simple, but often helpful, rule in the interview is to
remember that, when you as an interviewer become lost
or confused about what to do, *attend.* Simply ask the
client to comment further on something just said or
mentioned earlier in the interview. The use of
nonattention to discourage certain client talk and focus
the interview may be useful.

## PRACTICE EXERCISES AND SELF-ASSESSMENT

Attending behavior is a simple set of skills. Yet it is awareness of and competence in these skills that form the foundation of effective interviewing, counseling, or therapy.
You can never stop bettering your skill in attending; there
is always room for improvement.

The following steps have proven most helpful as a systematic framework for mastering attending behavior.

1. *Individual practice.* Can you identify the presence or absence of
   attending? A short series of practice and observation exercises will
   provide the opportunity to test your ability to understand the central
   aspects of attending behavior (p. 27).
2. *Systematic group practice.* Practice by yourself is a good beginning,
   but you will need to work with someone else in a role-played interview if you are to obtain precise feedback on your use of attending
   behavior (p. 29). If no group is available, adapt the systematic practice exercise for practice with a friend or family member.
3. *Self-assessment and follow-up.* At the conclusion of the chapter you'll
   find a self-assessment form where you can evaluate your performance
   on this skill and assess its value to you (p. 34).

*INDIVIDUAL PRACTICE*

**Exercise 1. Generating alternative attending and nonattending
statements.**

A client comes to you saying:

I just got fired. It wasn't my fault. It just wasn't fair. The
boss gave me a bad time. I wasn't late very often, and I
did a good job. I'd like to fix him. But . . . I need a job.
What ideas do you have for me?

Write below three things you might say, each of which could lead the client in a different direction, yet all of which are attending responses.

1. _____

2. _____

3. _____

The most important gift you can give a client is attending. At the same time, it is important to be aware of the impact of nonattending; at times it can be useful. Write below one potentially effective and one potentially ineffective nonattending statement.

Potentially effective _____

Potentially ineffective _____

### Exercise 2. Behavioral counts.

Observe an interview. This could be a role-played counseling practice session, a television talk-show, or simply an interaction between friends or family. Use the following form to count the behaviors:

_____ Number of eye contact breaks
_____ Number of distracting nonverbal gestures
_____ Number of distracting vocal hesitations/changes
_____ Number of topic jumps

The same dimensions may be counted in a positive way. Observe another interview and complete the following form.

_____ Percentage of time (approximate) appropriate eye contact maintained
_____ Number of facilitating nonverbal gestures
_____ Number of helpful vocal changes, emphasis, underlining
_____ Number of times person stayed on the same topic

Both observations provide useful data. What did you discover from this experience?

_____

_____

_____

_____

_____

_____

**Exercise 3. Deliberate attending.**

During a conversation with a friend or acquaintance deliberately attend and listen more carefully than usual. Maintain eye contact and an open, attentive posture, and stay on that person's topic. Note the reaction of the other person. What happens to her or his body posture? Language patterns?

You may wish to contrast deliberate attending with nonattending. What happens when your eye contact wanders, your body posture becomes more tight, or you change the topic?

Note your reactions to this exercise below:

_____

_____

_____

_____

_____

_____

_____

_____

_____

*SYSTEMATIC GROUP PRACTICE*

The instructions below are designed for groups of four, but may be adapted for use with pairs, trios, and groups up to five or six in number. Ideally, each group has access to video- or audiorecorders. However, careful observers using the feedback sheets provided can still offer involving and successful practice sessions without the benefit of equipment.

**Step 1. Divide into practice groups.** Get acquainted with each other informally before you move further.

**Step 2. Select a group leader.** The leader's task is to ensure that the group follows the specific steps of the practice session. It often proves helpful if the least experienced group member serves first as leader.

## Step 3. Assign roles for the first practice session.

▲ Role-played client. The role-played client will be cooperative, talk freely about a selected topic, and not give the interviewer a "hard time."

▲ Interviewer. The interviewer will demonstrate a natural style of attending behavior with the client and practice the basic skills.

▲ Observer I. The first observer will fill out a feedback form (see page 33) detailing some aspects of the interviewer's attending behavior.

▲ Observer II. The second observer will time the session, start and stop any equipment, and fill out a second observation sheet as time permits.

## Step 4. Planning.[2]    The members of the group should take time to plan the role-play.

The interviewer should plan to open and to facilitate client talk. An increased percentage of client talk-time on a single topic will indicate a successful session. The interviewer may also plan to close off client talk and then open it again.

The suggested topic for the attending practice session is "my current work setting." The role-played client talks about his or her current work setting while the interviewer demonstrates attending skills. Other possible topics for the session include:

A job I had in the past that I liked, and one I didn't like

Attitudes and experiences in school

Thoughts about current political or social situations

Favorite books or hobbies

The topics and role-plays are most effective if you talk about something real for you. You will also find it helpful if the entire group works on the same topic. In that way you can compare styles and learn from one another more easily.

While the interviewer and interviewee plan, the two observers should review the feedback sheets and plan their own practice session to follow.

## Step 5. Conduct a three-minute practice session using attending skills.
The interviewer practices the skills of attending, the client talks about the current work setting or other selected topic, and the two observers complete the feedback sheets. Do not go beyond three minutes. If possible, record the interview.

---

[2]The importance of planning as part of microskills practice was brought to my attention by Kevin Heath, Health Commission of South Australia. Heath suggests that it is essential to think through what we will do *before* we do it. Then, after having attempted the task, we must evaluate and review whether we did what we said we would do (see Step 6).

**Step 6. Review the practice session and provide feedback to the interviewer for 12 minutes.**    As a first step in feedback, the role-played client will often want to give her or his impressions of the session. This may be followed by interviewer self-assessment and comments by the two observers. As part of the review, ask yourselves the key question, "Did the interviewer achieve his or her own planning objective?" This is critical for assessing the level of mastery obtained.

In reviewing the audio- or videotapes of the interview, *start and stop the tape periodically*. Replay key interactions. Only in this way can you gain the full value of recording media.

Note both verbal and nonverbal behaviors and their varied impressions on the client and the observers.

Giving useful, specific feedback is particularly critical. Note suggestions for feedback in Box 2-2.

**Step 7. Rotate roles.**    Everyone should have a chance to serve as interviewer, role-played client, and observer. Divide time equally!

**Some general reminders.**    It is not necessary to have a complete interview in three minutes. Behave as if you expected the session to last a longer time. The timer can break in after three minutes. The purpose of the role-play sessions is to observe skills in action. Thus, you should attempt to practice skills, not solve problems. Clients often took years to develop their interests and concerns, so do not expect to solve their problems in a three-minute role-play session. Written feedback, if carefully done, is an invaluable part of a program of interview skill development.

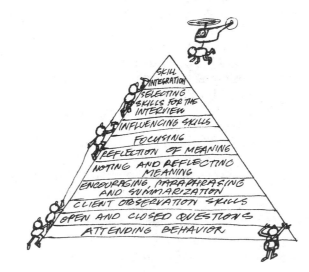

**Box 2-2  Guidelines for effective feedback**

To see ourselves as others see us,
To hear how others hear us,
And to be touched as we touch others . . .
These are the goals of effective feedback.

Feedback is one of the skill units of the basic attending and influencing skills program; it is discussed in more detail in Chapter 9. However, if you are to help others grow and develop in this program, you must provide feedback to them now on their use of the skills in practice sessions.

Some guidelines for effective feedback include:

▲ *The person receiving feedback should be in charge.* Let the interviewer in practice sessions determine how much or how little feedback is provided.

▲ *Feedback should focus on strengths*, particularly in the early phases of the program. If negative feedback is requested by the interviewer, add positive dimensions as well. People grow from strength, not from weakness. Feedback should be helpful, not harmful.

▲ *Feedback should be concrete and specific.* Not "your attending skills were good," but "you maintained eye contact throughout; however, you broke eye contact once when the client seemed uncomfortable." Make your feedback factual, specific, and observable.

▲ *Feedback should be relatively nonjudgmental.* Feedback often turns into evaluation. Stick to the facts and specifics. Though the word *relatively* recognizes that judgment inevitably will appear in many types of feedback, the nonjudgmental attitude often expressed in vocal qualities should appear in other skills of interviewing as well. Avoid the words "good" and "bad" and their variations.

▲ *Feedback should be lean and precise.* It does little good to suggest that a person change 15 things. Select one to three things the interviewer might actually be able to change in a short time. You'll have opportunities to make other suggestions later.

## ATTENDING BEHAVIOR FEEDBACK SHEET

_____ (Date)

_____     _____
(Name of Interviewer)                (Name of Person Completing Form)

_____

*Instructions:* Provide written feedback that is specific and observable,
nonjudgmental, and supportive.

_____

1. *Eye contact*   Facilitative? Staring? Avoiding? Specific feedback? At
   what points, if any, did the interviewer break contact? Eye contact
   breaks may be facilitative or disruptive.

2. *Body language*   Trunk lean? Gestures? Facial expression? At what
   points, if any, did the interviewer shift the trunk or make a marked
   change in body language? Number of facilitative body language
   movements?

3. *Vocal qualities*   Summarize here your impression of vocal tone, speech
   rate, volume, and accent. Again, are there points where any of these
   changed in response to client actions? Number of major changes or
   speech hesitations?

4. *Verbal tracking and selective attention*   Was the interviewer able to
   stay on the client's topics? If shifts occurred, what specific topics
   seemed to be indicators of interviewer interest patterns? Did the
   interviewer demonstrate any patterns of selective attention in selecting one item rather than another? Number of major topic jumps?

5. *Cite specific positive aspects of the interview*

*SELF-ASSESSMENT AND FOLLOW-UP*

The purpose of this section is to encourage you to examine your own patterns of attending. Special attention will be given to your level of mastery of attending. The mastery levels may prompt additional suggestions for practice in this basic skill.

**1. What one single idea stood out for you from all those presented in this chapter?**

_____

_____

_____

**2. What is your natural style of attending?** Are you able to understand a problem or concern from the other person's point of view, or do you typically try very early to provide an answer or solve a problem? What are your natural nonverbal styles of attending?

_____

_____

_____

_____

_____

_____

**3. To what topics are you most likely to attend easily?** What topics do you find more difficult? What topics might you overemphasize?

_____

_____

_____

_____

**4. Mastery of attending skills.** Attending behavior may be identified as having four levels of mastery—identification, basic mastery, active mastery, and teaching mastery. Indicate the competencies you have mastered below. Those you find more difficult, you may wish to practice for further mastery. In each

case on the lines provided give brief and specific evidence that you have mastered the competency.

**Identification.**   You will be able to identify and count eye contact breaks, major shifts in body posture, patterns of vocal qualities, and major topic jumps in the interview on the part of counselor and client. You will be able to demonstrate beginning awareness of cultural differences on these dimensions.

———   Ability to identify the presence and absence of attending behavior on the part of an interviewer.

_____

_____

———   Ability to write attending and nonattending statements.

_____

_____

———   Identification, through observation, of specific individual and cultural differences in attending styles of clients and other people.

_____

_____

**Basic mastery.**   You will be able to demonstrate basic attending skills in the interview. You will be able to maintain culturally appropriate eye contact, body language, and vocal tone. In particular, you will be able to stay on the client's topic rather than introducing a new topic of your own. Your talk-time will be reduced while the client's increases.

———   Ability to demonstrate culturally appropriate eye contact, body language, vocal qualities, and verbal tracking.

_____

_____

———   Ability to increase client talk-time while reducing your own.

_____

_____

———   Ability to stay on a client's topic without introducing any new topics of your own.

_____

_____

**Active Mastery.**   You will be able to use attending skills intentionally to facilitate client talk or to discourage it. You will be able to encourage clients to talk about specific topics and issues through selective attention. The effectiveness of your skill usage is measured by what your client does, not by your behavior.

_____ Through inattention, topic changes, and nonverbal behavior, assisting clients to talk about topics that are more productive and growth producing.

_____

_____

_____ Increased awareness of the client's patterns of attending. What topics does the client attend to or ignore?

_____

_____

_____ Modifying your own patterns of attending to establish rapport with an individual of a different style, background, or culture. Eye contact is not always appropriate!

_____

_____

_____ Your own additional definition of mastery of attending skills.

_____

_____

**Teaching mastery.**   The ability to teach attending to others may be defined as the highest level of mastery. The effectiveness of your teaching can be measured by your students' ability to achieve identification, basic mastery, and active mastery levels of competence. Ideas for teaching attending behavior are outlined in the final chapter of this book.

_____

_____

**5. Read the story "Becoming a Samurai Swordsman" (page 37).**   How does this story and its concepts relate to your own experience of learning single skills of the interview?

_____

_____

_____

_____

_____

**6. Given your experience with attending behavior, what one personal goal might you set for yourself in the future?**

_____

_____

_____

_____

## BECOMING A SAMURAI SWORDSMAN[3]

 Japanese master swordsmen learn their skills through a complex set of highly detailed training exercises. The process of masterful swordsmanship is broken down into specific components studied carefully, one at a time. In this process of mastery the naturally skilled person often suffers and finds handling the sword awkward. The skilled individual may even find his performance dropping during the practice of single skills. _Being aware of what one is doing can interfere with coordination and smoothness._

Once the individual skills are practiced and learned to perfection, the Samurai retire to a mountaintop to meditate. They deliberately forget about what they have learned. When they return, they find that the distinct skills have naturally been integrated into their style or way of being. The Samurai then seldom have to think about skills at all. They have become Samurai swordsmen.

The same holds true for ballet, tennis, golf, cooking, and many other activities of life. Rehearsal and practice of basic skills builds mastery, which later becomes integrated into our own natural style. The new, unique whole is often larger than the sum of the distinct parts.

You likely found discomfort in practicing the single skills of attending. Later you'll find the same problem with other skills. This happens to both the beginner and the advanced counselor. Improving and studying our natural skills often results in a temporary and sometimes frustrating drop in performance just as it does when we learn single skills like the Samurai.

_____

[3] I am indebted to Lanette Shizuru, University of Hawaii, for the example of the Samurai Swordsman.

Consider driving. When you first sat at the wheel, you had to coordinate many tasks, particularly if you drove a car with a shift lever. The clutch, the gas pedal, the steering wheel, and the gear ratios had to be coordinated smoothly with what you saw through the windshield. When you gave primary attention to the process of shifting, you might have lost sight of where you were going.

But practice and experience soon led you to forget the specific skills, and you were able to coordinate them automatically and give full attention to the world beyond the windshield. The mastery of single skills led you to achieve your objectives.

**3**

# Questions: Opening Communication

---

### How can questions help you and your clients?

*Major Function*

If you use open questions effectively, you can expect the client to talk more freely and openly. Closed questions will elicit shorter responses and provide you with information and specifics.

Like attending behavior, questions may encourage or discourage client talk. With questions, however, the stimulus comes more from the interviewer. The client is often talking from your frame of reference.

*Secondary Functions*

Knowledge and skill in questioning results in:

▲ Bringing out additional specifics of the client's world.
▲ Effective diagnosis of a client's concern or issue.
▲ Determining the manner in which a client talks about an issue. For example, *what* questions often lead to talk about facts, *how* questions to feelings or process, and *why* questions to reasons.
▲ The ability to open or close client talk according to the individual needs of the interview.

---

## INTRODUCTION

While attending and client observation form the foundation of the microskills hierarchy, it is helpful to learn questioning skills before attempting the more complex client observation skills. Questions help an interview begin and move along smoothly. They open new areas for discussion, assist in pinpointing and clarifying issues, and aid in client self-exploration. However, some theorists do not like questions and suggest that the interviewer never ask them. Your central task in this chapter is to examine this skill and to determine where you stand on the issue of questions in the interview.

Why do some people object to questions? Take a minute to recall and explore some of your own experiences with questions in the past. Perhaps you had a teacher or a parent who used questions in a certain manner that resulted in your feeling a particular way. Write below one of your own negative experiences with questions and the feelings and thoughts the questioning process brought out in you.

My experience with questions was: _____

_____

_____

_____

The thoughts and feelings this experience brought out in me were:

_____

_____

_____

Many people respond to this exercise with situations where they were "put on the spot" and "grilled" by someone else. They may associate questions with anger and guilt. Many of us have had negative experiences with questions. Furthermore, questions may be used to direct and control client talk. If your objective is to enable clients to truly find their own way, questions may slow that process, particularly if they are used ineffectively. It is for these reasons that some authorities, particularly in the humanistic orientation to helping, object to questions in the interview. In addition, in many non-Western cultures, questions are inappropriate and may be rude and intrusive.

Nevertheless, questions remain a fact of life in our culture. We encounter them everywhere. The physician or nurse, the salesperson, the government official, and many others find questioning clients basic to their profession. Most counseling theories use questions extensively. The issue, then, is using questions wisely and intentionally. The goal of this section is to explore some aspects of questions and to provide you with an opportunity to examine their properties and, eventually, to determine their place in your communication skill repertoire.

The basic focus of this questioning skill unit is on open and closed questions:

**Open questions** are those that can't be answered in a few short words. They encourage others to talk and provide you with maximum information. Typically, open questions begin with *what, how, why,* or *could*. An example is "Could you tell me what brings you here today?"

**Closed questions** can be answered with a few short words or sentences. They have the advantage of focusing the interview and obtaining information, but the burden of talk remains with the interviewer. Closed questions often begin with *is, are, do*. An example is "Are you living with your family?"

## EXAMPLE INTERVIEWS

 In the following examples we see counseling skills used in management. In the first example the manager uses closed questions almost exclusively to achieve his objective; in a contrasting example he uses open questions to achieve a different objective. The open questions are used to clarify the situation and assist the other person to resolve her own problems.

### CLOSED QUESTION EXAMPLE

*Don:* Hi, Suzie. What's up?

*Suzie:* Well, I'm having a problem with Jo again.

*Don:* Is she arguing with people again?

*Suzie:* Yes, she's having a difficult time getting along with the other people.

*Don:* Does she get to work on time?

*Suzie:* She gets to work on time. That's not the problem. (Suzie appears somewhat frustrated and confused. Don is leaning forward, taking some of her space. Suzie, having experienced this type of behavior before, holds her own ground.)

*Don:* Does she try hard?

*Suzie:* She tries hard. That's not the problem.

*Don:* So, it's a personality problem?

*Suzie:* Yeah. (Said with some relief as Don has finally heard what she wanted him to hear. Don, however, is working much harder to get that information than is really necessary.)

*Don:* Does she get along with Jane?

*Suzie:* Well, some of the time. I mean, not really . . . ah . . . I mean, everybody has a hard time with Jane.

*Don:* Do you get along . . . how about Sam?

*Suzie:* Not really anybody. Anytime she has to do something for some-body else she, you know, she can't follow through, she has a hard time.

*Don:* Does she follow your orders?

*Suzie:* (Surprised) Not my orders as much as I'd like . . .

*Don:* Are you being clear when you give her orders, Suzie?

*Suzie:* . . . I try to be . . . I . . .

*Don:* Sometimes you're pretty vague.

*Suzie:* Probably that's right. I expect her to . . . you're right . . . I prob-ably expect her to do things on her own a little bit more than she's able. She needs more direction . . . (Don is playing the game of "Who's got the monkey?" Rather than take time to search out via open ques-tions what is really happening, he uses closed questions to validate his own prior assumptions and is placing the blame, or "monkey," with Suzie. While this may often be effective, it doesn't allow Suzie much room.)

*Don:* Do you think you maybe need to be a little bit more clear?

*Suzie:* Probably, but I wonder if she has a hard time hearing people. I often wonder if she misses things.

*Don:* Sounds like you need to give her clearer orders. Do you think *you* can do that?

*Suzie:* I think so . . .

Comment: Closed questions are helpful in obtaining specifics. This example should not deter you from their use. Overuse of closed ques-tions, however, is a distinct problem in many supervisory and counsel-ing interviews.

## OPEN QUESTION EXAMPLE

*Don:* Hi, Suzie, what's up?

*Suzie:* Hi, Don. I'm having a problem with Jo—you know, the woman I hired this fall to work for me. (Attending behavior serves as a solid foundation for this interview. Suzie is more relaxed and attentive her-self. Throughout the session there is an atmosphere of respect and ease between the interviewer and the interviewee.)

*Don:* Oh, yeah. Could you tell me generally what's been going on? (An open question beginning with the maximally open *could*.)

*Suzie:* Well, Jo's been just having a hard time working with everybody, everybody on our staff. You know . . . she'll often interrupt them. Jo talks incessantly and, you know, takes a lot of time. People are very busy and have to stop and listen to her. And, to give her instructions, I have to do it over and over again. Then *I* have to listen to what she has to say about something. It's taking a great deal of time, and people find it offensive.

*Don:* How do you feel about her, Suzie? (Open question dealing with feelings beginning with *how*.)

*Suzie:* Well, she's a nice woman and she means well, but I have a hard time listening to her. She's just . . . she seems to talk so much about everything, and it's difficult. I don't have all that much time, too, you know, and I have to keep moving. I have lots to do and don't have time to sit and listen to her all the time.

*Don:* Repeating the question, Suzie, how do you feel about her? I do hear you think *she* is nice. (Don has a prior solid relationship with Suzie and so can force the issue a bit more. Suzie and he both know she often avoids talking about her feelings. Feelings can be important in determining action. Without a solid relationship this string of questions would be too intrusive.)

*Suzie:* She's just hard to work with. She makes me feel a bit sad and even angry. She means well, though, but I have a hard time relating to her. I have a hard time liking her, too, because she's so intrusive.

*Don:* Uh-huh.

*Suzie:* Also, her voice is very difficult to listen to.

*Don:* Why do you think she does this? (*Why* questions tend to bring out reasons and interpretations of the situation. However, *why* often puts people on the defensive, and many authorities argue against *why* questions. How often did your parents ask you the same question?)

*Suzie:* I think she probably wants to do a good job, and she has a need to control. At the same time, she wants to be in charge and therefore seems to want to direct and talk to people all the time. I think she's going to go about getting her way no matter what, even if it means talking to everybody until they are absolutely sick of her . . . and then, finally, she gets her way.

*Don:* So far, Suzie, I've heard you say that you're having trouble with Jo and that it's kind of an ongoing problem.

*Suzie:* Uh-huh.

*Don:* Ah . . . it seems to be that one of the important things is that she isn't getting along too well with others. She talks a lot and is intrusive. At the same time, you feel angry with her, particularly her intrusiveness. You have a hard time liking her. I gather that you feel she needs to control. Am I hearing you accurately so far? (This is a *summarization*, a skill that is discussed in more detail in Chapter 4. Questions bring out considerable data, and you will find it helpful if you summarize what you are hearing from time to time. The closed question at the end is a *perception check or check-out*. This is an important aspect of the interview. In the microskills system, this provides room for the client or other person to react to what you have said. It is a way of sharing ownership of the interview.)

*Suzie:* Yes, that's exactly accurate. (She smiles.)

*Don:* Now, maybe it would help if you could give a very specific example. Could you give me a specific example of one situation where she caused this type of conflict? (To this point Suzie has talked in generalities about Jo. Asking the client for a specific example is an important interviewer skill. It brings concreteness to the interview. The phrase *hard time*, for example, means different things to different people. But when we get a concrete description of observable behavior, we have something both interviewer and counselee can agree to. The question "Could you give me a specific example of . . . ?" may be the most useful skill of this entire book.)

*Suzie:* Okay, she was assigned work with the R and D department, in which she had to do some purchase plans with the supervisor. She had her own ideas for the project. She wanted to change the design of the form while the R and D super wanted quicker feedback from us. I suppose Jo had a good idea, but she ended up arguing with the super and caused a lot of dissension between the two groups. Sure, we need the new form, but we also need to get along with R and D. And . . . she didn't schedule the appointment either. You know, Bill, the R and D super, wants the status treatment. Jo thinks that's foolish, and she insists on doing it her way.

Comment: This interview illustrates the use of just a few open questions. Extensive data comes in a relatively short time. Note that the responsibility rests with the client in this session and with the supervisor in the closed question session. Client talk-time is higher with open questions.

## INSTRUCTIONAL READING

Clients come to the interview seeking to say something about their interests and concerns. If it is an employment interview, they want to talk about their positive assets and make a good impression. In many sales, management, or medical situations, the client wants to express ideas clearly and concisely so that help may be obtained for some problem or need. Clients in counseling and therapy want to express themselves also, but they sometimes find it difficult.

In all these diverse situations skill with open and closed questions can facilitate client self-disclosure and enable interviews to achieve their objectives more completely. At the same time, a barrage of probing, insensitive questions may put the client on guard and impede open communication. Several basic points about open and closed questions are noted below:

### 1. Questions help begin the interview.

With verbal clients the open question facilitates free discussion and leaves plenty of room to talk. Some examples include:

"What would you like to talk about today?"

"Could you tell me what you'd like to see me about?"

"How have things been since we last talked together?"

"The last time we met we talked about your tension while watching the baseball game. How did it go this week?"

The first three open questions provide considerable room in that the client can talk about virtually anything. The last question is open but provides some focus for the session, building on material from the preceding week.

Such open questions may be more than a nontalkative client can handle. In such cases a gentle series of closed questions—"Did you go to the baseball game last week?" "Who won?" "Were you tense once again?" and the like—may provide structure for the interview. These can be followed by more open questions as the client begins to talk more freely.

## 2. Open questions help elaborate and enrich the interview.

A beginning interviewer often asks one or two questions and then wonders what to do next. Even more experienced interviewers at times find themselves hard-put to know what to do. An open question on some topic the client presented earlier in the interview helps the session start again and keep moving:

"Could you tell me more about that?"

"How did you feel when that happened?"

"Given what you've said, what would be your ideal solution to the problem?"

## 3. Questions help bring out concrete specifics of the client's world.

If there is one single open question that appears to be useful in most theoretical persuasions or in most practice situations, it is the open question that aims for concreteness and specifics in the client's situation. Again, the model question "Could you give me a specific example?" is the most useful open question available to any interviewer. Many clients tend to talk in vague generalities, and specific, concrete examples enrich the interview and provide data for action. Some additional open questions that aim for concreteness and specifics are illustrated below:

*Client:* George makes me so mad.

*Counselor:* Could you give me a specific example of what George does? *or*

What does George do specifically that brings out your anger? *or*
What do you mean by "makes me mad"? *or*

Could you specify what you do before and after George brings about the angry reaction?

Closed questions, of course, can bring out specifics as well, but they place more responsibility on the interviewer. However, if the interviewer knows specifically the desired direction of the interview, closed questions such as "Did George show his anger again by striking you?" "Does George tease you often?" "Is George on drugs?" and so on may prove invaluable. Yet even well-directed closed questions may take the initiative away from the client.

## 4. Questions are critical in diagnosis and assessment of a problem.

Physicians must diagnose their client's physical symptoms. Managers may have to diagnose a problem on a production line. Vocational counselors wish to diagnose a client's vocational history. Questions are the meat of effective diagnosis. George Kelly, the personality theorist, has suggested for general client problem diagnosis the following set of questions, which roughly follow the *who, what, when, where, how, why* of newspaper reporters:

*Who* is the client? What is the client's personal background? Who else may be involved?

*What* is the client's problem? What is happening? What are the specific details of the situation?

*When* does the problem occur? When did it begin? What immediately preceded the occurrence of the problem?

*Where* does the problem occur? In what environments and situations?

*How* does the client react to the problem? How does the client feel about it?

*Why* does the problem occur?

Needless to say, the *who, what, when, where, how, why?* series of questions also provides the interviewer with a ready system for helping the client elaborate or be more specific on an issue at any time during a session.

## 5. The first word of certain open questions partially determines client verbalizations.

Often, but not always, key question stems result in predictable outcomes.

*What* questions most often lead to facts. "What happened?" "What are you going to do?"

*How* questions often lead to discussion about processes or sequences or to feelings. "How could that be explained?" "How do you feel about that?"

*Why* questions most often lead to discussion of reasons. "Why did you allow that to happen?" "Why do you think that is so?"

*Could* questions are considered maximally open and contain some of the advantages of closed questions in that the client is free to say "No, I don't want to talk about that." *Could* questions contain less control and command than others. "Could you tell me more about your situation?" "Could you give me a specific example?" "Could you tell me what you'd like to talk about today?"

## 6. Some additional problems with questions.

While questions can have immense value in the interview, we must not forget their potential problems. Among their problems are the following:

*Bombardment/grilling.* Too many questions will tend to put many clients on the defensive. They may give too much control to the interviewer.

*Multiple questions.* Interviewers may confuse their clients by throwing out several questions at once. This is another form of bombardment, although at times it may be helpful to some clients.

*Questions as statements.* Some interviewers may use questions as a way to sell their own point of view. "Don't you think it would be more helpful if you studied more?" "What do you think of trying relaxation exercises instead of what you are doing now?" This form of question, just like multiple questions, can be helpful at times. Awareness of the nature of the question, however, may suggest alternative and more direct routes toward reaching the client. If you are going to make a statement, it is best not to frame it as a question.

*Questions and cultural differences.* The rapid-fire questioning style of this culture is often received less favorably in non-Western groups. If you are working with a person of a different cultural group in this country, excessive use of questions sometimes results in distrust of the counselor.

*Why questions.* Most of us experienced some form of "Why did you do that?" as children. *Why* questions often put interviewees on the defensive and cause discomfort. This same discomfort can be produced by any question that produces a sense of being grilled.

*Questions and control.* The person who asks the questions is usually in control of the interview. He or she is determining who talks about what, when the talk will occur, and under what conditions it will occur. At times, questions can be helpful in bringing out-of-control

**Box 3-1 Key points**

*Why?*

Questions help begin the interview, open new areas for discussion, assist in pinpointing and clarifying issues, and assist the client in self-exploration.

*What?*

Questions can be described as open or closed:

*Open questions* are those that can't be answered in a few short words. They encourage others to talk and provide you with maximum information. Typically, open questions begin with *why*, *how*, or *could*. One of the most helpful of all open questions is "Could you give me a specific example of . . . ?"

*Closed questions* are those that can be answered in a few short words or sentences. They have the advantage of focusing the interview and bringing out specifics, but they place the prime responsibility for talk on the interviewer. Closed questions often begin with *is*, *are*, or *do*. An example is "Where do you live?"

It is important to note that a question, open or closed, on a topic of deep interest to the client will often result in extensive talk-time *if* it is interesting enough and important enough. If an interview is flowing well, the distinction between open and closed questions is less important.

*How?*

A general framework for diagnosis and question asking is provided by the newspaper reporter framework of *who, what, when, where, how, why?*

*Who* is the client? What are key personal background factors? Who else is involved?

*What* is the problem? What are the specific details of the situation?

*When* does the problem occur? What immediately preceded and followed the situation?

*Where* does the problem occur? In what environments and situations?

*How* does the client react? How does he or she feel about it?

*Why* does the problem occur?

**Box 3-1 continued**

|  |  |
|---|---|
|  | Interviewing is about more than problems. The same set of questions could be asked to discover what events and issues surround a positive situation or accomplishment. Too much of interviewing training emphasizes problems and difficulties. A positive approach is needed for balance. |
| *With whom?* | Questions may turn off some clients. Some cultural groups find North American rapid-fire questions rude and intrusive. Yet questions are very much part of our culture and provide a way to obtain information that most clients find helpful. |
| *And?* | The first word of open questions often leads to a variety of results. For example, *what* questions often lead to facts, *how* to feelings and process, *why* to reasons. *Could* is often the most open: "Could you tell me more?" "Could you give me an example?" |

interviews under control and direction. At the same time questions can be used unfairly and intrusively for the interviewer's gain rather than the client's.

**7. A final word on interviewing comfort and pace.**

Questions, used effectively, can help the counselor or interviewer pace the session. If a client finds him- or herself revealing too much and the counselor senses this discomfort, a series of closed questions can help the client slow down and regain composure. Similarly, open questions can provide room for the client to open up and explore things in more depth. The skilled, intentional use of questioning can help produce an interview that meets the client's needs and wishes.

## PRACTICE EXERCISES AND SELF-ASSESSMENT

How are you going to use questions in your own interviewing practice? The following exercises are designed to increase your mastery of questioning skills and to encourage you to decide if and how you want to use questions.

*INDIVIDUAL PRACTICE*

### Exercise 1. Which of the following questions are open? Closed?

Open Closed

_____ _____ Do you come here often?

_____ _____ Where does your daughter live?

_____ _____ Do you get along with Joe?

_____ _____ What important things have happened during the week?

_____ _____ Could you tell me more about your family?

_____ _____ How do you imagine she feels about that?

_____ _____ Why do you think Harry quit his job?

### Exercise 2. Writing questions that may be expected to impact client talk.

A client tells you the following:

My check is lost. I think I left it on the bureau, but I looked there, and it is still gone. I worry that my son might have taken it and used it for drugs.

Write below open questions that will tend to bring about general information, specific facts, feelings, and reasons.

Could _____?

What _____?

How _____?

Why _____?

Now, generate three closed questions that might bring out some specifics of the situation.

Do _____?

Are _____?

Where _____?

Finally, what questions might be used to get specific examples and details that might enlarge and make the problem more concrete?

_____?

_____?

### Exercise 3. Observation of questions in your daily interactions.

This chapter has talked about the basic question stems, *what, how, why,* and *could,* and how clients respond differently to each. During a conversation with a friend or acquaintance try sequentially these four basic question stems:

*Could* you tell me generally what happened?

*What* are the critical facts?

*How* do you feel about the situation?

*Why* do you think it happened?

Record your observations below. Were the predictions of the book correct?

_____

_____

_____

_____

_____

_____

_____

_____

## SYSTEMATIC GROUP PRACTICE

Two systematic exercises are suggested for practice with questions. The first focuses on the use of open and closed questions, the second on diagnosis of a client's concern or problem. The instructional steps for practice are abbreviated from those described in Chapter 2 on attending behavior. As necessary, refer to those instructions for more details on the steps leading toward systematic practice.

**Exercise 1. Systematic group practice on open and closed questions.**

**Step 1. Divide into practice groups.**

**Step 2. Select a group leader.**

**Step 3. Assign roles for the first practice session.**

Role-played client
Interviewer
Observer I
Observer II, who runs equipment and keeps time

**Step 4. Planning.** The observer should plan to use both open and closed questions. It is important in the practice session that the key what, how, why and could questions are used.

In active mastery, planning should include efforts to produce specific client results as indicated in the active mastery list of competencies.

The suggested topic for this role-play is a real situation in which the client did something he or she felt good about. To repeat an important point, counseling and interviewing are too often focused on negative behaviors and problems. Some time given to assets in the interview will provide an opportunity to balance negative thinking.

Suggested alternative topics include:

A friend or family member who does something well.

A problem I find interesting and stimulating.

A positive addiction I have (such as jogging, health food, biking, team sports).

Observers should take this time to examine feedback forms and to plan their own sessions.

**Step 5. Conduct a three-minute practice session using only questions.** The interviewer should practice open and closed questions and may wish to have handy a list of suggested question stems (*could, what, how, why*). The client should be relatively cooperative and talkative, but not respond at such great length that the interviewer has only a limited opportunity to ask questions.

**Step 6. Review the practice session and provide feedback to the interviewer for 12 minutes.** Be sure to use the feedback forms (page 57) to ensure that the interviewer's questions have been recorded accurately. Feedback on impressions is not nearly as valuable as feedback on specific, observable data. The interviewer should examine performance— was he or she able to achieve planned objectives?

Remember to stop the audio- or videotape periodically and listen to or view key happenings several times for increased clarity. Generally speaking, it is wise to provide some feedback before reviewing the tape, but this sometimes results in a failure to view or listen to the tape at all!

**Step 7. Rotate roles.**

**A reminder.** The question "Could you give me a specific example?" tends to be one of the most helpful of all questions as it helps the client or other person become much more specific and concrete. Too much interviewing works in broad generalities rather than in behavioral specifics understandable to all. You will often find that this question changes your impression of the client and the client's problem in an important fashion.

### Exercise 2. Systematic practice in elementary assessment.

This exercise focuses on the use of the newspaper formula (*who, what, when, where, how,* and *why*) as a system for obtaining a basic summary of a client's problem or issue. The steps of the exercise are identical to the preceding series of seven steps. The same feedback form may be used.

An assessment interview will, of necessity, require more than three minutes. The broad questions of the newspaper formula will need amplification by more open and closed questions. The key question "Could you give me a specific example?" will often prove useful. As such, the assessment interview may run in practice session as long as 15 minutes or more.

Suggested topics for the assessment practice interview include:

Difficulty with a past or present academic course

Work problems, past or present

A past illness or experience with a family member who was ill

Views on alcohol, drugs, sexuality

### SELF-ASSESSMENT AND FOLLOW-UP

How do you feel and think about questions? The purpose of this section is to help you think through your position on questions and examine your level of mastery of questioning skills.

**1. Questions are a controversial skill in the helping professions. Do you want to use them at all? If so, how?**

_____

_____

_____

_____

_____

_____

_____

_____

**2. What is your position on the use of _why_ questions in the interview?**

_____

_____

_____

_____

**3. Mastery of questioning skills.**  What specific competencies have you mastered with questioning? Give evidence for each level of mastery in the space provided.

**Identification.**  You will be able to identify and classify open and closed questions and note the specific impact in the interview.

_____ Ability to classify questions as open or closed.

_____

_____

_____ Ability to note the impact of open and closed questions and specific question stems on clients and other persons.

_____

_____

**Basic mastery.**  You will be able to demonstrate the use of open and closed questions in a role-played interview and be able to use these questions deliberately in daily life.

_____ Demonstration of questions in a role-played interview.

_____

_____

_____ Demonstration of ability to use questions in daily life situation.

_____

_____

**Active mastery.**  You will be able to use questioning skills to achieve specific, demonstrable impact on client talk in the interview. At issue is what the client does in response to your questioning skills, not your use of skills.

Check below those skills you have demonstrated in a practice session or in your own interviewing. Use this list as a set of guidelines for future development of questioning skills. At this point, aim to produce a specific result from your verbal intervention. Evidence of your ability can be provided by audiotapes and/or written journal examples.

_____ Use of open questions to enable clients to bring out more data.

_____ Use of closed questions to close off and/or direct client talk to specifics.

_____ Use of *could* questions to bring out the general picture or a summary of a situation.

_____ Use of *what* questions to bring out facts and information.

_____ Use of *how* questions to enable clients to talk about feelings and/or process.

_____ Use of *why* questions to bring out reasons.

_____ Ability to assist clients to bring out specifics via the "Could you give me a specific example?" type of question.

_____ Use of the newspaper formula to bring out the basic facts of a client's problem for an elementary assessment.

_____ Use of questions to enable a client to talk about facts, then feelings, then facts again, thus providing a change of pace and demonstrating your ability to facilitate client talk in a variety of directions.

_____ Ability to start a client talking about a subject, then stop and move to another subject via questioning.

**Teaching mastery.**  The ability to teach questions to clients and other persons. The impact of your teaching will be measured by your students' achievement on the above criteria.

_____

_____

**4. Given your experience with questioning skills, what one single goal for increasing your mastery might you set for yourself at this point?**

_____

_____

_____

_____

_____

_____

## QUESTIONS FEEDBACK SHEET

_____ (Date)

_____     _____

(Name of Interviewer)       (Name of Person Completing Form)

_____

*Instructions:* List below the questions asked by the interviewer as completely as possible. At a minimum, indicate the first key
words of the question (*what, why, how, do, are,* and so on).
Indicate whether each question was open or closed.

_____

_____ open _____ closed  1. _____

_____ open _____ closed  2. _____

_____ open _____ closed  3. _____

_____ open _____ closed  4. _____

_____ open _____ closed  5. _____

_____ open _____ closed  6. _____

_____ open _____ closed  7. _____

_____ open _____ closed  8. _____

_____ open _____ closed  9. _____

_____ open _____ closed 10. _____

1. Which questions seemed to provide the most useful client information?

2. Provide specific feedback on the attending skills of the interviewer.

3. General impressions of the interview.

# CHAPTER 4

# Client Observation Skills

---

**How can client observation skills help you and your clients?**

*Major Function*  Client observation skills enable you, as an interviewer or counselor, to note and understand the client and how he or she thinks and behaves in relation to other people and situations. This understanding will help you to choose useful interviewing skills and counseling interventions to facilitate client growth and development.

*Secondary Functions*  Knowledge and skill in client observation results in increased ability to note:

▲ Client nonverbal behavior.
▲ Client verbal behavior.
▲ Client discrepancies, conflicts, and incongruities.

---

## INTRODUCTION

The skilled interviewer is concerned with assisting and understanding clients. It is important that you be able to observe client behaviors in your interviewing sessions. This chapter is concerned with sharpening your powers of observation. You will find the basic skills of attending and questioning useful in this process.

What should you observe about client behavior in the interview? From your own life experience you are already aware of many things that are important for a counselor or interviewer to notice about other people and clients. Brainstorm from what you already know and make a list below:

_____

_____

_____

_____

_____

_____

_____

_____

_____

_____

There is an almost infinite array of things you can observe about clients. How can you organize all these data in a meaningful way? Some organizing principles are necessary if we are to make sense out of the client's often confusing world. Psychological theories help us make sense of and organize our own understanding of client behavior. However, this chapter does not deal with theory. Rather, it presents three key underlying dimensions that will help you to understand the client's world *before* you start applying a formal theory or your own viewpoint to the client's situation.

Three organizing dimensions for understanding client behavior are stressed in this chapter.

▲ *Client nonverbal behavior.* Some authorities have claimed that 85% or more of client communication of meaning is nonverbal. Client eye contact patterns, body language, and vocal qualities should be observed. Supplementary information on body language will also be presented in this chapter.

▲ *Client verbal behavior.* Words form the basis of most interviewing and counseling sessions. Clients tend to focus on certain key words and constructs through selective attention and verbal tracking. It is important to note these key words and constructs as they often form patterns that provide the interviewer with important clues as to how the client understands and represents the world.

▲ *Client discrepancies.* Incongruities, mixed messages, contradictions, and conflict are often the reason clients come to the interview. Clients tend to come for help because of some discrepancy within themselves or in relation to someone or something else. Careful observation of client verbal and nonverbal behavior will provide the counselor or interviewer with extensive data on conflict and discrepancies in the client's world, and thus often provide a central focus for the session.

More information will be presented in this chapter than most readers will be able to use immediately. The concepts will be repeated and used throughout the remainder of this book to enable further practice.

You will now have an opportunity to read a transcript of the early stages of an interview where the counselor uses exclusively attending and questioning skills to bring about a basic discrepancy in a client. The task at this point is not to problem solve, but rather to understand where the client is "coming from," or how she or he views the world. Important here is observing key aspects of verbal and nonverbal communication.

## EXAMPLE INTERVIEW

Our task in examining the following interview is different from that in the preceding two chapters. There we examined interviewer behavior  with minimal attention on the client. In this session, at a community mental health center, a set of questions proposed by the interviewer will provide data for us to examine client response. As you read the transcript, give primary attention to the client. This interview has been edited extensively and condensed to provide the most examples.

*Jane:* You were saying that you are troubled by your relationship with your parents, that they aren't satisfied with your job or your relationship with Carol. I sense anger, frustration, and hurt. Could you tell me a little more about it?

*Ralph:* Yeah . . . It seems that they are always on me. Dad is a driver . . . uh . . . he's made a mint in sales. He thinks I should do as well as he did at the same age. (As Ralph talks, he looks at the floor, he sits in a slumped, dejected fashion, his speech is slow and deliberate. There is one speech hesitation. There are no gestures.)

*Jane:* Could you give me a specific example of where you and your father disagreed?

*Ralph:* Well, last night I was going to go out with Carol. We were going to go to the movies. He saw me backing the car out of the driveway and came running up. I can see the fire in his eyes. He started shouting, saying that I hadn't asked permission. And it just looked impossible, and I couldn't say anything. (Ralph looks up and talks more animatedly while discussing this concrete example. At the end, when he talks about his inability to say anything, his eyes drop, his face flushes, and his right hand clenches in a fist. Note that Ralph is using visual imagery in his statements "*saw* me backing . . .", "*see* the fire . . .", "looked impossible . . .").

*Jane:* So things *looked* impossible to you. How did you feel when that happened? What do you *visualize* was happening inside your gut? (Note that Jane has matched Ralph's visual imagery. She is now searching for feelings.)

*Ralph:* I *see* myself as *focusing* on tension, my *image* is of tight muscles, moving away. (Ralph closes his eyes, and his hands move to cover his stomach.)

*Jane:* You felt tense. What *perspective* or meaning does this have for you? What sense do you make out of it? (Jane is searching here for the meaning of the situation to Ralph.)

*Ralph:* I do want to please my father, but he makes it impossible for me to meet the *picture* he demands of me. I've got my own *image* of myself. (As Ralph talks, his right hand is tense and closed, his left hand open.)

*Jane:* So what I *see* is that you have been saying that the *pictures* you have of yourself and those of your father conflict. There seem to be different *perspectives* on what you are and want to be. (Jane points out the incongruity or discrepancy between the son's and the father's pictures of the situation. It is these discrepancies that provide data for the bulk of the interview.)

*Ralph:* Yeah . . . that *looks* right, the *picture* is fuzzy, but we sure do have different ideas of what I seem to *look like* and need. It gets to me. (At this point, Ralph seems a bit more relaxed, his eye contact is more frequently on the interviewer. His body is somewhat more congruent, although he is sitting toward the edge of the chair with his shoulders slightly hunched.)

Comment: So far in the interview you should be able to see, hear, and feel that a considerable amount of client data has been produced. Making sense of all those data is one skill of the successful interviewer or counselor. The conflict with the father is the major discrepancy that has been identified. While it may need further honing (for example, "Tell me more about your father" or "Describe some other interactions with him.") and exploration of feelings and meanings, a basic problem definition has been established. Ralph's key words (verbal descriptors) should also be noted. The father is described as a driver who made a mint in sales. Ralph's brief description of himself includes some important key words including *impossible, couldn't say anything*, and *moving away*. Key descriptive words used by clients usually indicate their understanding of a person or situation and may indicate the meaning the situation has to them. A task of the interviewer is to note the meaning behind the descriptors and help the client develop alternative meanings and actions.

*Jane:* It would help if you could describe a situation where you and your father were able to *see* each other *clearly* and perhaps had more feelings in tune with each other. (The interviewer is still within Ralph's visual imagery, but is adding feeling and auditory images or concepts as well. The search for a positive experience may reveal strengths in the client.)

*Ralph:* One thing Dad and I have been able to work together on is when we do something around the house, like paint or build a new closet. (Ralph talks with a little more animation, his body is more relaxed. No nonverbal discrepancies may be observed.)

*Jane: Looks and sounds* like you were able to do something. Tell me more about it. (Jane has matched Ralph's visual system and adds a secondary system of auditory listening to strengthen the impression. She has also picked up on the word *able*. Note that *able* is a contrast to the words *impossible* and *moving away* mentioned earlier as key descriptors.)

*Ralph:* For example, when we built the closet, I was able to meet my father's demands. In fact, it was fun . . . we both enjoyed the *appearance* of the end product. We were able to work together. (Ralph continues to appear more relaxed and evidences a slight smile.)

*Jane:* So, when you were working together with mutual goals, things went differently . . . it *looked* and *felt* good, it *sounds* to me. Remember that positive *feeling* and *image*. Now put it together with the feelings of inadequacy and impossibility you were talking about as you gave me the picture of the two of you driving out the driveway. What sense do you make of the two images?

*Ralph:* Hummmm . . . I *see* myself in one situation doing what Dad and I wanted to do together. It really *felt good*. But now it seems that he wants me to do everything he says. Yet he always stressed the importance of me "being my own man." It seems confusing and impossible. (Ralph starts slowly with a major speech hesitation. His shoulders hunch again, and his eyes squint. When he says *felt good*, he relaxes for a moment and smiles slightly. A tone of bitterness and frustration enters when he talks about being his own man and his feelings of confusion.)

*Jane:* What do those words *confusing* and *impossible* mean to you? (At this point, Jane is searching for the underlying deeper meanings of two key words.)

Comment: There are extensive data in this condensed interview even though it is very brief. The task of the beginning interviewer and counselor at the first stage is simply to note the data and organize it into verbal and nonverbal dimensions. Later, concepts of discrepancy, incongruity, and conflict can be added. There is always room for increased sophistication and awareness of the behavior of the client. Those verbal and nonverbal data give us specific suggestions as to when to open the interview further, to narrow or focus it, or even to change topic completely.

## INSTRUCTIONAL READING

Three central organizing principles for understanding client behavior are stressed in this chapter: nonverbal behavior, verbal behavior, and discrepancies or incongruities. Over time, considerable skill in drawing out and working with the client's view of the world can be gained. The material here is designed as a beginning in this direction toward client empathy.

### NONVERBAL BEHAVIOR

The central concepts of attending behavior are important to observe in clients. Clients may be expected to shift eye contact, exhibit bodily movement, and change vocal qualities when they are talking about top-

ics of varying levels of comfort to them. You may observe clients crossing their arms or legs when they want to close off a topic, rapid shifts of eye contact during periods of confusion, or increased stammering or speech hesitations on difficult topics. This chapter includes a nonverbal behavior observation form that you may use to increase your awareness of these and other factors.

Facial behavior is particularly important to observe. The eyebrows may furrow, lips may tighten or loosen, flushing may occur, a client may smile at an inappropriate time. Even more careful observation will reveal subtle color changes in the face as blood flow changes with emotional reactions. Breathing may change or stop temporarily. The lips may swell, and pupils may dilate or contract. These seemingly small behaviors are important clues as to what a client is experiencing. To notice them takes work and practice beyond general understanding of nonverbal communication.

Particularly important are discrepancies in nonverbal behavior. When a client is talking casually about a friend, for example, one hand may be tightly clenched in a fist and the other relaxed and open, possibly indicating mixed feelings toward the friend.

Dramatic and interesting patterns of movement exist between people. It is useful to observe the degree of harmony of movement with others. Often people who are communicating well will mirror each other's body language. They both may sit in identical positions and even make complex hand movements together, as if in a ballet. This is termed *movement synchrony*. The movements may not be identical, but still be in harmony in *movement complimentarity*. For instance, one person talks, and the other person nods in agreement. You may observe a hand movement at the end of one person's statement that is answered by a related hand movement as the other takes "the conversational ball" and starts talking.

Needless to say, patterns of *movement dissynchrony* should also be observed. Lack of harmony in movement may often be observed in people who disagree markedly or even have subtle conflicts they may not be aware of. You as interviewer will want to observe your degree of bodily harmony with your clients. How do your movements relate to theirs? *Discreetly* but deliberately assuming their posture and some of their movements may help you to become more in touch with their experience.

## *VERBAL BEHAVIOR*

 Many clients will demonstrate problems of verbal tracking and selective attention. They may either stay on a single topic to the exclusion of other important issues or change the topic subtly or abruptly when they want to avoid talking about a difficult issue. Perhaps the most difficult task of the beginning counselor or interviewer is to assist the client in staying on the topic without being overcontrolling. Observing client changes in topic is particularly important. At times, it may be helpful to comment, for instance, "A few minutes ago we were talking about *X*, which seems important, and now we are talking about the weather. Would you please tell me more about *X*?" Another possibility is to make the same observation and to ask how the client might explain the shift in topic.

Clients often have key words or sentences you may note as particularly important. These sentences may be stated rather clearly and take the form of "I statements" (for example, "I am depressed." "I am pregnant." "I can't get along with Bob."). "I statements" may be implicit and/or confused ("I don't know what's wrong with me." "I feel lost, I don't know what to say."). The task of the interviewer in both cases is to note key sentences and to help clients explore the facts and concrete specifics of the situation, the way the client feels about them, and what they mean to the client. For example:

*Client:* I'm having a terrible time getting along on the production line. I can't make my quota, and the foreman is pushing me. I'm afraid I'll be fired.

*Counselor:* (Searching for more facts underlying the key sentence) Could you tell me *specifically* what the foreman said to you?

(Listening for feelings about the situation) How do you feel toward the foreman?

(Determining meaning to the client) And what does this all mean to you personally?

If you listen carefully to clients, you will find that certain words appear again and again in their description of situations. Noting these key words and helping the client explore the facts, feelings, and meanings underlying these words may be useful. Key descriptive words are often the constructs by which a client organizes the world and may relate to underlying meanings. *Verbal underlining* through vocal emphasis is a most helpful aid in determining what is most important to a client. Through vocal intonation and volume clients tend to stress single words or phrases that are most important to them.

## STYLES OF PERCEIVING THE WORLD

Finally, clients have individual ways of receiving information from the world. Some of us obtain our data primarily through visual means—we need to "see the situation." Others may be mainly auditory and "hear what is happening." Still others are kinesthetic and need physical representations before full understanding is gained—they may need to "feel out the situation." You will find it helpful to note the words used by your client and to match your language to facilitate expression. Some example words follow:

| *Visual* | *Auditory* | *Kinesthetic* |
|---|---|---|
| see | hear | feel |
| perceive | sounds | touch |
| view | in tune | wrap around |
| visualize | harmony | let's dance |
| imagine | that rings a bell | swinging |
| draw a picture | dissonant | blow away |
| flat | sharp | sharp |
| dull | flat | that grabs me |
| flaming | noisy | cool |
| sunny | quiet | warm |

In addition, some people may use taste words ("A sweet person") or olfactory words ("that smells wrong").

The concept of individual verbal style is rooted in a long tradition of education that children have different learning styles. Some children learn to read best by looking at words, others by sounding them out, and some by touching cloth cut-outs of words and letters. Apparently, these learning styles remain in adult life and are illustrated in language usage. Many people have mixed styles, however, and such concepts cannot be relied on consistently. With some experimentation you will find that matching language systems with the client truly helps the development of rapport and understanding. However, to make your counseling interventions successful, you will find it often helps if you use all modalities rather than just the client's prime language system. For example, "Can you *picture* an ideal outcome to your problem? How would it *feel*? What would it *sound* like?"[1]

Recently, it has been discovered that eye movements roughly correspond to perception systems. See Box 4-1 for an illustrative summary. (For more information on these perception concepts, see Lankton, 1980).

## DISCREPANCIES

The variety of discrepancies clients may manifest is perhaps best illustrated by the following statements:

"My son is perfect, but he just doesn't respect me."

"I really love my brother." (Said in a quiet tone with averted eyes)

"I can't get along with Charlie."

"I deserve to pass the course." (From a student who has done no homework and just failed the final examination)

"That question doesn't bother me." (With a flushed face and a closed fist)

Once the client is relatively comfortable and some beginning steps have been made toward rapport and understanding, a major task of the counselor or interviewer is to identify basic discrepancies, mixed messages, conflicts, or incongruities in the client's behavior and life. A common goal in most interviews, counseling, and therapy is to assist clients in working through discrepancies and conflict, but first these have to be identified clearly.

Discrepancies can be of several types:

*Between nonverbal behaviors.* A client may be talking smoothly on a topic, but careful observation may reveal that a smile is coupled with a tightly closed fist. Mixed messages are often conveyed when the body is incongruent.

*Between two statements.* In a single sentence a client may express two

---

[1]Gumm, Walker, and Day (1982) sharply criticize the concept of an individual client having a single primary perceptual system and provide data indicating that the reliability of identifying these systems may be poor. As such, it is recommended that you: (a) use all three systems to increase your interviewing impact; and (b) match your language usage to the words used by the client. Eye-movement patterns are perhaps the least reliable method of assessment.

completely contradictory ideas ("My son is perfect, but he just doesn't respect me." "This is a lovely office you have, but isn't the furniture just a bit seedy?") Over a long time, a positive statement about one's job may be qualified with an extensive discussion of problems. Most of us have mixed feelings toward our loved ones, our work, and other situations. It is helpful to aid others in understanding their ambivalences.

*Between what one says and what one does.* A parent may talk of love for a child but be guilty of child abuse. A student may say that he or she deserved a higher grade than the test score.

*Between statements and nonverbal behavior.* "That question doesn't bother me." (With a flushed face and a closed fist.)

*Between people.* Conflict can be described as a discrepancy between people. Noting interpersonal conflict is a key task of the interviewer, counselor, or therapist.

*Between the client and a situation.* "I want to be admitted to medical school, but I didn't make it." "I just found out I have beginning arthritis." "I can't find a job."

Most clients are aware at some level of the conflicts and discrepancies in their life. Moreover, they are usually not fully attuned to the full dimensions of these discrepancies. The skilled counselor does not necessarily attack client discrepancies immediately but may hold back and observe verbal and nonverbal behavior carefully so that other discrepancies, perhaps even more important, may be noted. In certain forms of time-limited interviewing and in certain counseling theories (such as Gestalt) immediate direct confrontation of discrepancies may be essential.

## SUMMARY

The interviewer seeks to observe client verbal and nonverbal behavior with an eye to identifying discrepancies, mixed messages, incongruity, and conflict. Counseling and therapy, in particular, but even interviewing, frequently focus on problems and their resolution. A discrepancy is often a problem. At the same time, discrepancies in many forms are part of life and may even be enjoyed. Humor, for example, is based on conflict and discrepancies. It is wise for counselors and interviewers to work on client problems, but with that emphasis often comes a tendency to view life as a problem to be solved rather than as an opportunity to be enjoyed. Even while working with the most complex case, it is wise to focus on client assets and strengths from time to time. The basic exercise used in the preceding chapter on questions ("Talk about something you feel good about") is ideally part of every interview. The focus on positive assets is necessary to combat the tendency to search constantly for problems and difficulties. People solve problems with their strengths, not with their weaknesses!

## Box 4-1· Determining a client's primary representational system

A primary representational system **(PRS)** is the person's main way of handling and processing information from the world. We receive data through visual, auditory, and kinesthetic means. Bandler and Grinder (1979) have suggested, and Falzett (1981) has tentatively confirmed, that clients are most comfortable when the interviewer uses language systems in accord with the client's primary representational system.

Closely related to **PRS** are perceptual systems. How does your client perceive the world? Different people have different perceptual systems or maps for experiencing the same event. A major counselor task is to enter the perceptual system or map of the client.

Observation of key words is perhaps the most reliable and important route toward determining client **PRS**, and example words are discussed in the text. However, eye movements indicate roughly the **PRS** of some individuals, as the following chart indicates:[2]

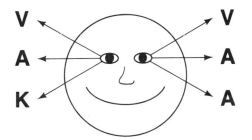

Eye movement chart for normally organized right-handed person. (V = visual; A = auditory; K = kinesthetic; eyes closed or straight ahead with pupils dilated = visual.) Falzett, 1981, p. 307.

Following are some questions you can use to observe client eye movements. Falzett (1981) suggests example sentence stems for use with clients after you have determined the **PRS** of the client:

[2]From "Matched Versus Unmatched Primary Representational Systems and Their Relationship to Perceived Trustworthiness in a Counseling Analog," by W. Falzett. In *Journal of Counseling Psychology*, 1981, *28*(305). Copyright 1981 by the American Psychological Association. Reprinted by permission.

## Box 4-1 continued

### Questions for Eye Movements[3]

The client is asked to remain silent and only think of the answer.

1. How did you get here today?
2. Describe a favorite pet.
3. Think about the last time you were truly comfortable and at ease.
4. Think about a happy time in your childhood.
5. Think about something you enjoy touching.
6. Think about your favorite TV program.
7. What is your favorite song? Can you hear it?

The client is asked to respond with words.

8. Tell me about a special person to you.
9. Tell me about a time when you felt someone truly helped you.
10. Tell me about someone who instills a feeling of trust in you.

### Phrases for Interviewer Use

Visual condition:
  I see . . .
  Your view is . . .
  You're seeing . . .
  Show me . . .
  Repeat any visual-sounding phrases mentioned by the subject.
Auditory condition:
  I hear . . .
  You're sounding . . .
  It sounds like . . .
  Tell me . . .
  Am I hearing . . .
  Repeat any auditory-sounding phrases.
Kinesthetic condition:
  That feels . . .
  Are you in touch with . . .
  You're feeling . . .
  Put me in touch with . . .
  Your sense of . . .
  Repeat any kinesthetic-sounding phrases.

Not all clients follow these examples. Left-handed people may be expected to be opposite. Some people use one system almost exclusively, whereas others may use several. Some people sequence the systems, for example, by first looking up (visual) and then down (kinesthetic). For others, the system simply doesn't work. In many cases it will help to use multiple systems. For most clients, however, listening for verbal style will be most helpful.

If you observe skilled counselors, you will note that many use all three modalities to enhance client experiencing of an event. For example, a client may be *asked* to recall an important life event and to *see* that event in "the mind's eye," then to *hear* the voice of a person featured in that event. Finally, the client may be asked to describe emotions welling up inside.

[3]The questions for eye movements were developed by the author following a format in Falzett's article. This format was originally generated by Darcy Shaw and Lee Owens at Ball State University.

**Box 4-2 Key points**

*Why?*

The most effective interviewer is constantly aware of the client. Clients tell us about their world by nonverbal and verbal means. What you say or do has an effect on the other person. Client observation skills focus on the importance of determining how the client interprets the world.

*What?*

Client observation skills may be organized in three areas:

1. *Client nonverbal behavior.* Client eye contact patterns, body language, and vocal qualities are, of course, important. Shifts and changes in these may be indicative of client interest or discomfort. A client may lean forward, indicating excitement about an idea, or may cross arms to close it off. Facial behavior (eyebrow furrowing, lips tightening or loosening, flushing, pulse rate at the temples) is especially important. Large trunk shifts may mean changes in client reactions, thoughts, or topics.

2. *Client verbal behavior.* Noting patterns of verbal tracking is particularly important. At what point do clients change topic, and to what topics do they shift? Clients tend to use certain key words to describe their behavior and situations. Noting these descriptive words and repetitive themes is helpful. Some clients use primarily auditory (*hear, sounds like*), visual (*see, looks like*) or kinesthetic (*feel, touch*) words to describe their way of interacting with the world. It is helpful to match the client's key words. Using all three sensory modalities will strengthen the impact of many interviews.

3. *Client discrepancies.* Incongruities, mixed messages, contradiction, and conflict are manifest in many interviews. The effective interviewer is able to identify these discrepancies and name them appropriately and, sometimes, feed them back to the client. These discrepancies may be between nonverbal behaviors, between two statements, between what one says and

**Box 4-2 continued**

|  | what one does, or between statements and nonverbal behavior ("That question doesn't bother me" said with a closed fist and flushed face). They may represent conflict between people, or between a client and a situation. |
| --- | --- |
| *How?* | Simple, careful observation of your client is basic. What can you see, hear, and feel from the client's world? Further, note your impact on the client. How does what you say change or relate to the client's behavior? Use those data to change your microskill or interviewing technique. |
| *With whom?* | All clients. Note individual and cultural differences in verbal and nonverbal behavior. |
| *And?* | Movement harmonics are particularly interesting and provide a basic concept to explain much verbal and nonverbal communication. When two people are talking together and communicating well, they often exhibit movement symmetry or movement complimentarity in that their bodies move together in a harmonious fashion. When people are not communicating clearly, movement dissynchrony will appear; body shifts, jerks, and movements away are readily apparent. |

## PRACTICE EXERCISES AND SELF-ASSESSMENT

Many concepts have been presented in this chapter; it will take time to master them and make them a useful part of your interviewing. As such,  the exercises here should be considered introductory. Further, it is suggested that you continue to work on these concepts throughout the time that you read this book. For example, in the next chapter on paraphrasing you will want to continue to practice observing the primary representational system of your role-played client. In reflection of feeling (Chapter 6) you will want to observe nonverbal expressions of emotion. In reflection of meaning (Chapter 7) you will again have the opportunity to note "I statements." If you keep practicing the concepts in this chapter throughout the book, material which now might seem confusing will gradually be clarified.

*INDIVIDUAL PRACTICE*

**Exercise 1. Observation of client nonverbal patterns.**

Observe a counseling interview, a television interview, or two people talking. Give special attention to the person being interviewed or the person who seems to be talking less. Note the following:

*Eye contact patterns:* Do people maintain eye contact more while talking or listening? Does the "client" break eye contact on certain subjects more than others? Can you observe changes in pupil dilation as an expression of interest?

*Body language:* Note gestures, shifts of posture, trunk lean, patterns of breathing, use of space. Give special attention to facial expressions such as changes in skin color, flushing, lip movements. Note appropriate and inappropriate smiling, furrowing of eyebrows.

*Vocal qualities:* Note speech rate, changes in intonation or loudness. Give special attention to speech "hitches" or hesitations.

With each of these variables use the following format to present your data and impressions: The Client Observation Form (page 76) provides space for you to record these observations.

| Context | Observation | Impression |
|---|---|---|
| Describe the situation in which the observations occur. | Describe in clear, behavioral terms what you see or hear during the observation. | At this point you may give your speculation about what you observe. |
| For example: Viewing an interview in which the client is talking about vocational history. | For example: Eye contact break accompanied by sitting back in chair, and a shortness of breath coupled with a raised vocal tone in response to counselor question "Are you married?" | For example: Client feels anxious in some way around issue of marriage. |

**Exercise 2. Observation of movement harmonics.**

Observe an interview or conversation, but this time note the behavior of both people. Give your primary attention to examples of movement harmonics. Note places and examples where the bodies of the two communicators mirror one another. You may find complex movement patterns being mirrored. At the same time, you will also likely note examples of dissynchronous movements. Record your observations using the Client Observation Form (page 76) or use the space provided below.

For example, consider the following context, observation, and impression:

| *Context* | *Observation* | *Impression* |
|---|---|---|
| Counselor and client are talking about sexual difficulties experienced during the last week. | The counselor and client were sitting in mirror positions until this topic came up. The counselor sat back, put hand to chin, his vocal tone lowered. The client in turn hesitated, moved back, the voice raised in tone with more rapid speech. | The counselor and client appeared to be in harmony until this topic came up. The counselor may be uncomfortable in this area. Clearly, they are not communicating as well as they were earlier in the session. |

_____

_____

_____

_____

_____

_____

_____

_____

_____

**Exercise 3. Observation of nonverbal communication discrepancies.**

After you have observed a variety of situations in which you demonstrate your ability to note nonverbal communication and movement harmonics, give special attention to discrepant nonverbal behavior. You may note the picking of lint off one's clothes as if to brush off the other person's comments, inappropriate smiling, sitting back in a chair as if to distance oneself from another, and the like. The nonverbal discrepancies may be within one person (for example, a closed fist in one hand and an open palm in the other) or between two people. Again, it is important to separate context, observation, and impression.

### Exercise 4. Observation of client verbal tracking and selective attention.

Listen carefully to clients (or other people in your daily interactions) and note when they change topics. Do those to whom you listen have varying abilities and interests in staying on certain topics? Are some topic changes abrupt and others more subtle?

It is particularly important to note selective attention patterns. Some clients, for example, will selectively attend only to negative elements in their life situation, while others attend only to positive strengths. Some people attend only to discussions where sexuality is an issue, whereas others will avoid the same topic.

Using the same format of context, observation, and impression, summarize your observations of others either in an interview or in conversations.

### Exercise 5. Noting "I statements" descriptive of the self.

Clients tell you much about themselves if you listen carefully. Much of counseling and interviewing can be focused on understanding client self-statements, or "I statements." Clients will often present clear statements about their condition: "I am depressed," "I am lonely," "I feel sad," "I am pregnant." Note that these key sentences are often the issue around which the interview or counseling session will focus. Further, the sentences often (though not always) follow a form in which the subject is the self (*I*), followed by a verb of being (*am*), and ending with an adjective descriptor referring to the self (*depressed*).

One task of the interviewer or counselor is, through the process of counseling, to change the "I statements" from negative to positive self-descriptors—for example, to change "I am lonely" to "I have friends and am a happy person."

Once an "I statement" has been identified, the task of the interviewer is to clarify its meaning and obtain more specifics. Note in the following example how a sequence of questions can discover more data underlying the original "I statement."

*Client:* Joan really bugs me. I don't know what to do. ("I statement" = "I don't know what to do.")

*Counselor:* Could you tell me generally what is going on between you? (Search for general summary via the *could* question.)

Could you give me a specific example where the conflict occurred? What did she do? What did you do? (Search for concrete facts.)

How did you feel when that happened? (Search for feelings.)

What does all this mean to you? (Search for meaning.)

The data generated by this series of questions clarify for the interviewer the total situation in which the client is living. Armed with more concrete specifics and facts derived from the original "I statement," the counselor may aid the client in a search for alternative solutions. The effectiveness of the interview may be determined by the "I statement" of the client as he or she leaves the session and actually determines a new action (for instance, "I am going to do *X*") with an affirmative voice.

Note a negative "I statement" of a client or another person and use the questioning sequence suggested here to clarify the situation that brought about the negative "I statement." Summarize your experience below:

Negative "I statement": _____

Result of systematic questioning: _____

_____

_____

_____

_____

Positive "I statement" that might be generated by the client after successful interviewing or counseling: _____

Client observation form

| Context | Observation | Impression |
|---|---|---|
|  |  |  |

**Exercise 6. Noting client modes of receiving information.**

Some clients tend to use primarily visual ways of describing their environment, others auditory, and still others kinesthetic. Some people have blended ways of perceiving the world and may use combinations. Refer back to page 65 for lists of sample words in each category. Give 15 minutes a day for at least four days to noting other peoples' modes of receiving information. Deliberately match their reception mode through use of vocabulary. Alternatively, deliberately mismatch mode and note the difficulties that tend to arise in communication when reception modes are discrepant. Summarize your discoveries below:

_____

_____

_____

_____

_____

**Exercise 7. Observation of discrepancies in your daily life.**

The skilled counselor and interviewer will be able to note discrepancies, mixed messages, incongruity, and conflicts as a central part of any interview. The six types of discrepancies discussed are: between nonverbal behaviors (see Exercise 3), between two statements, between what one says and what one does, between statements and nonverbal behavior, between people, and between people (clients) and situations. For three days give special attention to observation of discrepancies among those you meet. Summarize some of the observations below:

_____

_____

_____

_____

_____

*SYSTEMATIC GROUP PRACTICE*

Several client observation skills have been discussed in this chapter:

Observation of client nonverbal patterns

Observation of movement harmonics

Observation of discrepancies in nonverbal communication

Observation of client verbal tracking and selective attention

Noting "I statements"

Noting client modes of receiving information

Observation of discrepancies

It is obviously not possible to master all these concepts in one single role-played interview. However, practice in these dimensions can serve as a foundation for elaboration at a later time. The exercise here has been selected to summarize the central ideas of the chapter.

**Step 1. Divide into practice groups.**

**Step 2. Select a group leader.**

**Step 3. Assign roles for the first practice session.**

Role-played client, who responds naturally and is talkative. The client may give the interviewer a "hard time," but should be talkative.

Interviewer, who follows a set list of questions.

Observer I, who observes nonverbal communication.

Observer II, who observes verbal communication.

**Step 4. Planning.**   As the central task is observation, the interviewer should give primary attention to asking the stock questions listed in Step 5. After the role-play is over, the interviewer should report personal observations of the client made during that time, and demonstrate basic or active mastery skills.

The suggested topic for the practice role-play is "something or someone with whom I have a present conflict or have had a past conflict." Alternative topics include:

My positive and negative feelings toward my parents or other significant person.

The mixed blessings (pro and con) of my work, home community, or present living situation.

The two observers may use this session as an opportunity for providing feedback to the interviewer, and for sharpening their own observation skills.

**Step 5. Conduct a six-minute practice session.**   The interviewer should follow a stock set of open questions in this session, using each one in order. It will be useful to have the questions available in one's lap and to use language relatively close to the following questions. The feedback emphasis this time will be on client verbal and nonverbal behavior, not on the interviewer. The suggested questions are:

1. "Could you give me a general summary of your conflict situation?" (Or positive and negative feelings about parents, work, home community, or area of country.)
2. Search for facts. "Could you give me a specific example where the conflict occurred? What did they say? What did you do?" (Or ask for an example of a positive thing one's parents did and/or a negative thing. Similar specific examples could be sought for work, home community, or area of country.)
3. Search for feelings. "How did you feel when that happened?" "What feelings or emotions did the positive event bring out in you?"
4. Search for meaning. "What does all this mean to you?" "What kind of sense does this make to you?" "What do your thoughts and feelings about this situation say about you as a person?"

**Step 6. Review the practice session and provide feedback for 14 minutes.** Remember to stop the audiotape or videotape periodically and listen to or view key items several times for increased clarity. Observers should give special attention to careful completion of the feedback sheet throughout the session.

**Step 7. Rotate roles.**

**Some general reminders.** Again, it is important that the interviewer feel free to have notes on his or her lap and refer to them when desired. This session is about bringing out client facts, feelings, and meanings and then examining client behavior, not about counselor behavior.

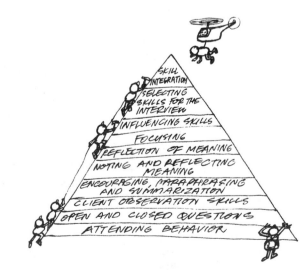

## CLIENT OBSERVATION FEEDBACK SHEET

_____ (Date)

_____     _____
(Name of Interviewer)                                  (Name of Person Completing Form)

_Instructions:_  Observe the client carefully during the role-played session and immediately afterward complete the nonverbal feedback portion of the form. As you view the videotape or listen to the audiotape, give special attention to verbal behavior and note discrepancies. If no recording equipment is available, one observer should note nonverbal behavior and the other verbal behavior during the interview itself.

1. _Nonverbal behavior checklist_

   Eyes:  At what points do eye contact breaks occur? Staring? Does the client maintain eye contact more when talking or when listening? Changes in pupil dilation?

   Face: At what points do changes in expression occur? Do you note changes in skin color, flushing, swelling or contracting of lips? Appropriate or inappropriate smiling? Head nods? Eyebrow furrowing?

   Body language: General style and changes in hands and arms, trunk, legs? Open or closed gestures? Tight fist? Playing with hands or objects? State of physical tension—relaxed or tight? Body oriented toward or away from interviewer? Sudden body shifts? Twitching? Distance? Breathing changes?

   Vocal qualities: Where do speech hesitations occur? Changes in tone and volume? What single words or short phrases are emphasized?

   Movement harmonics: Examples of movement complimentarity, synchrony, or dissynchrony? At what times did these occur?

Nonverbal discrepancies:  Is one area of the body saying something different from another? With what topics does this occur?

2. *Verbal behavior checklist*

Verbal tracking and selective attention:  At what points did the client fail to stay on topic? What topics did the client give most attention to?

Client "I statements":  In the process of discussing the conflict or confusing situation, what self-statements did the client make about her- or himself? List them below. Which statements might be desirable to change over a longer interview?

Client mode of receiving information:  Is this client visual, auditory, or kinesthetic? How well did the interviewer track the language system of the client?

3. *Client discrepancies*

Write here observations of discrepancies between two statements, between what was said and what the client did, between statements and nonverbal behavior, between people, and between the client and situations. Nonverbal discrepancies are to be presented under point 1.

_____

_____

_____

_____

_____

_____

_____

_____

*SELF-ASSESSMENT AND FOLLOW-UP*

Observation of client verbal and nonverbal behavior is a central skill of effective interviewers and counselors. As you progress over time, you will find it possible to increase your skills. Do not expect to be fully conversant with the concepts of this chapter after one reading and a few practice exercises. Even the most skilled individual after years of experience is constantly learning new ways to understand and interpret client behavior.

Use the self-assessment and follow-up ideas here as beginning steps toward eventual mastery of the complex art of observing others.

**1. What single dimension stood out for you in this chapter as either a significant learning or an interesting and helpful concept?** Use this knowledge and interest as *your* base for further study of client verbal and nonverbal behavior.

_____

_____

_____

_____

_____

**2. Which single concept stands out for you as least relevant and least helpful?** Could you summarize your reasons here? It is important that you develop your own position on these issues.

_____

_____

_____

_____

_____

**3. Mastery of client observation skills.** What specific competencies have you mastered? Provide specific evidence of your mastery of each level below. Additional evidence may be provided by tapes, transcripts, and case studies.

_____

_____

_____

_____

_____

**Identification.**   You will be able to note a wide variety of nonverbal behavior and verbal behavior in clients and other people. You will be able to identify discrepancies among these behaviors.

_____ Ability to note eye contact patterns, particularly changes in patterns.

_____

_____

_____ Ability to note facial expression and body language, particularly shifts or changes in relation to certain topics.

_____

_____

_____ Ability to note vocal qualities, particularly changes and hesitations.

_____

_____

_____ Ability to note movement harmonics.

_____

_____

_____ Ability to note client verbal tracking and selective attention.

_____

_____

_____ Ability to note explicit and implicit client "I statements."

_____

_____

_____ Ability to note client mode of receiving information (auditory, visual, kinesthetic).

_____

_____

_____ Ability to note discrepancies in verbal and nonverbal behavior.

_____ Between nonverbal behaviors.

_____

_____

_____ Between two verbal statements.

_____

_____

_____ Between statements and nonverbal behavior.

_____

_____

_____ Between people.

_____

_____

_____ Between people and situations.

_____

_____

_____ Between what one says and what one does.

_____

_____

**Basic mastery.** You will be able to demonstrate the same observation skills in your own interviewing practice. For example, you will note body shifts, changes in eye contact or skin coloration, use of repetitive verbal patterns. Provide one specific example of your own in-interview observations for nonverbal, verbal, and discrepant behavior. (As time permits, provide specific examples from your interviews for each of the above general observation criteria.)

_____ Ability to note nonverbal behavior.

_____

_____

_____

_____ Ability to note verbal behavior patterns.

_____

_____

_____

_____ Ability to note client discrepancies.

_____

_____

_____

**Active mastery.**  You will be able to note client verbal and nonverbal behaviors in the interview and be able to match your behavior to the  client's. Where necessary, you will be able to mismatch behaviors to promote client movement. You will be able to note your own verbal and nonverbal responses to the client. You will be able to note discrepancies between you and the client and work to resolve these discrepancies.

One route toward demonstrating this level of mastery is to take each of the specific observation areas in *Identification* and provide evidence that you are able to use these concepts effectively in the interview. At the first stages of active mastery, the following competencies are suggested as most important for beginning active mastery:

_____ Ability to mirror nonverbal patterns with the client. The interviewer mirrors body position, eye contact patterns, facial expression, and vocal qualities.

_____

_____

_____

_____

_____ Ability to identify client patterns of selective attention and use those patterns either to bring the topic back to the original topic *or* to move knowingly with the new topic provided by the client

_____

_____

_____

_____ Ability to identify key client "I statements" and feed them back to the client accurately, thus enabling the client to describe and define what they mean more fully. (Helpful in this exercise is the series of questions identified in Exercise 5.)

_____

_____

_____

_____

_____ Ability to match your language system with the client's mode of processing the experience (auditory, visual, kinesthetic).

_____

_____

_____

_____

_____ Ability to note client discrepancies and feed them back to the client accurately. Note that this is an important skill termed *confrontation;* it is discussed in detail in Chapter 9. The client, in turn, will be able to accept the confrontation and use this feedback for further effective self-exploration.

_____

_____

_____

_____

**Teaching mastery.** You will demonstrate your ability to teach others client observation skills. (The level of your mastery of teaching can be determined by how well your students perform on the basic competencies of this self-assessment form.)

_____

_____

_____

_____

**4. Given your experience with client observation skills, what one single goal might you set for yourself at this point?**

_____

_____

_____

_____

# REFERENCES

Bandler, R., and Grinder, J. *Frogs into princes.* Moab, Utah: Real People Press, 1979.

Falzett, W. Matched versus unmatched primary representational systems and their relationship to perceived trustworthiness in a counseling analog. *Journal of Counseling Psychology*, 1981, *28*, 305–308.

Gumm, W., Walker, M., and Day, H. Neurolinguistic programming: Method or myth? *Journal of Counseling Psychology*, 1982, *29*, 327–330.

Lankton, S. *Practical magic.* Cupertino, Calif.: Meta Publications, 1980.

CHAPTER **5**

# Encouraging, Paraphrasing, and Summarizing: Hearing the Client Accurately

---

**How can these three skills help you and your clients?**

*Major Function*

Clients need to know that the interviewer has *heard* what they have been saying, *seen* their point of view, and *felt* their world as they experience it. Encouragers and restatements, paraphrases, and summarizations are perhaps most basic to helping a client feel understood.

*Secondary Functions*

Knowledge and skill in these dimensions result in:

▲ Clarifying for the client what he or she has said.
▲ Clarifying for the interviewer what the client has said. By feeding back what you have heard, you can check on the accuracy of your listening.
▲ Helping clients to talk in more detail about issues of concern to them.
▲ Helping an overly talkative client stop repeating the same facts or story over and over again, thus speeding up and clarifying the interviewing process.

---

## INTRODUCTION

Attending, questioning, and client observation skills form the basis of this training program. They all help bring the client out to share concerns and issues. Yet simply opening the client is not enough; clients need to know they have been *heard*. And the more accurate the listening process, the more likely the client is to continue exploring issues in greater depth.

Encouraging, paraphrasing, and summarizing are all concerned with communicating to clients that they have indeed been heard. In these accurate listening skills you do not mix your own ideas with what the client has been saying. You may feed back the client's ideas in your own words, which distill, perhaps shorten, and clarify what the client has said. Even then, however, it is wise to use the client's main words and ideas for particularly delicate topics.

Hearing another person accurately is not easy. A simple exercise will illustrate this fact. Ask a friend to tell you about a recent life event. Ask a series of open questions so that considerable information is generated. Then, feed back what the friend told you and ask how accurate your summary was. Note, too, how your friend felt about your feedback. Use this space for observations about your friend's reactions:

_____

_____

_____

_____

_____

_____

Paraphrasing and summarizing communicate to clients that they have been listened to. Encouraging helps clients explore their thoughts and feelings more completely. A brief definition of each of these skills follows:

**Encouragers** are a variety of verbal and nonverbal means the counselor or interviewer can use to prompt clients to continue talking. They include head nods, an open-handed gesture, a phrase such as "uh-hum," and the simple repetition of key words the client has uttered.

**Paraphrases** feed back to the client the essence of what has just been said by shortening and clarifying client comments. Paraphrasing is *not* parroting; it is using some of your own words plus the important main words of the client.

**Summarizations** are similar to paraphrases but they cover a longer time span and more information. Summarizations may be used to begin or end an interview, to act as transition to a new topic, or to clarify lengthy and complex client issues.

## EXAMPLE INTERVIEW[1]

With this example, we again return our attention to the options open to the counselor. In the following excerpt, note how the counselor uses the three skills of this chapter, while at the same time remaining aware of needed client observation skills. The counselor begins with a summary of the last interview. Note that the three skills are often helpful in clarifying issues more precisely for both the client and the counselor.

*Marsha:* The last time we talked, Jesse, you were saying you weren't sure what you wanted to do. You had this interesting job possibility way across the country, but there were some things holding you here, too. We were discussing some details of the job, and I noted how pleased and excited you were about it. Could you go on and tell me what's been happening this week?

(This is a summary of the main points discussed earlier followed by an open question to keep the dialogue going and to open the discussion more fully.)

*Jesse:* Well, what's been happening since we last talked, Marsha, is that I did get the job offer . . . and it's exciting. The salary is higher, and it's in Florida, and I've always wanted to be in a place with more sun, and it really sounds great. On the other hand, the family isn't too enthused about it. Ah . . . May likes the idea of being here in the Rockies. It's the type of life she likes. She likes horses and all that. The kids didn't seem too enthused either . . . they are running around in the dumps. I came home with big news, and no one responded. It's kind of a downer.

*Marsha:* So, you're pretty excited about making this move, but there are some other issues that need to be addressed.

(This brief paraphrase catches the essence of the conflict, at least as discussed thus far. It also contains elements of a basic confrontation in that incongruity between Jesse and his family is identified.)

*Jesse:* Yes, there seem to be two things happening. The job looks good, but the family is really down. I've been thinking about it, too. I've enjoyed being on the bowling team here . . . ah, I have a lot of friends. I understand housing is going to be more expensive down there. And . . . there are a lot of things to decide . . . and then the family comes in and complicates it.

*Marsha:* Complicates it?

(This single-word encourager may be expected to produce more talk from Jesse about his meaning and understanding of his words. Single-

---

[1] Several of the paraphrases and summaries in this transcript contain reflections of feeling, a skill that relates closely to paraphrasing and is discussed in the next chapter.

word encouragers stated in a questioning tone facilitate client talk in more depth.)

*Jesse:* Yeah . . . complicates it in that I thought the decision was made last week. If I got the offer, we'd go. Now it seems more complex.

*Marsha:* So, it's really hard to go ahead and make this move.

(This paraphrase catches the essence of what Jesse has been saying so far in the interview. There are some dimensions of reflection of feeling—"it's really hard"—in the paraphrase.)

*Jesse:* Yeah, I think you've got it right on target. I've thought a lot about it, but . . . I really want to go . . . I don't really feel comfortable about the move. I did before.

(Jesse talks in a less certain tone of voice. He is seeing the decision as more complex than he originally thought. Note that almost every counselor statement has resulted in a "yeah," indicating that the counselor is closely accurate in her paraphrases. You will note clients using affirmatives frequently when your paraphrasing is effective.)

*Marsha:* Could you tell me more of these thoughts?

*Jesse:* I'm getting older, and the kids are almost through high school. I like the house here, and it's expensive down in Florida. I not sure we'd be happy down there.

*Marsha:* You're not sure you'd be happy down there.

(An encourager in the form of a restatement.)

*Jesse:* Yes, it'd be very disruptive. Yet, on the other hand, I'm awfully bored with this job. I feel I could do it blindfolded.

*Marsha:* Blindfolded?

(Encourager.)

*Jesse:* Yeah, It's a snap. I feel like I'm going to seed and am stuck. There just isn't a lot of opportunity here. The salary is OK, but there isn't much of a challenge anymore.

*Marsha:* So, you've got to weigh the potential disruption of your life with some of the boredom and repetitiveness you feel right now on the job.

(This paraphrase again catches a basic dilemma and involves elements of a confrontation in that the conflict is distilled and clarified.)

*Jesse:* Exactly! That's exactly how I feel. And the decision is really tough. I almost feel like it comes down to a chance to do something new. The more bored I get, the harder I get to live with around the house. That isn't so good; that might get us into trouble.

(Note that, as the paraphrasing continues, Jesse continues to expand on the complexity of the decision.)

*Marsha:* So, while you're worried about your life being disrupted, sounds like you're very worried about being bored where you are now.

(This paraphrase is a little less effective than the previous one as it misses the possible dimension of conflict between husband and wife.

However, this omission may be deliberate, and even wise, as the conflict may be discussed later.)

*Jesse:* Yeah . . . (hesitant), I think so.

(Jesse indicates the paraphrase wasn't fully on target through vocal tone and speech hesitation.)

*Marsha:* Could you give me an idea of what might be needed to make the job here more interesting to you?

(This open question follows up on Jesse's need to stay in the Rockies and opens the discussion for new options.)

*Jesse:* Well, I don't get along too well with the guy across the hall. He's always disagreeable. He's in good with the boss. I get along OK, but not as well as I would like.

*Marsha:* What you're saying now is that difficulties on the job may be as much a motivator to leave as the attractions of Florida. At the same time, you find your family wants to stay here. Perhaps it might be worthwhile to explore for a while some of these new dimensions you're talking about. But before I go on, let me check out if I have been hearing you accurately so far.

Last week, you talked quite definitely that, if the job came, you'd take it. Now, it seems that you have the job offer you wanted, but a set of new issues has come up. Important among them are your family's reactions and your own reactions to leaving a place and people you like. Issues of boredom on the job and the guy across the hall seem to be strong motivators to leave. Now we've started talking a bit about what might be done to make the job here more comfortable. Have I heard you correctly? Shall we take a look at the setting here?

Comment: This summary brings together two interviews to this point and focuses potential discussion for the next stage of the interview. As often happens, a "simple" choice has become increasingly complex as the deeper issues underlying the move are explored. Still to be considered are the possible family conflict, ways in which the current setting could be made more satisfactory, and further exploration of the positive and negative aspects of the potential move.

This particular excerpt may strike some as unrealistic as it uses so many of the reflective listening skills. In fact, it is a portion of an actual interview. It is possible to engage a client rather fully using only encouraging, paraphrasing, and summarizing. The questions used help to open up new areas where, again, the three skills can be helpful in clarifying. In your own practice sessions you may at first find it difficult to paraphrase even once in a brief interview. Work to build up your skill, and you will be surprised at the power you have to facilitate others making their own decisions—and with relatively little input from you. The counselor or interviewer who paraphrases seeks to tread as lightly as possible on the client's world.

# INSTRUCTIONAL READING

Most valuable in communicating to clients that they have been heard, encouraging, paraphrasing, and summarizing help the client clarify issues and move more deeply into exploration of issues and concerns. The three skills are related, but each has special advantages and purposes, which are discussed below.

## *ENCOURAGING*

Encouragers have been defined as head nods, open gestures, and positive expressions that encourage the client to keep talking. Minimal verbal

utterances such as "Ummm" and "Un-huh" have the same effect. Silence accompanied by appropriate nonverbal communication can be another type of encourager. All these types of encouragers affect the direction of client talk only minimally; clients are simply encouraged to keep talking. Restatement and repetition of key words, on the other hand, have more influence on the direction of client progress.

Consider the following client statement:

> "And then, it happened again. The grocery store clerk gave me a dirty look and I got angry. It reminded me of my last job, where I had so much trouble getting along. Why are they always after me?"

There are several key words in the above statement. Repetition of any one of them would tend to lead the interview in very different directions. The counselor could use a variety of short encouragers in a questioning tone of voice ("Angry?" "Last job?" "Trouble getting along?" "After you?"), and in each case the client would move in a different direction and talk about different topics. These short encouragers are forms of selective attention on the part of the interviewer and direct the interview much more than casual observation would suggest. It is important that you as an interviewer note your patterning of single-word encouraging responses. You may be directing clients more than you think.

A restatement is another type of encourager in which the counselor or interviewer repeats back short phrases ("The clerk gave you a dirty look?" "You got angry." "You had trouble getting along in your last job?" "You wonder why they are always after you."). Like short encouragers, different types of restatements lead the client in differing directions. Restatements can be used with a questioning tone of voice; they then function much like the single-word encourager. When they simply parrot the client's words, they function more as brief paraphrases. In this case they highlight points noted by the counselor or interviewer and tend to close off discussion. Vocal tone may determine the difference.

All types of encouragers facilitate client talk unless they are overused or used badly. Excessive head nodding or gestures and excessive parroting can be annoying and frustrating to the client. Observation of many interviewers suggests that too many encouragers are wooden and unexpressive. Well-placed encouragers help maintain flow and communicate continuously that the client is being listened to. Single-word encouragers often facilitate client talk about deeper meaning.

## PARAPHRASING

At first glance, paraphrasing appears to be a simple skill, only slightly more complex than encouraging. In restatement and encouraging exact words and phrases are fed back to the client. In paraphrasing the entire content is repeated back to the client, but in a shortened and clarified form. If you are able to give an accurate paraphrase to a client, you are likely to be rewarded with a "That's right" or "Yes . . ." and the client will go on to explore the issue in more depth. Further, accurate paraphrasing will help the client stop repeating a story. Some clients have complex problems that no one has ever bothered to hear accurately, and they literally need to tell their story over and over until someone indi-

cates they have been heard clearly. Once clients know they have been heard, they can then move on to new topics. The goal of paraphrasing is the facilitation of client exploration and the clarification of issues. The tone of your voice and your body language accompanying the paraphrase indicate to the client as well whether you are interested in listening in more depth or wish the client to move on.

How do you paraphrase? Client observation skills are important in accurate paraphrasing. You need to hear the client's important words and use them in your paraphrase much as the client does. Other aspects of the paraphrase may be in your own words, but the main ideas and concepts should reflect the client's view of the world, not yours!

An accurate paraphrase, then, usually consists of four dimensions:

1. A *sentence stem* using, insofar as possible, some aspect of the client's mode of receiving information. Visual clients tend to respond best to visual words ("*Looks* like you're saying you *see* the situation from this *point of view* . . ."); auditory clients respond best to tonal words ("As I *hear* you, *sounds* like . . . does that *ring a bell*?"); and kinesthetic clients respond to feeling words ("So the situation *touches* you like . . . and how does that *grab you*?"). With many clients a mixture of visual, auditory, and kinesthetic words will be even more powerful. A stem, of course, is not always necessary.
2. *The key words and construct systems used by the client to describe the situation or person.* Again, drawing from client observation skills, the effort is to include main ideas that come from the client and use the client's exact words. This aspect of the paraphrase is sometimes con-

fused with the encouraging restatement. A restatement, however, is almost entirely in the client's own words and covers only limited amounts of material.

3. *The essence of what the client has said in summarized form.* It is here that the interviewer's skill in transforming the client's sometimes confused longer statements into succinct, meaningful, and clarifying statements is most manifest. The counselor has the difficult task of keeping true to the client's ideas, but not repeating them exactly.

4. A *check-out for accuracy.* The check-out is a brief question at the end of the paraphrase, asking the client for feedback on whether or not the paraphrase (or summary or other microskill) was relatively correct and useful. Some example check-outs include "Am I hearing you correctly?" "Is that close?" "Does that ring a bell?" and "Does that touch the situation?" It is also possible to paraphrase with an implied check-out by raising your voice at the end of the sentence as if the paraphrase is a question.

Following is a client statement with sample key-word encouragers, restatements, and a paraphrase:

"I'm terribly concerned over my wife. She has this feeling she has to get out of the house, see the world, and get a job. I'm the breadwinner, and I imagine I have a good income. The children view Sally as a picture-perfect mother, and I do too. But last night, we really saw the problem differently and had a terrible argument."

▲ Key word encouragers: "Argument?" "Terribly concerned?"
▲ Restatement encouragers: "You're terribly concerned over your wife." "She's a picture-perfect mother." "You had a terrible argument."
▲ Paraphrase: "Let me *see* if I can *visualize* what the situation is. You're concerned over your *picture-perfect* wife who wants to work even though you have a good income, and it resulted in a terrible argument. Is that how you *see* it?"

The above example shows that the key-word encourager, the restatement, and the paraphrase are all different points on a continuum. In each case the emphasis is on hearing the client and feeding back what has been said. Both short paraphrases and longer key-word encouragers will resemble restatements. All can be helpful in an interview, or they can be overdone. A long paraphrase is close to a summary.

## SUMMARIZING

Summarizations fall on the same continuum as the key-word encourager, restatement, and paraphrase. Summarizations, however, encompass a longer period of conversation—at times they may cover an entire interview or even points discussed by the client over several interviews.

In a summarization the interviewer attends to verbal and nonverbal comments from the client over a period of time and then selectively attends to key concepts and dimensions, restating them for the client as accurately as possible. A check-out at the end for accuracy is an important part of the summarization.

The following are examples of summarizations.

(To begin a session) "Let's see, last time we talked about your feelings toward your mother-in-law and we discussed the argument you had with her around the time the new baby arrived. You saw yourself as guilty and anxious. Since then you haven't got along too well. We also discussed a plan of action for today. How did that go?"

(Midway in the interview) "So far, I've seen that the plan didn't work too well. You felt guilty again when you saw the idea as manipulative. Yet one idea did work. You were able to talk with her about her garden, and it was the first time you had been able to talk about anything without an argument. You visualize the possibility of following up on the plan next week. Is that about it?"

(At the end of the session) "In this interview we've reviewed your feelings toward your mother-in-law in more detail. Some of the following things seem to stand out: First, our plan didn't work completely, but you were able to talk about one thing (the garden) without yelling. As we talked, we identified some behaviors on your part that could be changed. They include better eye contact, relaxing more, and changing the topic when you start to see yourself getting angry. I liked your idea at the end of talking with your father-in-law. Does that sum it up?"

## SUMMARY

The skills of encouraging are particularly important in helping a client to keep moving, open up, and talk more freely. Paraphrasing and summarization will communicate that the client has been heard, enabling further exploration in depth. Using a delicate balance of the client's words and your own is essential. If you are too close to what the client is saying, you may be guilty of excessive parroting and very little is gained. If you are too far from what the client has said, you may be guilty of imposing your own ideas on the client's world. An accurate style of paraphrasing is critical for the counselor or interviewer who seeks to develop empathy with clients.

---

**Box 5-1   Key points**

*Why?*               Clients need to know they have been *heard*. Attending, questioning, and other skills help the client open up, but accurate listening through the skills of encouraging,

**Box 5-1  continued**

paraphrasing, and summarizing, is needed to communicate that you have indeed heard the other person fully.

*What?*

Three skills of accurate listening help communicate your ability to attend:

1. *Encouragers* are a variety of verbal and nonverbal means the counselor or interviewer can use to encourage others to continue talking. They include head nods, an open palm, "uh-huh," and the simple repetition of key words the client has uttered.
2. *Paraphrases* feed back to the client the essence of what has just been said by shortening and clarifying client comments. Paraphrasing is *not* parroting; it is using some of your own words plus the important main words of the client.
3. *Summarizations* are similar to paraphrases except that a longer time and more information are involved. Summarizations may be used to begin or end an interview, for transition to a new topic, or to provide clarity in lengthy and complex client issues or statements.

*How?*

Encouragers are described above. It is important to add that the so-called "simple" repetition of key words is more important than appears at first glance. Key words repeated back to the client usually lead to the client elaborating in greater detail on the meaning of that word to him or her. Interviewers and counselors find it interesting and sometimes challenging to note their own selective attention patterns as they use this at first "simple" skill.

Paraphrasing involves four dimensions:

1. *A sentence stem* using, insofar as possible, some of the client's mode of receiving information (auditory, visual, kinesthetic). "You appear to be saying . . ."
2. *The key descriptors* and concepts of the client used to describe the situation or person. Use the client's own words for the most important things.
3. *The essence of what the client has said in summarized form.* The interviewer transforms a confusing longer statement or series of statements into a relatively brief form.

**Box 5-1 continued**

4. *A check-out for accuracy.* Implicitly or explicitly, the interviewer checks to see if hearing has been accurate. "Am I hearing you correctly?"

The summarization is similar to the paraphrase, but covers a longer time span.

*With whom?*    Virtually any client. However, some find repetition tiresome and may ask "Didn't I just say that?" Consequently, when you use the skill, you should pay attention to your client observation skills.

*And?*    All these skills involve active listening, encouraging others to talk freely. They communicate your interest and help clarify the world of the client both for you and the client. This skill set is one of the most difficult in the microtraining framework for many people.

## PRACTICE EXERCISES AND SELF-ASSESSMENT

The three skills of encouraging, paraphrasing, and summarizing are much less controversial than questions. Virtually all interviewing theories recommend and endorse these key skills of active listening.

*INDIVIDUAL PRACTICE*

### Exercise 1. Identification of skills.

Which of the following are most likely identified as encouragers (E), restatements (R), paraphrases (P), or summarizations (S)? Keep in mind that restatements are considered a variation of encourager.

| E | R | P | S | |
|---|---|---|---|---|
| _____ | _____ | _____ | _____ | "Uh-huh . . ." |
| _____ | _____ | _____ | _____ | Silence, with facilitative body language |
| _____ | _____ | _____ | _____ | "Fearful?" |
| _____ | _____ | _____ | _____ | "Change your mind?" |
| _____ | _____ | _____ | _____ | "You'd like to return to college." |
| _____ | _____ | _____ | _____ | "I hear you saying that you've changed your mind, that you are considering returning to college, but that finances may be a real problem. Is that right?" |

———— ———— ———— ————  "In the last interview, we talked about returning to college, and some of your mixed feelings about it, and we agreed that you'd try a visit to your sister's campus to look at it again."

### Exercise 2. Generating written encouragers, restatements, paraphrases, and summarizations.

A client comes to you, saying:

"I've just broken up with Dan. I couldn't take his drinking any longer. It was great when he was sober, but it wasn't that often he was. Yet, that leaves me alone. I don't know what I'm going to do about money, the kids, or even where to start looking for work."

Write three different types of minimal encouragers: _____

_____

Write a restatement: _____

Write a paraphrase (include a check-out): _____

_____

_____

Write a summarization (generate imaginary data from previous interviews): _____

_____

_____

_____

_____

_____

### Exercise 3. Observation.

Use the Feedback Sheet on page 103 to observe an interview. During the coming week observe conversations for the use of encouragers, paraphrases, restatements, and summarizations. One thing you may expect to find is that these skills are not used very frequently in conversations, though TV talk shows make use of them at times. Note below your observations and the impact of the skills on the "client."

_____

_____

_____

_____

_____

_____

**Exercise 4. Practice of skills in other settings.**

**Encouraging.**   During conversations with friends or in your own interviews, deliberately use single-word encouragers and brief restatements. Note their impact on your friends' participation and interest. You may find that the flow of conversation changes in response to your brief encouragers. Summarize some of your observations below.

_____

_____

_____

_____

_____

_____

_____

_____

**Paraphrasing and summarizing.**   Continue practicing client observation skills from Chapter 4. Note the key words the other people use and their primary mode of processing information (visual, auditory, kinesthetic) and then paraphrase to them what they have been saying. Sometimes the paraphrase will produce further talk and elaboration, while at other times it may close off a topic and lead to a change in the discussion. The tone of the paraphrase may be critical here. A questioning tone at the end of a paraphrase tends to bring out further talk. By contrast, a lowered vocal tone (particularly if coupled with the check-out) tends to close off discussion, with the other person feeling accurately heard. The check-out may provide you with useful data on the accuracy of your paraphrases and summarizations. Summarize your important observations below.

_____

_____

_____

_____

_____

_____

_____

_____

_____

_____

*SYSTEMATIC GROUP PRACTICE*

Experience has shown that the skills of this chapter are often difficult to master. It is easy to try to feed back what another person has said, but to do it *accurately* so that the client feels truly heard is another matter.

**Step 1. Divide into practice groups.**

**Step 2. Select a group leader.**

**Step 3. Assign roles for the first practice session.**

Role-played client

Interviewer

Observer I

Observer II

**Step 4. Planning.**   The interviewer should plan a role-play in which open questions are used to bring the client's problem out. Once this is done, use encouragers to help bring out details and deeper meanings. Use more open and closed questions as appropriate, but give primary attention to both the paraphrase and the encourager. End the interview with a summary. This is often forgotten. Check the accuracy of your summary with a check-out ("Am I hearing you correctly?").

For real mastery, seek to use only the three skills of this chapter and use questions only as a last resort. Further note the list of competencies in active mastery and seek to demonstrate that you can achieve these specific client objectives.

Ideally, the role-play topic for this practice session should be continued again in the next chapter practice session on reflection of feeling. Thus, you will have the opportunity to work through the same problem or concern emphasizing two different skill areas. Select the topic for practice with particular care. Consider the following topics as each involves observation of interpersonal or intrapersonal discrepancies:

Something or someone I have a present or past conflict with.

Positive and negative feelings toward my parents or other significant persons.

Mixed blessings of my work setting, home community, or area of the country.

A conflict around a decision regarding work, school, or a major purchase.

Observers may use planning time to examine feedback forms and to plan their own interviews.

**Step 5. Conduct a three-minute practice session.**

**Step 6. Review the practice session and provide feedback to the interviewer for 12 minutes.** Be sure to use the Feedback Sheet to ensure that the interviewer's statements are available for discussion. This sheet provides a helpful log of the session which greatly facilitates discussion. If you have audio- or videotape, stop and start the tape periodically and rewind it to hear and observe important points in the interview. Did the interviewer achieve his or her goals and what mastery level was demonstrated?

**Step 7. Rotate roles.**

**Some general reminders.** It is important that clients talk freely in the role-plays. As you become more confident in the practice session, you may want your clients to become more difficult so you can test your

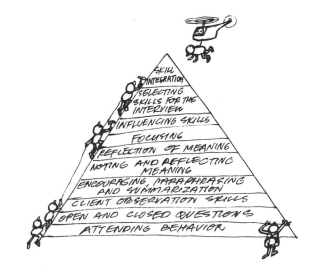

## ENCOURAGING, PARAPHRASING, AND SUMMARIZING FEEDBACK SHEET

_____ (Date)

_____     _____
(Name of Interviewer)              (Name of Person Completing Form)

_____

_Instructions:_ Write below as much as you can of each counselor statement. Then classify the statement as a question, an encourager, a paraphrase, a summarization, or other. Rate each of the three skills for its accuracy.

| Counselor statement | Open question | Closed question | Encourager | Paraphrase | Summarization | Other | Accuracy of encourager, paraphrase, or summarization Rate from 1–5 (5 high) |
|---|---|---|---|---|---|---|---|
| 1. _____ | | | | | | | |
| 2. _____ | | | | | | | |
| 3. _____ | | | | | | | |
| 4. _____ | | | | | | | |
| 5. _____ | | | | | | | |
| 6. _____ | | | | | | | |
| 7. _____ | | | | | | | |
| 8. _____ | | | | | | | |
| 9. _____ | | | | | | | |
| 10. _____ | | | | | | | |

1. What were the key discrepancies demonstrated by the client?

2. General interview observations.

skills with more stressful situations. You'll find that difficult clients are often easier to work with after they feel they have been heard.

## SELF-ASSESSMENT AND FOLLOW-UP

**1. Is paraphrasing a skill you had from the past?** Were you aware of it and its impact? Encouraging? Summarizing?

_____

_____

_____

_____

_____

**2. Mastery of encouraging, paraphrasing, and summarizing.** What specific competencies have you mastered? Provide evidence for each level of mastery in the space provided or via audio-or videotapes, case studies, or related demonstrations.

**Identification.** You will able to identify and differentiate between encouragers, restatements, paraphrases, and summarizations in the interview. You will note their impact on the client.

_____ Ability to classify and differentiate the skills.

_____

_____

_____ Ability to note the impact of these skills on the client.

_____

_____

**Basic mastery.** You will be able to demonstrate the use of encouragers, paraphrases, and summarization in the interview.

_____ Demonstration of the skills in a role-played interview.

_____

_____

_____ Demonstration and ability to use these skills in daily life situations.

_____

_____

**Active mastery.** You will be able to use these skills in the interview  and (1) through the use of encouragers and restatements facilitate further client talk on a topic; (2) paraphrase accurately what the client has said and, through your use of the skill encourage either further talk or introduction of a new topic; (3) summarize what the client has been saying accurately and, through the summarization, begin the interview, provide structure at key points in the session, and wrap up the interview at the end.

Provide evidence of mastery by supplementary written or taped materials.

_____ Are you able to use a variety of nonverbal encouragers (head nods, gestures, and the like) in such a way that they encourage client talk?

_____ Can you, through the single-word encourager and the restatement, assist clients in talking in more depth and detail about specific topic areas?

_____ By changing the single-word encourager or brief restatement, can you change the content of client talk?

_____ Through accurate paraphrasing can you encourage a client to talk further about a topic?

_____ Through accurate paraphrasing can you assist a client to stop unnecessary repetition and move on to new topics of discussion?

_____ Are you able to distinguish between an accurate and an inaccurate paraphrase and change your paraphrase when you discover inaccuracies?

_____ Are you able to summarize the main strands of a client's conversation over time accurately and use these data to provide:

_____ a. A summary at the beginning of the interview when necessary?

_____ b. A periodic summary to clarify and organize what the client has said?

_____ c. Summaries to close off sections of the interview or organize the entire interview itself?

**Teaching mastery.** Are you able to teach these skills to others with demonstrable competence on their part?

_____

_____

**3. Do you agree with this chapter's strong emphasis on the importance of hearing other people accurately and encouraging them to talk in more depth on the topic?** In review, how do you feel this skill fits with your natural style?

_____

_____

CHAPTER **6**

# Noting and Reflecting Feelings: A Foundation of Client Experience

---

**How can reflection of feeling help you and your clients?**

*Major Function*

Underlying client words and behaviors are feelings and emotions. The purpose of reflection of feeling is to make these implicit (or partially implicit) feelings explicit and clear to the client.

*Secondary Functions*

Knowledge and skill in reflection of feeling results in:

▲ Bringing out additional specifics of the client's emotional world.
▲ Noting that most clients have mixed or ambivalent feelings toward significant events and others. You can use the skill to help clients sort out these varied feelings and thoughts.
▲ Grounding the counselor and client from time to time in basic experience. There is a tendency in much interviewing to intellectualize and move away from deeper goals and feelings.

---

## INTRODUCTION

"I'm feeling down right now. I just got word that I got turned down by graduate school. Now I *really* don't know what to do. It just seems that I've tried everything. If only Professor Jones hadn't treated me so unfairly, I might have made it. He really ticks me off!

107

But maybe I should have worked harder. I just feel so confused about what to do next."

Paraphrasing is concerned with feeding back to the client the essence of what has been said. Reflection of feeling deals with client emotions and feeds back to the client key feelings the interviewer has observed. To clarify the distinction, take a moment right now and write a paraphrase of the client statement above:

_____

_____

_____

When you reflect feelings, you *add* to the paraphrase those affective, or feeling, words that tune in with the client's emotional experience. Before reading further, write down the client's expressed feeling words and your impressions of what some of the client's unspoken feeling words might be if they were expressed:

| Client expressed feelings (explicit feelings) | Unexpressed feelings the client may have (implicit feelings) |
| --- | --- |
| _____ | _____ |
| _____ | _____ |
| _____ | _____ |
| _____ | _____ |
| _____ | _____ |

Feelings that were explicit in the client's statement are "feeling down," "ticked off," and "confusion." The unexpressed, implicit feelings could be sadness, depression, worry, anxiety, anger, guilt, fear, and many others.

In a reflection of feeling the counselor focuses on client emotion(s). In this case the counselor could say, "You feel down and confused, and I sense some anger there as well." As emotions form the base of much of life experience, noting key feelings and helping the client clarify them can be one of the most facilitative things an interviewer can do. This is particularly so in situations where client emotions are confused or mixed. It often helps if we know how we feel before we act.

Paraphrasing is concerned with the essence of what has been said, reflection of feeling is concerned with the emotions. In practice the two skills are often used together, and this chapter will present many illustrations of how the two skills relate.

Before continuing it would be helpful if you generated your own personal list of feeling words. If you are to reflect feelings, you need a vocabulary of emotional labels. Words such as *happy*, *glad*, *sad*, and *confused* may give you a start. Also think of different intensities of the same emotion—for example, *annoyed*, *angry*, *furious*.

————————————   ————————————   ————————————

————————————   ————————————   ————————————

————————————   ————————————   ————————————

————————————   ————————————   ————————————

————————————   ————————————   ————————————

————————————   ————————————   ————————————

————————————   ————————————   ————————————

————————————   ————————————   ————————————

## EXAMPLE INTERVIEW

The following transcript illustrates reflection of feeling in action.

*Sylvia:* So, Beth, how are things with your mother?
(Open question)

*Beth:* Well, the tests that she had taken recently came back looking pretty good. But with cancer you never can tell. I'm just really worried. It's hard to feel relaxed about her illness.

*Sylvia:* You sound like you feel tight and worried.
(Reflection of feeling. Note kinesthetic mode used by Beth.)

*Beth:* Well, since she had her first bout with cancer . . . ah . . . I've just felt real concerned. She just doesn't look as well as she used to, and she seems to need a lot more rest. I guess I keep worrying that it's all going to, you know, turn out badly for her.

*Sylvia:* I can sense you felt upset and concerned. At the same time, are

there any positives in the situation? Anything at all encouraging?
(The reflection of feeling was followed by an open question oriented toward the search for something positive in the situation. Some counselors and interviewers focus solely on the negative and can literally cause depression and immobility. Some attention to positive dimensions is essential.)

*Beth:* Well . . . the doctors seem to feel that she's doing real well. She's basically made a good recovery. Most of my worry about her, Sylvia, is that I never know when it's going to hit again. You know . . .

*Sylvia:* Um-hum . . .

*Beth:* It's the unknown that's really leaving me up in the air.

*Sylvia:* So you do feel a little bit optimistic about the fact that she has recovered so quickly, is that right?

(The reflection of feeling focuses on positive feelings. This seems important so that the counselor and client can attack problem areas from a base of strength rather than pessimism.)

*Beth:* Yeah, I feel good about that.

*Sylvia:* At the same time, you feel a lot concerned about the fact that you don't know just what's going to happen.

(This reflection is a return to Beth's real concerns of the moment.)

*Beth:* You know, ah . . . I've always seen her as a healthy person and now this thing has come up, I just worry about her all over the place. You know, little things that I never used to think about get me pretty jumpy.

*Sylvia:* You've got real deep feelings of caring about her.

(This reflection of feeling differs from earlier reflections in that the words *deep feelings of caring* come more from the counselor than from the client. This reflection potentially "adds" to Beth's understanding and again emphasizes positive assets on her part.)

*Beth:* Yes, that's really correct. It made me realize that . . . how much I love her and how much she means to me. And . . . it's all real crazy 'cause that makes me worry about her even more.

*Sylvia:* It's almost as if the more you care, the more you worry. This feeling becomes very powerful.

(In this reflection the positive feelings are pointed out to be part of the problem. Specifically, positive feelings toward a person can lead to even more anxiety than if you didn't care a lot. This, of course, is a basic human issue. The price of the joy of caring for another is possible loss, a real issue underlying the difficulty many people find in being committed to each other.)

*Beth:* That's right; it's like a vicious circle. I just . . . you know . . . realize how much she means to me and then I worry more . . . and I think you're right—there isn't that much to worry about.

(Note that Beth continuously begins her statements with affirmations of the counselor's reflections, such as "Yes," "That's right." Beth's last sentence comes from Beth, not from the counselor. Through the process of working through feelings, she is beginning to resolve issues: "But . . . ah . . . it's just real hard right now.")

*Sylvia:* So in one sense you feel there's really not that much to worry about. But there is . . . and there's not much you can do about it. Is that correct?

(This reflection of feeling is particularly important as Sylvia has reflected in summary form the main feelings that Beth has talked about so far. The feelings are mixed—that is, a desire to do something and anxiety and worry about not being able to, feelings of deep caring and love, and Beth's beginning awareness that she will have to *accept* things as they are. That acceptance is the beginning of some emotional relief in the situation.)

*Beth:* Yeah, it's the helplessness I feel. It's that, if she is really sick, it's out of my hands . . .

*Sylvia:* Ummmm . . .

*Beth:* Maybe that's what's really bothering me . . . that I used to think I had a lot of control over my life and her life, and now I realize that . . . ah . . . there's nothing I really can do anything about.

*Sylvia:* Sounds like it's a deeply troubling thing, but it's something that you're beginning to accept. Am I hearing you correctly there?

(The reflection of feeling focuses on the mixed feelings of being bothered or troubled and the beginning of acceptance. As the counselor is now in more murky or difficult areas, the check-out or perception checks at the end of her last two reflections of feeling are important to ensure accuracy and more open communication. The perception checks were not consciously planned in this interview, but at times they should be deliberately planned.)

*Beth:* That's right. I guess I'm having to learn how to do that right now.

Comment: The counselor in this case did not plan to use almost exclusively reflections of feeling. Yet this particular topic segment was such that the client seemed to want and need deeper exploration of feelings. Out of that exploration the client developed a new awareness. Now that this phase is completed, it would be appropriate to bring in other skills and work more concretely toward thinking through content issues or deciding on specific actions.

In your own reflection of feeling practice, attempt to use the skill as frequently as possible. In the early stages of mastery it is wise to combine the skill with questioning, encouraging, and paraphrasing. Most people find it awkward to use a single skill at a time. Full mastery of a skill will appear when a person can conduct a long segment of an interview effectively using any one skill almost constantly. Over the years the most effective interviewer, counselor, or therapist often develops—consciously or unconsciously—a level of skill such that the specific skill area being used (questions, paraphrasing, reflection and so on) makes relatively little difference. Each is used so well that positive client benefits can be produced. Effectiveness and competence, then, do not necessarily depend on the particular skill, but on the art of using it effectively. Nonetheless, being aware of and competent in each skill facilitates general personal and professional development as an interviewer.

## INSTRUCTIONAL READING

Many authorities argue that our thoughts and actions are only extensions of our basic feelings and emotional experience. The skill of reflection of feeling is aimed at assisting others to sense and experience the most basic part of themselves—how they really feel about another person or life event.

A basic feeling we have toward our parents, family, and best friends is love and caring. This is a deep-seated emotion in most individuals. At the same time, over years of intimate contact, negative feelings about the same people may also appear, possibly overwhelming and hiding positive feelings; or negative feelings may be buried. A common task of many counselors is to help clients sort out mixed feelings toward significant people in their lives. Many people want a simple resolution and want to run away from complex mixed emotions. However, ideally the counselor should help the client discover and sort out our many positive and negative feelings.

At another level our work and social relationships and the decisions we make are often based on emotional experience. In an interviewing situation it is often helpful to assist the client to identify feelings clearly. For example, an employee making a move to a new location may have positive feelings of satisfaction, joy, and accomplishment about the opportunity, but simultaneously feel worried, anxious, and hesitant about new possibilities. The effective interviewer notes both dimensions and recognizes them as a valid part of life experience.

At the most elementary level, the brief encounters we have with people throughout the day involve our emotions. Some are pleasant. Others can be fraught with tension and conflict even though the interaction may be only with a telephone operator about a bad connection, with a hurried clerk in a store, or with the police as they stop you for speeding. Feelings undergird these situations just as much as the more complex feelings we have toward significant others. Becoming aware of others' feelings can help you move through the tensions of the day more gracefully and can be helpful to other individuals in many small ways. Rather than reflecting feelings in these situations, you may find a brief acknowledgment of feeling helpful.[1] The same structure is used in an acknowledgment as in a full reflection, but much less emphasis is given to feeling, and interaction moves on quickly.

If you use client feelings and emotions in an interview, the following specifics are important.

## NOTING CLIENT VERBAL AND NONVERBAL FEELINGS

When a client says, "I feel sad" or "glad" or "gloomy" and supports this statement with appropriate nonverbal behavior, identifying emotions is easy. However, many clients present subtle or discrepant messages, for

---

[1]The concept of brief acknowledgment of feeling was developed by Robert Marx. It is especially useful in teaching reflection of feeling to groups such as police officers, salespeople, and managers who do not wish to delve deeply into emotion.

often they are not sure how they feel about a person or situation. In such cases the counselor will have to identify and label the implicit feelings.

The most obvious technique for identifying client feelings is simply to ask the client an open question (for instance, "How do you feel about that?" "Could you explore any emotions that come to mind about your parents?" "What feelings come to mind when you talk about the loss?"). With some more quiet clients a closed question in which the counselor supplies the missing feeling word may be helpful (such as, "Does that feel hurtful to you?" "Could it be that you feel angry at them?" "Are you glad?").

At other times the counselor will want to infer, or even guess, the client's feelings through observation of nonverbal or verbal cues such as discrepancies between what the client says about a person and his or her actions, or a slight movement of the body contradicting the client's words. As many clients have mixed feelings about the most significant events and people in their lives, inference of unstated feelings becomes one of the important observational skills of the counselor. A client may be talking about caring for and loving parents while maintaining a closed fist. The mixed emotions may be obvious to the observer though not to the client.

The intentional counselor does not necessarily respond to every emotion, congruent or discrepant, that has been noted. Reflections of feeling must be timed to meet the needs of the individual client. Sometimes it is best simply to note the emotion and keep it in mind for possible comment later.

## THE TECHNIQUES OF REFLECTING FEELING

Somewhat like the paraphrase, reflection of feeling involves a typical set of verbal responses that can be used in a variety of ways. The classic reflection of feeling consists of the following dimensions:

1. A *sentence stem* using, insofar as possible, the client's mode of receiving information (auditory, visual, kinesthetic) often begins the reflection of feeling ("I hear you saying you feel . . ." "Sounds like you feel . . ." "Feels like . . ."). Unfortunately, these sentence stems have been used so often that they can become almost comical or stereotyped. As you practice, you will want to vary sentence stems and sometimes omit them completely. Using the client's name and the pronoun *you* helps soften and personalize the sentence stem.
2. A *feeling label* or emotional word is added to the stem ("John, you seem to feel badly about . . ." "Looks like you're happy," "Sounds like you're discouraged today; you look like you feel really down."). With mixed feelings more than one emotional word may be used ("Sally, you appear both glad and sad . . .").

3. A *context or brief paraphrase* may be added to broaden the reflection of feeling. (Using the examples in #2 above: "John, you seem to feel badly about *all the things that have happened in the past two weeks.*" "Sally, you appear both glad and sad *when leaving home.*"). The words *about*, *when*, and *because* are only three of many that add a context to a reflection of feeling.

4. *The tense* of the reflection may be important. Reflections in the present tense ("Right now, you *are* angry.") tend to be more useful than those in the past ("You felt angry then.") Some clients will have difficulty with the present tense, whereas others may need more of it.

5. A *check-out* may be used to see if the reflection is accurate. This is especially helpful if the feeling is implicit. ("You appear angry today. Am I hearing you correctly?")

## SUMMARY

Reflection has been described as basic to the counseling process, yet it can be overdone. Many times a short and accurate reflection may be the most helpful. With friends, family, and fellow employees, a quick acknowledgement of feeling ("If I were you, I'd feel angry about that . . ." "You must be tired today.") followed by continued normal conversational flow may be most helpful in developing better relationships. In an interaction with a harried waiter or salesperson, an acknowledgement of feeling may change the whole tone of a meal or business interchange. Similarly, with many clients a brief reflection may be more useful than the more detailed emphasis outlined here. Identifying implicit feelings can be helpful, and as clients move toward complex issues, the sorting out of mixed feelings may be the central ingredient of successful counseling, be it vocational interviewing, personal decisions, or in-depth individual counseling and therapy.

Nevertheless, it is important to remember that not all people will appreciate or welcome your noting their feelings. Clients will prefer to disclose feelings after rapport and trust have developed. Less verbal clients may find reflection puzzling at times or may say, for instance, "Of course I'm angry. Why did you say that?" With some cultural groups reflection of feeling may be inappropriate and represent cultural insensitivity. Male blue-collar workers, for example, may believe that expression of feelings is "unmanly," yet the brief reflection may be helpful to them. As empathic reflection can sometimes have a confrontational quality that causes clients to look at themselves from a different perspective, it may be intrusive to some clients. Though noting feelings in the interview is essential, acting on your observations may not always be in the best interests of the client. Timing is particularly important with this skill.

**Box 6-1  Key points**

*Why?*

Emotions undergird our life experience. Out of emotions spring many of our thoughts and actions. If we can identify and sort out client feelings, we have a foundation for further action.

*What?*

Emotions and feelings may be identified through labeling client behavior with affective words such as *angry, happy, sad, scared,* or *confused*. The counselor will want to develop an array of ways to note and label client emotions. Important in labeling client feelings are noting:

1. Emotional words used by the client.
2. Implicit emotional words not actually spoken.
3. Nonverbal emotions seen through observation of body movement.
4. Mixed verbal and nonverbal emotions, which may represent a variety of discrepancies.

*How?*

Emotions may be observed directly, you may ask questions to draw out emotions ("How do you feel about that?" "Do you feel angry?"), or you may reflect feelings directly through the following steps:

1. Begin with a sentence stem such as "You feel," "Sounds like you feel," "Could it be you feel," and so on. Use the client's name.
2. Feeling word(s) may be added (*sad, happy, glad*).
3. The context may be added through a paraphrase or a repetition of key content. "Looks like you feel happy *about the excellent rating*."
4. In many cases a present tense reflection is more powerful than past or future tense. "You feel happy right now" rather than "you felt" or "will feel" happy.
5. Following an implicit identification of feeling, the check-out may be most useful. "Am I hearing you correctly?" "Is that close?" This lets the client correct you if you are either incorrect or uncomfortably close.

*With whom?*

Brief reflections of feeling may be particularly helpful with friends, family, and people met during the day. Deeper reflections and a stronger emphasis on this skill may be appropriate in many counseling situations, but they require a relatively verbal client. The skill may be inappropriate with clients of some cultural backgrounds and personal experience.

**Box 6-1 continued**

*And?*        The client observational skills of Chapter 4 will prove especially helpful in improving your skill in reflecting feeling. The concept of concreteness (see Chapter 10) may be useful to add to reflection of feeling. For example, "You seem to be angry toward your spouse. Could you give me a specific example of a situation where you feel this anger?" Following this, other feelings and thoughts may be identified, and the question "What does this mean to you?" may be helpful. Just because you observe a feeling does not mean it must be reflected. Too much reflection may overintensify the feeling. Some counselors focus too much attention on negative feelings. Accentuate the positive too! Where you discover a strong negative feeling, there is frequently an unseen positive contrasting feeling as well.

## PRACTICE EXERCISES AND SELF-ASSESSMENT

Feelings are basic to human experience. Although we may observe them in daily interaction, we usually ignore them. In counseling and helping situations, however, they can be central to the process of understanding another person. Further, you will find that increased attention to feelings and emotions may enhance the richness of your daily life and bring you closer understanding of those with whom you live and work.

*INDIVIDUAL PRACTICE*

### Exercise 1. Increasing your feeling vocabulary by categorizing feelings.

Return to the list of affective words you generated at the beginning of this chapter. Take some more time and add to that list. One way to make that list of feeling words even more extensive is to consider five categories of feeling words that give you some idea of how the client thinks about the world.

The first category is words that represent mixed or ambivalent feelings. In such cases the feelings are often very unclear, and your task will be to help the client sort out the deeper emotions underlying the surface word. List below words that represent confused or vague feelings (for instance, confused, anxious, ambivalent, torn, ripped, mixed). Mixed, vague feeling words include:

_____  _____  _____

_____  _____  _____

_____  _____  _____

_____  _____  _____

_____  _____  _____

_____  _____  _____

_____  _____  _____

   A common mistake is to assume that these words represent the root feelings. Most often, they cover deeper feelings. "Anxiety" is especially important to consider in this context. Anxiety sometimes is a vague description of mixed feelings. If you accept client anxiety as a basic feeling, counseling may proceed slowly. An important task of the interviewer is to note these mixed feeling words and use questions and reflections of feeling to help the client discover the deeper feelings underlying the surface ambivalence. Underlying confusion, for example, you may find anger, hurt, love, and concern over financial need.

   The next three categories of emotional words were suggested by Osgood, Suci, and Tannenbaum (1957), who categorize adjectives into bipolar opposites (good–bad, wise–foolish, strong–weak, and such). Emotional words used in reflection of feeling can likewise be categorized. You will

find that more words can be generated to increase your feeling vocabulary via the process below. *Also you will find that identifying client words that fit into the pattern of opposites provides you with a map of the client's feelings.*

   List feeling words into three main categories. Take your list of words from earlier in the chapter and categorize them below by which words seem to represent activity, potency, or evaluation. In some cases, you will find words repeated in more than one category. Space has also been provided for you to place *opposite* feeling words.

**Feelings of activity (such as active–passive, fast–slow, depressed–hyper):**

Active Word                        Passive Opposite

_____   _____

_____   _____

_____   _____

_____   _____

_____   _____

|              Active Word              |           Passive Opposite           |
| ------------------------------------- | ------------------------------------ |
| _____   | _____   |
| _____   | _____   |
| _____   | _____   |

**Feelings of potency (such as potent–impotent, strong–weak, skillful–clumsy):**

|              Potency Word             |           Impotency Opposite         |
| ------------------------------------- | ------------------------------------ |
| _____   | _____   |
| _____   | _____   |
| _____   | _____   |
| _____   | _____   |
| _____   | _____   |
| _____   | _____   |
| _____   | _____   |

**Feelings of evaluation (such as good–bad, bored–interested, nice–awful):**

|              Positive Word            |           Negative Opposite          |
| ------------------------------------- | ------------------------------------ |
| _____   | _____   |
| _____   | _____   |
| _____   | _____   |
| _____   | _____   |
| _____   | _____   |

Finally, feelings are often presented through metaphor, concrete examples, and similes. It is often more descriptive of emotions to say that you feel like a limp dishrag than to say you are tired and exhausted. Other examples might include dry as a desert, empty as a dish, wheeling along, proud as a lion, birdlike. Metaphors can also represent confused, active, evaluative, or potency emotions. Metaphors are often masks for more complex feelings. At times, it is appropriate to accept a metaphorical feeling as presented. At other times, you may want to search for the underlying feelings. After you have developed a list of at least ten metaphors, you may wish to generate a list of opposite metaphors and examples.

**Metaphors, similes, and concrete examples of feelings:**

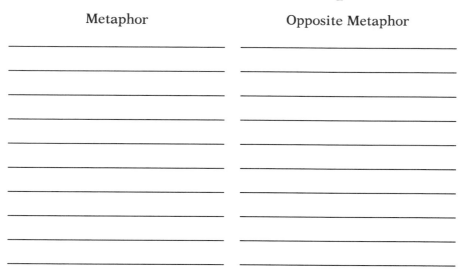

|  Metaphor  |  Opposite Metaphor  |
| --- | --- |

### Exercise 2.  Observation of feelings.

It is important to realize that different clients will have different patterns of feeling word constructs. These word patterns provide you with important information about how the client constructs and thinks about the world. For example, Beth, the client in the example interview in this chapter, used the following feeling words: *worried, relaxed, real concerned, good, jumpy, love, helplessness, out of my hands, control*. *Worry* was used in many of the client's statements, and, although it has some negative evaluative connotations, it is best considered a mixed feeling representing a synthesis of all the other more specific words. The other words may be categorized into feelings of activity–passivity (*real concerned, relaxed, jumpy*), potency–impotency (*helplessness, out of my hands, control*), and positive or negative evaluation (*good, love*). Some possible goals for Beth would be to acknowledge and validate the general worry; to become more relaxed; to accept the fact that in some ways she cannot control her mother's illness, though she can control other aspects of the situation; and to give more weight to her positive feelings.

Observe an interview or listen to a discussion and note below the feeling words used by the client. Develop polar opposites that may give you some idea of how the client constructs the world. Keep in mind that the polar opposites are *your* words, not those of the other person.

| Feeling Words | Polar Opposite |
|---|---|
| _____ | _____ |
| _____ | _____ |
| _____ | _____ |
| _____ | _____ |
| _____ | _____ |
| _____ | _____ |
| _____ | _____ |
| _____ | _____ |

Given the concepts of activity, potency, and evaluation, what concepts or ideas can you generate to describe the client and possible goals to help the client develop?

_____

_____

_____

_____

_____

_____

_____

_____

_____

_____

_____

_____

_____

**Exercise 3. Distinguishing a reflection of feeling from a paraphrase.**

The key feature that distinguishes a reflection of feeling from a paraphrase is the affective word. Many paraphrases contain reflections of feeling. These counselor statements are classified both as a paraphrase and reflection of feeling. Consider the two examples below. In the first example, you are to indicate which of the leads is a paraphrase (P), which is a reflection of feeling (RF), and which is an encourager (E).

*Client:* I am really discouraged. I can't find anywhere to live. I've looked at so many apartments, but they are all so expensive. I'm tired and don't know where to turn.

Mark the following with an E, P, or RF, or combination if more than one skill is used.

_____ "Where to turn?"

_____ "Tired . . ."

_____ "You feel very tired and discouraged."

_____ "Searching for an apartment simply hasn't been successful, they're all so expensive."

_____ "You look tired and discouraged; you've looked hard but haven't been able to find an apartment you can afford."

In the second example, write an encourager, a paraphrase, a reflection of feeling, and a combination of paraphrase and reflection of feeling in response to the client.

*Client:* Right, I do feel tired and frustrated. In fact, I am really *angry*. One place they treated me like dirt!

Encourager _____

Paraphrase _____

_____

Reflection of feeling _____

_____

Combination paraphrase and reflection of feeling _____

_____

## Exercise 4. Acknowledgment of feeling.

We have seen that the brief reflection of feeling (or acknowledgment of feeling) may be useful in your interactions with busy and harried people during the day. At least once a day, deliberately tune in with a waitress, a teacher, a service station attendant, a telephone operator, or a friend, and give a *brief* acknowledgment of feeling (such as "You seem terribly busy and pushed."). Follow this with a brief self-statement ("Can I help?" "Should I come back?" "I've been pushed today myself as well.") and note below what happens:

_____

_____

_____

_____

_____

**Exercise 5. Examining your own feeling vocabulary.**

Write a 200-word essay on any topic of interest to you. Alternatively, examine a letter you have written to a friend or family member. List below your feeling words and metaphors:

_____     _____

_____     _____

_____     _____

_____     _____

_____     _____

_____     _____

   Now classify your feeling words in terms of activity, potency, and evaluation. What do you discover?

_____

_____

_____

_____

_____

*SYSTEMATIC GROUP PRACTICE*

One of the most difficult skills for people in our culture to learn is the reflection of feeling. Mastering this skill is critical to effective counseling and interviewing.

**Step 1. Divide into practice groups.**

**Step 2. Select a group leader.**

**Step 3. Assign roles for the first practice session.**

Role-played client

Interviewer

Observer I gives special attention to noting client feelings

Observer II gives special attention to interviewer behavior

**Step 4. Planning.** A useful way for the interviewer to begin (if the topic is the same as in the paraphrasing practice session) is with a summary of the past interview. This can be followed with questioning, paraphrasing, and encouraging to bring out data. Periodically, the interviewer should reflect feelings. This may be facilitated by one-word encouragers that focus on feeling words, and by open questions ("How did you feel when that happened?"). The practice session should end with a summarization of both the feelings and the facts of the situation. Examine the basic and active mastery goals of self-assessment and follow-up, and determine your personal objectives for the interview.

It is critical that the client talk about feelings if the interviewer is going to reflect them. The same topics are suggested as those recommended for paraphrasing:

Something or someone I have a present or past conflict with.

Positive and negative feelings toward my parents or other significant persons.

Mixed blessings of my work setting, home community, or area of the country.

A conflict regarding a decision around work, school, or a major purchase.

The observers should use this time to plan their feedback and their own sessions.

**Step 5. Conduct a five-minute practice session using this skill.**

**Step 6. Review the practice session and provide feedback to the interviewer for ten minutes.** How well did the interviewer achieve goals

## NOTING AND REFLECTING FEELINGS FEEDBACK SHEET

_____ (Date)

_____    _____
(Name of Interviewer)           (Name of Person Completing Form)

_____

*Instructions:* Observer I will give special attention to client feelings via verbal and nonverbal notations. Observer II will write down the wording of interviewer reflections of feeling as closely as possible and comment on their accuracy and value.

_____

1. Verbal feelings expressed by the client (list all *words* that relate to emotions here):
2. Nonverbal indications of feeling states in the client (facial flush, body movements, and the like at certain times):
3. Implicit feelings not actually stated by the client (check these out with the client later for validity):
4. Reflections of feelings used by the interviewer (as closely as possible use the exact words of the interviewer):
5. Comments on the reflections of feeling (What typical sentence stems were used? Were the feeling words used by the interviewer implicit or explicit from the client? Was the interviewer's use of the skill accurate and valid? Was the check-out used?)

1. _____

_____

2. _____

_____

3. _____

_____

4. _____

_____

5. _____

_____

and mastery objectives? As skills and client role-plays become more complex, you'll find that time is not sufficient for in-depth practice sessions. Contract for practice time outside the session with your group. Again, it is particularly important that the observers and interviewer note the level of mastery achieved by the interviewer. Was the interviewer able to achieve specific objectives with specific client impact?

**Step 7.  Rotate roles.**

**A reminder.**   The role-played client may be difficult if he or she wishes, but must be talkative. This may help generalize learning to real situations. Remember that this is a practice session, and unless affective issues are discussed, the interviewer will have no opportunity to practice the skill.

### SELF-ASSESSMENT AND FOLLOW-UP

The questions and self-assessment items presented below are designed to help you determine your present mastery level of reflection of feeling and to determine possible directions for the future.

**1.  Reflection of feeling is seen by many interviewers and counselors as the interviewing central skill, enabling the interviewer to reach and understand client emotional experience.** Without understanding of emotional experience and feelings, many say, no real counseling or effective interviewing can exist. Do you agree or disagree with this statement? Explain your position.

_____

_____

_____

_____

_____

_____

**2.  Mastery of reflection of feeling.** What specific competencies have you mastered with this skill? Give evidence of each level of mastery in the space provided and/or information from tapes, transcripts, or case studies.

**Identification.**   You will be able to classify the skill of reflection of feeling as it is shown in the interview. You will be able to develop an extensive list of affective words to assist you in reflecting feelings.

_____ An extensive list of affective words has been generated.

_____

_____

_____ These affective words have been categorized into mixed and metaphorical feelings and classified into activity, potency, and evaluation.

_____

_____

_____ Ability to classify reflection of feeling as it is demonstrated in an interview.

_____

_____

_____ Ability to acknowledge feelings briefly in daily interaction with people outside of counseling (restaurant, grocery store, and the like).

_____

_____

**Basic Mastery.**  You will be able to demonstrate the skill of reflection of feeling in a role-played interview.

_____ Demonstration of use of the skill in a role-played interview.

_____

_____

_____ Demonstration of skill in real interviews.

_____

_____

**Active mastery.**  You will be able to use this skill in the interview and to identify client feelings accurately. A client may be expected to say "that's right . . ." at times in response to your reflection. Through the careful use of this skill, you may open a client to more expression of personal feeling and emotion, or, given the need in a particular situation, you may close off an overly extensive discussion of emotion. You may combine reflection of feeling with paraphrasing and summarization. You will enable a client to talk about emotions and to sort through mixed emotions.

Provide evidence of your mastery of each of the following with tapes, transcripts, or case studies.

———— In response to your reflections of feeling, do clients often say "that's right . . ." and continue their talk?

———— Through reflection of feeling (often coupled with questioning) can you facilitate exploration of feelings?

———— Can you match the client's auditory, visual, or kinesthetic system?

———— Through the skill (often coupled with closed questions) can you close off discussion of feelings?

———— Can you use activity, potency, and evaluative dimensions to classify feelings more accurately in the session?

———— Can you sort out and discover the feelings underlying words such as *confused* and *ambivalent*?

———— In a problem-solving interview or in a session where a client talks about an important relationship, can you bring out the positive and negative feelings about each alternative or about the relationship?

———— Most of us have mixed feelings toward our significant relationships or important issues in our lives. Either in a role-played practice session or in a real interview or personal interaction, can you help the other person sort out confused feelings through questions, paraphrasing, encouragers, and reflection of feeling?

**Teaching mastery.**   Are you able to teach the skill of reflection of feeling to clients and other persons? The impact of your teaching will be measured by the achievement of your students on the above criteria.

_____

_____

**3. What one single goal would you set for yourself with the skill of reflection of feeling?**

_____

_____

_____

_____

## REFERENCE

Osgood, C., Suci, G., and Tannenbaum, P. *The measurement of meaning.* Urbana, Ill.: University of Illinois Press, 1957.

CHAPTER **7**

# Eliciting and Reflecting Meaning: Helping Clients Explore Values and Beliefs[1]

"He who has a why to live for can bear with almost any how." (Nietzsche)

**How can reflection of meaning help you and your clients?**

*Major Function*

Two people may both have had a vacation on the beach. But whereas one talks about the glorious sun and the wonderful experience, the second talks about the sunburn and the problems that occurred. People experience the same event, but it *means* something different to each of them. A small gift may be given to two people. One experiences the gift joyfully, but the other thinks, "Now I've got to give them something," and misses the joy of the moment.

Reflection of meaning is concerned with finding the deeply felt thoughts and feelings (meanings) underlying life experience. If you use reflection of meaning, you may expect clients to search into deeper aspects of their life experience.

*Secondary Functions*

Knowledge and skill in reflection of meaning results in:

▲ Facilitating clients' interpretation of their own experience. Reflection of feeling and the skill of

---

[1]Conversations with Otto Payton of the Medical College of Virginia were important in the development of this skill for the microtraining framework. The initial stimulus came from a meeting in the summer of 1979 with Viktor Frankl, whose logotherapy offers a critical and central ingredient missing from much current theory. This chapter is dedicated to Viktor Frankl.

interpretation are closely related. However, clients can use reflection of meaning to interpret for themselves what their experience means.

▲ Assisting clients to explore their values and goals in life.
▲ Understanding deeper aspects of client experience.

## INTRODUCTION

Consider the following statement: "I just got divorced, and I have plenty to do." What does this statement mean? The words are clear and explicit, but to different people the same words may have vastly different meanings. For example, for client A this means feelings of guilt and the need to restructure life through psychotherapy, for client B it means anger and the need for revenge, for client C it means that new housing must be found and new child-care arrangements developed for simple survival, and for client D it may mean a turn to a more playful, hedonistic life. The same words may mean different things to different people. Our task in this chapter is to assist clients in finding meanings that underlie their feelings, thoughts, and actions.

Two levels of speech and action may be identified. Thus far, we have been working primarily with *explicit*, observable levels. Attending, questioning, encouraging, paraphrasing, and summarizing all focused on reacting specifically to what a client says and does. In reflection of feeling we introduced the concept of explicit and implicit feelings. We know that our feelings may sometimes run deeper than our own awareness of them. As deep as, and sometimes deeper than, feelings are meanings, which provide basic organizing constructs for a person's life. The skill of noting and reflecting meaning often operates at an *implicit* level.

It is important, at this point, to consider the relationship of reflection of meaning to other skills, such as paraphrasing and encouraging. Figure 7-1 provides a pictorial representation of meaning behaviors, thoughts, and feelings. The following points are important in relating the figure and its concepts to your own practice.

1. All four dimensions are operating simultaneously and constantly in any individual or group. We are systems, and any change in one part of the system affects the total.
2. As a rough rule, paraphrases speak to thoughts, reflections of feelings to feelings, attending behavior and client observation to behaviors, and reflection of meaning to meaning. Different helping methods view differing areas of the model as most important.

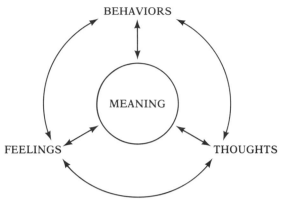

**FIGURE 7–1.** Pictorial representation of the relation between behaviors, thoughts, feelings, and meaning

3. In using these attending skills, we attempt to break down the complex behavior of the client into component parts. It is possible that attacking only one dimension (for instance, thoughts through paraphrasing) will lead to a change in client behavior, which in turn affects changes in feelings and meaning. *A change in any one part of the system may result in a change in other parts as well.* Even though, for practical purposes, we divide the client and the counseling interview into component parts, we cannot escape the interaction of the parts.

4. For many clients meaning is the central issue, and it is here that the most profound change may occur. For other clients, however, change in thoughts (rational-emotive therapy, cognitive behavior modification) may be most helpful. Still others may change behavior (behavior modification, reality therapy) or work on feelings (Rogerian, encounter therapy). Meaning-oriented therapies include psychoanalysis, logotherapy, and certain types of cognitive behavior modification.

5. A multimodal approach (see Lazarus, 1976) may involve using all the skills and concepts in an effort to maximize change and personal growth.

To get some sense of how meaning may differ among people, consider the concept of divorce. Write below what divorce means to you.

_____

_____

_____

_____

_____

Now compare your personally felt and stated meanings with those of others. How are you similar, and how are you different?

_____

_____

_____

_____

The world around us is often complex and confusing. We process the data of the world through our auditory, visual, and kinesthetic senses and organize it into meaningful patterns (for instance, what divorce means to us). Some of those patterns of organization come from society and culture, others come from parents and close friends, and some are totally unique to us. Some suggest we use a form of *inner speech* in which we metaphorically talk to ourselves and make sense of things. All of us seem to have some system of meaning, concepts, and judgments, but with varying levels of clarity.

Counseling can help individuals clarify underlying meanings. It is, of course, helpful to assist a client explore a divorce or the death of a significant person through questioning, paraphrasing, and reflecting feeling. But the thoughts and feelings are not usually worked through until they are organized into some meaningful value pattern, which often provides reasons for what happened. "Death, I guess, is part of life." "Through dying, I know my loved one is in heaven." "I guess my extreme reaction is partly because I feel guilty and afraid of dying myself." These are just three responses, representing organized meaning systems in the client's life, that may be facilitated by attending and listening skills.

Noting and reflecting meaning may at times be a difficult skill. Yet used sparingly and effectively, it can help clients find themselves and their direction more clearly.

In practice, the skill of reflection of meaning looks and sounds very much like a reflection of feeling or a paraphrase. However, it is distinctly different in tone and purpose. You will often find the reflection of meaning following a "meaning probe" or question (such as, "What does that mean to you?") or an encourager focusing on an important single key word (such as "Divorce . . ."). The reflection of meaning is structured like the reflection of feeling with the exception that "You feel . . ." becomes "You mean . . ." The reflection of meaning then paraphrases the important ideas of meaning expressed by the client. The skill is particularly important in cognitive behavior modification, existential approaches to counseling, and logotherapy.

The following transcript illustrates the skill in action.

## EXAMPLE INTERVIEW

In the following interview the client is talking about feelings surrounding a past divorce.

*Jay:* So, Carl, you're thinking about the divorce again . . .
(Encourager-restatement)

*Carl:* Yeah, that divorce has really thrown me for a loop, I tell ya. I really cared a lot about Dolores and . . . ah . . . we got along well together. But there was something missing.

*Jay:* Uh-huh . . . something missing?
(Single-word or short-phrase encourager. Note that clients often talk about what these words mean in more depth. Encouragers appear to be closely related to meaning in many cases.)

*Carl:* Uh-huh, we just never really shared something very basic. You know . . . it was like the relationship didn't have enough depth to go anywhere. We liked each other, we amused one another, but beyond that . . . I don't know . . .

*Jay:* I think I can feel that. Uh . . . as I listen, there seem to be a lot of different things going on. What sense do you make of it?
(A mild self-disclosure is followed by an open question searching for Carl's meaning in the situation.)

*Carl:* Well, in a way, it seems like the relationship was somewhat shallow. When we got married, there just wasn't much . . . ah . . . depth there that I had hoped for in a meaningful relationship.

*Jay:* Mm-hmmm . . . you seem to be talking in terms of shallow versus meaningful relationships. What does a meaningful relationship feel like to you?
(Encourager followed by a reflection of meaning. Note that Carl's personal constructs for discussing his past relationship center on the word *shallow* and the contrast *meaningful*. This polarity is likely one of Carl's significant meanings around which he organizes much of his experience. The open question is designed to further the exploration of meaning.)

*Carl:* Well, I guess . . . ah . . . that's a good question. I guess for me, in order to be married, there has to be some real, you know, some real caring beyond just on a daily basis. It has to be something that goes right to the soul. You know, you're really connected to your partner in a very powerful way.

*Jay:* So, connections, soul, deeper aspects strike you as really important.
(Reflection of meaning. Note that this reflection is also very close to a paraphrase, and Jay uses Carl's *main words*. The distinction centers around issues of meaning. A reflection of meaning could be described as a special type of paraphrase.)

*Carl:* That's right. If I'm married to somebody, I have to be more than just a roommate. There has to be some reason for me to really want to stay married, and I think with her . . . ah . . . those connections and that depth were missing, and we didn't miss each other that much. We liked each other, you know, but when one of us was gone, it just didn't seem to matter whether we were here or there.

*Jay:* So there are some really good feelings about a relationship that is meaningful even when the other person is gone. That relationship didn't have that. It didn't have those values for you.

(Reflection of meaning plus some reflection of feeling. Note that Jay has added the word *values* to the discussion. In reflection of meaning it is likely that the counselor or interviewer will add words such as *meaning, understanding, sense,* and *values.* Such words seem to produce a very different discussion and lead the client to interpret experience from her or his own frame of reference. A reflection of meaning comes from the client's frame of reference. An interpretation is derived from the counselor's frame of reference or theoretical ideology.)

*Carl:* Uh-huh.

*Jay:* Ah . . . could you fantasize how you might play out those thoughts, feelings, and meanings in another relationship?

(Open question oriented to meaning.)

*Carl:* Well, I guess it's important for me to have some independence from a person, but I'd like that independence such that, when we were apart, we'd still be thinking of the other one.

*Jay:* Um-humm.

*Carl:* In other words, I don't want a relationship in which we are always tagging along together. You know, the extreme of that is where you don't care enough whether you are together or not. That isn't intimate enough. I guess what it boils down to is that I really want the intimacy in a marriage. My fantasy is to have a very independent partner whom I care very much about and who cares very much about me, and we can both live our lives and be individuals and have that bonding and that connectedness.

*Jay:* Let's see if I can put together what you're saying. The key words seem to be independent with intimacy and caring. It's those concepts that can produce bonding and connectedness, as you say, whether you are together or not.

Comment: This reflection of meaning becomes almost a summarization of meaning. Note that the key words and constructs have come from the client in response to questions about meaning and value. A logical place to move from this point is further exploration of meaning or, more specifically, to actions in life the client could take to actualize these deeply felt meanings. The counseling would seek to bring behavior in accord with thoughts. Current relationships could be explored for how well they achieve the client's important meanings as well as for behaviors that illustrate or do not illustrate the meaning in action. Meaning often operates at a deep level and determines what people think and do. Incongruities and discrepancies between meanings and actions can be very troublesome to many clients. Further, meanings themselves can conflict within the client's world.)

## INSTRUCTIONAL READING

 The most direct way to determine what a situation or a relationship means to a client is to ask a question. Skilled questioning can uncover underlying, implicit meanings. Some useful questions include:

"What does that mean to you?"

"What sense do you make of it?"

"What values underlie your actions?"

"Why is that important (or unimportant) to you?"

"Could you give me examples of some values that are important in your life decisions? How have those values been implemented in your life?"

"What are some of the reasons you think that happened?"

"Which of your personal values support/oppose that behavior/thought pattern/feeling?"

"Why?" (by itself, used carefully)

Once the implicit meaning is brought forward, it is relatively easy to reflect meaning. Simply change "You feel . . ." to "You *mean*. . . ." Other variations could include "You value . . . ," "You care . . . ," "Your reasons are . . . ," or "Your intention was. . . ." Distinguishing between a reflection of meaning and a paraphrase or reflection of feeling may at times be most difficult. Often the skilled counselor will blend the three skills together. For practice, however, it is useful to separate out meaning responses and develop an understanding of their import and power in the interview. Noting the key words that relate to meaning (*meaning, value, reasons, intent, cause,* and the like) will help distinguish reflection of meaning from other skills.

Reflection of meaning becomes vastly more complicated when meanings or values conflict. Just as clients may express mixed and confused feelings about an issue, so may explicitly or implicitly conflicting values underlie their statements. A client may feel forced to choose between loyalty to family and loyalty to a spouse, for instance. Underlying meanings of love for both parties may be complicated by a value of dependence fostered by the family and independence represented by the spouse.

In making a decision, it may be more important for the client to sort out these felt meaning constructs than the facts and feelings associated with the decision.

Similarly, a young person may be in a value conflict over a vocational choice. The facts may be paraphrased accurately and the feelings around each choice duly noted. Yet the meaning of each choice may be most important. The counselor can ask, "What does each choice mean for you? What sense do you make of each?" The client's answers provide the opportunity for the counselor to reflect back the meaning, eventually leading to a decision that involves not only facts and feelings, but also values and meaning.

Now that we have defined reflection of meaning, the remainder of this instructional reading will focus on the place of this skill in different theoretical frameworks. Many counseling and therapy theories give attention to issues of meaning. The following are a few examples of how this skill undergirds the helping process.

*REFLECTION OF MEANING AND LOGOTHERAPY*

If one person were to be identified with meaning and the therapeutic process, that individual would be Viktor Frankl, the developer of logotherapy. Frankl (1959) has pointed out the importance of a life philosophy that enables us to transcend suffering and find meaning in our existence. Frankl argues that our greatest need is for a core of meaning and purpose in our life.

Logotherapists search for meaning underlying behavior and action. Dereflection is a specific technique that logotherapy uses to uncover meaning. Many clients "hyperreflect" on a negative meaning of events in their lives and may overeat, drink to excess, or wallow in depression. They are constantly attributing a negative meaning to life. The direct reflection of meaning may assist such clients in continuing the negative thoughts and behavior patterns. Dereflection, by contrast, seeks to help clients discover the "multitude of values that lie beyond their own weak selves" (Lukas, 1980, p. 180). The goal is to help clients think of things *other* than the negative issue and to find alternative positive meaning in the same event. The questions listed at the beginning of this section represent first steps to help clients dereflect. The following abbreviated example illustrates this technique.

*Client:* I just can't stop abusing my child. I feel helpless.
*Counselor:* I understand that; we've talked about it in some detail. Could you explore for a while some of the things you have valued and enjoyed in the past? Or that even now you still like?

     . . . . . (dots indicate time lapse)

(Client and counselor explore via reflection of feeling and questions a range of activities that have been satisfying. The counselor particularly attends to positive values during the process.)

. . . . .

*Counselor:* (Reflecting meaning) So what is truly most meaningful to you is having some time to be yourself and to be alone. You seem to have found that you can feel best and can come out and be with others if you have time to explore what is most important to you. Let's carry that on further.

The dereflection process has only begun, but positive steps have been initiated. At issue here is finding something positive in a negative situation. This does not deny the negative aspects but seeks to find something positive in each individual on which a more positive approach to the problem may be developed. At a later point the issue of child abuse may be approached once again with a positive action plan.

## REFLECTION OF MEANING AND CLIENT-CENTERED THERAPY

Carl Rogers's client-centered therapy (see Rogers, 1961) is often characterized as predominantly paraphrasing and reflection of feeling, at least in the early stages. However, *meaning* plays perhaps an even more important part in his overall thinking and conceptualization. The following brief excerpt illustrates how use of reflection of meaning and reflection of feeling are closely intertwined:

*Client:* . . . I have all the symptoms of fear.
*Therapist:* Fear is a very scary thing. Is that what you mean? (Note reflection of feeling, followed by a meaning check-out.)
*Client:* Mm-hm. (Long pause)
*Therapist:* Do you want to say any more about what you mean by that? That it really does give you the symptoms of fear.

The pattern of encouraging, listening to the client, and searching for deeper meanings is quite similar to the reflection of meaning discussed in this chapter. Reflection of feeling, by contrast, would work more directly with the emotions themselves. Meaning is a deeper concept and area for talk.

Eugene Gendlin's (1979) focusing technique is a self-directed approach to the same process. In focusing, people pay attention in depth to their feelings, then associate to a specific problem situation, and then feel and experience that problem deeply through complete attention. This is followed by experiencing the same process with positive thoughts and feelings and new words. The positive and negative are then joined together, and the client (or oneself) often finds new meaning spontaneously.

The Gendlin framework is in many ways clearer than the Rogerian process, and it could be extended to the interview. Through the skills taught in this program, clients experience first negative events, and then positive events, rather fully. The basic discrepancy between the two events may be summarized by the counselor. This summary coupled with a basic meaning question such as "How do you put those two together?" "What sense/meaning do you get out of it?" or some similar statement often leads to a new meaning or new interpretation in the client's own words. The client's frame of reference has been honored.

## REFLECTION OF MEANING AND BEHAVIORAL APPROACHES

Cognitive behavior modification (see Beck, 1976; Meichenbaum, 1977) has become an important area for behavioral psychologists. Cognitive behavior modifiers talk in depth about cognitive structures and internal dialogue. They see underlying behaviors as internal thought processes (or "inner speech"), which often monitor and guide more observable behavior.

The typical behavior modification approach directs clients to specific activities to change or alter thought sequences and meaning—for example, thought-stopping, guided imagery, implosion, and other techniques. Cognitive behavioral approaches view cognitive structures as shaping the content of client internal dialogue. These structures may be best described as constructs that order and guide behavior. The search for these constructs in behavioral approaches matches closely those of logotherapists and client-centered theorists. However, behavioral psychologists add an additional armament of directives, techniques, and other skills to move some clients more rapidly into new patterns of cognition and meaning.

## HOW REFLECTION OF MEANING RELATES TO INTERPRETATION

Reflection of meaning may be confused with interpretation, an advanced skill of interpersonal influence. In an interpretation the counselor supplies the client with a new frame of reference or understanding. The words and meanings may be stimulated by the client, but they are the counselor's impressions. Reflection of meaning, by contrast, focuses on the client's frame of reference, even if the meanings and values are unclear. Through questioning and reflection, clients search for deeper ideas underlying their statements and behaviors and learn to reinterpret their experience from their own frame of reference.

## ADDITIONAL ISSUES

Meaning may be related to the practice exercise for reflection of feeling (Exercise 1 of Chapter 6). There, emotions were categorized into activity, potency, and evaluative types. If you take a feeling (for instance, *good*) and search with the client for its polar opposite (in this case, most likely *bad*), a major personal construct or idea of the client may have been generated. Many people in this culture organize the meaning of their life in terms of "good and bad." Identifying and clarifying such a construct may be a first step to helping a client more fully understand what an event means. The construct may be identified and then reflected to the client in a deeper search for meaning. Clients will not always be able to identify polar constructs, but counselors who search for them may help supply more complete understandings while staying within the client's frame of reference. Some exercises leading toward this direction are suggested in the following section.

To some, reflection of meaning will be the most valuable skill of this training program, whereas others may seldom use it. What are your impressions of its value?

_____

_____

_____

_____

_____

---

## Box 7-1 Key points

*Why?*

Meaning organizes life experience and often serves as a metaphor from which clients generate words, sentences, and behaviors at a more surface level. Clients faced with complex life decisions may make them on the basis of meaning, values, and reasons rather than on objective facts or on feelings. However, these meanings and values are often unclear to the client.

*What?*

Meanings may be identified through noting and observing client words and constructs that describe their values and attitudes toward important issues and people. As meaning is often implicit, it is helpful to ask questions that help clients explore and clarify meaning. For example:

1. What does this mean to you?
2. What sense do you make of it?
3. What values underlie your actions?
4. Why is that important to you?
5. Why? (by itself, used carefully)

**Box 7-1 continued**

*How?*                   Meanings are reflected through the following process:

1. Beginning with a sentence stem that contains the key words "You mean . . . ," "Could it mean that you . . . ," "Sounds like you value . . . ," or "One of the underlying reasons/intentions of your actions was. . . ."
2. Using the client's own words that describe the most important aspect of the meaning. This helps ensure that you stay within the client's frame of reference rather than using your own.
3. Adding a paraphrase of the client's longer statements that catches the essence of what has been said but, again, operates primarily from the client's frame of reference.
4. A check-out in the form of "Is that close?" "Am I hearing you correctly?" or the like may be helpful.

Meanings may be more complex in situations where two values or two meanings collide. Use of questions, reflections of feelings, and so on may be required to help clients sort through meaning and value conflicts.

*With whom?*             Reflections of meaning are for more verbal clients and may be found more in counseling than in general interviewing. It is a temptation to reflect negative meanings back to troubled clients. The issue with such clients, however, is to help them find positive meanings. This may be done through questioning about situations in the client's past where positive feelings existed and searching there for meanings that may be contrasted with the negative view. A reflection of meaning used skillfully may benefit virtually any client. It can help clarify cultural and individual differences *if* the client is willing to share them.

*And?*                   Reflection of meaning is a skill basic to logotherapy and client-centered therapy. It is an alternative that may be useful in cognitive-behavioral counseling. The skill has implications for other theories as well.

## PRACTICE EXERCISES AND SELF-ASSESSMENT

The concepts of this chapter build on previous work. If you have solid attending and client observation skills, can use questions effectively, and demonstrate effective use of the encourager, paraphrase, and reflection of feeling, you are well prepared for the exercises that follow.

*INDIVIDUAL PRACTICE*

### Exercise 1.  Identification of skills.

Read the client statement below. Which of the following counselor responses are paraphrases (P), reflections of feeling (RF), and reflections of meaning (RM)? List possible key words for an encourager.

"I feel very sad and lonely. I thought Bill was the one for me. After my divorce I saw a lot of people, but no one special. Bill seemed to care for me and make it easy for me. Before that I had fun, particularly with Bob. But it seemed to be at the end just foolish, alienated sex. It appeared Bill was it, we seemed so close."

P     RF     RM

_____ _____ _____ You're really hurting and feeling sad right now.

_____ _____ _____ Since the divorce you've seen a lot of people, but Bill provided the most of what you wanted.

_____ _____ _____ Looks like the sense of peace, caring, ease, and closeness meant an awful lot to you.

_____ _____ _____ You felt really close to Bill and are now sad and lonely.

_____ _____ _____ Peace, caring, a special one means a lot to you. Bill represented that to you. Bob seemed to mean mainly fun, but it ended up with feelings of alienation. Is that right?

List possible single-word encouragers below.

_____        _____

_____        _____

_____        _____

### Exercise 2.  Identifying client issues of meaning.

Affective words in the preceding client statement include *sad*, and *lonely*. Some other words in the client statement contain elements of emotion and closely resemble feeling words—*care, easy, fun, foolish, alienated sex,* and *close*. The feeling words represent the client's emotions about the current situation; the other words represent the meanings she uses to represent the world. Specifically, the client has given us a map of how she constructs the world of her relationships with men.

It would be possible to extend the feeling exercise from the preceding chapter to issues of meaning. This time, however, it is important to note *key descriptive words*. In most client comments they tell us immediately how clients construe and represent the world in their natural language. It is possible to generate a set of polar constructs using the client's key words. For example:

| *Client's Key Words* | *Polar Opposite* | *(Whose Opposite?)*[2] |
|---|---|---|
| caring | uncaring | counselor |
| easy | hard | counselor |
| close | far/distant | counselor |
| fun | boring | counselor |
| foolish, alienated | close | client |

From just this brief example, several things may be inferred: (1) The words used to describe the client's relationship with Bill are opposites of those we infer from her relationship with Bob. (2) Very likely the constructs and words will be used to describe other relationships she has had. (This can be tested by questioning her about past relationships and noting again the key descriptive words.) (3) It is possible to identify the important constructs around which counseling should proceed. The client's actual polar constructs can be developed over time (through observation or direct questioning); they may suggest treatment alternatives.

Now listen to one of your own past practice audiotapes, view a counseling session, or listen carefully during a conversation and generate the important constructs.

| Client's Key Words | Polar Opposite | (Whose Opposite?) |
|---|---|---|
| _____ | _____ | _____ |
| _____ | _____ | _____ |
| _____ | _____ | _____ |
| _____ | _____ | _____ |
| _____ | _____ | _____ |
| _____ | _____ | _____ |

---

[2]When you identify the opposite, you may find yourself in error. Watch for the danger of projecting your experience on the client.

_____    _____    _____
_____    _____    _____
_____    _____    _____
_____    _____    _____
_____    _____    _____
_____    _____    _____

What descriptive patterns do you observe in the above construct systems? For example, do the key words/meanings pattern themselves around a particular person, situation, or thing? Do you obtain some idea of how different people represent the same event with different meanings? Record here your pattern observations.

_____
_____
_____
_____
_____
_____

The patterns you have developed represent client constructs for organizing the world. As they are partially your organization, they are not necessarily accurate representations of the other person's world. Yet if you were to listen to this person over time, you would find these constructs and words reappearing, possibly in many different settings or widely varying topics. This reappearance of words and patterns forms the tip of the iceberg, providing a clue to underlying meanings and values.

**Exercise 3.  Questioning to bring out and elicit meanings.**

Assume a client comes to you and talks about an important issue in her or his life (for instance, divorce, death, retirement, a daughter who is pregnant). List five questions that might be useful in bringing out the meaning of the event.

1. _____

2. _____

3. _____

4. _____

5. _____

**Exercise 4. Observation.**

Use the Feedback Sheet for this chapter to observe meaning issues as they might be explored in a role-played or real interview. You will find that many effective communicators will elicit meaning from others through questions such as "What do you mean by that?" "What do you value?" and the like. Again, viewing a skilled talk-show host on TV may be helpful. Record your observations here.

_____

_____

_____

_____

_____

_____

_____

**Exercise 5.  Practice of skills in other settings.**

During conversations with friends or in your own interviews, practice eliciting meaning through a combination of questioning and single-word encouragers, and then reflect the meaning back. You will often find that single-word encouragers lead people to talk about meaning issues. Record your observations of the value of this practice here. What one thing stands out from your experience?

_____

_____

_____

_____

_____

_____

_____

_____

*SYSTEMATIC GROUP PRACTICE*

Two group exercises are suggested here. The first focuses on the skill of eliciting and reflecting meaning, the second on the dereflection process as it might be used in logotherapy.

**Exercise 1. Systematic group practice in eliciting and reflecting meaning.**

**Step 1. Divide into practice groups.**

**Step 2. Select a group leader.**

**Step 3. Assign roles for the first practice session.**

Role-played client

Interviewer

Observer I observes client descriptive words and develops polar opposites

Observer II notes interviewer behavior

**Step 4. Planning.** For practice with this skill, it will be most helpful if the interview starts with the client completing one of the following model sentences. The interview will then follow along, exploring the attitudes, values, and meanings to the client underlying the sentence.

"My thoughts about divorce are . . ."

"My thoughts about death are . . ."

"My thoughts about moving from this area to another are . . ."

"My thoughts about the value of an education are . . ."

"The most important event in my life was . . ."

A few alternative topics are "my closest friend," "someone who made me very angry (or happy)," "a place where I feel very comfortable and happy." Again, a decision conflict or a conflict with another person may be a good topic.

The task of the interviewer in this case is to elicit meaning from the model sentence and help the role-played client find underlying meanings and values. A useful sequence of microskills for eliciting meaning from the model sentence is: (1) The open question "Could you tell me more about that?" (2) Encouragers and paraphrases to help the client continue. (3) Reflections of feeling to ensure you are in touch with the client's emotions. (4) Questions that relate specifically to meaning and are summarized in Box 7-1. (It is quite acceptable to have those questions in your lap and refer to them during the interview practice session.) (5) Reflecting the meaning of the event back to the client using the framework outlined in this chapter.

Examine basic and active mastery competencies in the self-assessment and follow-up section and plan your interview to achieve specific goals.

Observers should study the feedback sheets especially carefully.

**Step 5.  Conduct a five-minute practice session using the skill.**

**Step 6.  Review the practice session and provide feedback for ten minutes.**   The feedback forms are useful. It is often tempting to just talk and forget to give the interviewer helpful and needed specific feedback. Take time to complete the forms before talking about the session. As always give special attention to mastery achievement by the interviewer.

**Step 7.  Rotate roles.**   Remember to share time equally.

**Some general reminders.**   This skill can be used from a variety of theoretical perspectives. It may be useful to see if an explicit or implicit theory is observable in the interviewer's behavior.

**Exercise 2.  Systematic group practice in dereflection.**

Follow the same steps as for Exercise 1. This exercise is to remind you of the power and importance of finding positive dimensions and meaning in negative situations. One of the purposes of dereflection is to prevent and balance the excessive attention given to the negatives in life experience by helping people find positive dimensions and strengths in difficult, troubling situations.

The task of the role-played client is to talk about something negative in her or his life. For example:

An illness

A death

Loss of job or inability to find work

An accident

A divorce or other significant loss

A friend who betrayed you

The task of the interviewer is to draw out the person's negative experience through eliciting and reflecting meaning (similar to Exercise 1). Then, however, the interviewer is to draw out a positive dimension in the experience via questioning. For example, in discussing illness, "Could you talk about some positive experiences or something you learned at the hospital?" "What situations have you learned to value more as a result of that experience?" "What do you value even more now as a result?" These positive value statements may be reflected to check on the accuracy of the interviewer's understanding.

As a final step the interviewer may summarize the negative experience and the positive meaning statements and feed them both back to the client via a summarization. (For instance, "You seem to feel that being ill and near death was your worst fright ever, but at the same time you seem to value your relationships with your children and family even more now. Does that make sense to you?") In this way the positive and negative elements in the situation may be joined in a new synthesis. Some clients find this experience useful in reframing their view, and their process of hyperreflection on the negative is balanced with the positive dimensions. This often can lead to new actions and behaviors.

Summarize here your findings about the concept of dereflection.

_____

_____

_____

_____

_____

_____

_____

_____

_____

_____

# REFLECTING MEANING FEEDBACK SHEET[3]

_____ (Date)

_____     _____
(Name of Interviewer)                (Name of Person Completing Form)

_____

_Instructions:_ Observer I completes the first half of this form, giving special attention to recording descriptive words the client
associates with _meaning_. Observer II notes the use of the
skill of reflection of meaning, giving special attention to
questions that appeared to elicit meaning issues.

_____

Observer I develops polar opposites to the meaning words described by
the client. Circle those polar opposites actually used by the client.

Meaning Word                    Opposite

_____      _____

_____      _____

_____      _____

_____      _____

_____      _____

_____      _____

_____      _____

What are the main meaning issues of the interview?

_____

_____

_____

_____

_____

[3]The structure of this form was suggested by Robert Marx.

Observer II lists questions and reflections of meaning using key words and concepts.

1. _____

2. _____

3. _____

4. _____

5. _____

6. _____

Comment on the effectiveness of the reflection of meaning skill.

_____

_____

_____

_____

_____

_____

_____

_____

_____

_____

_____

_____

_____

_____

_____

_____

_____

_____

_____

_____

_____

_____

*SELF-ASSESSMENT AND FOLLOW-UP*

**1. What did this chapter mean to you?** What constructs and ideas stood out for you personally?

_____

_____

_____

_____

_____

_____

**2. Words and constructs have been given real prominence in this chapter.** Are you able to match your interviewer style with the main meaning words of the client? Can you tell which words are yours and which are the client's? As the interview progresses, who gradually adopts the other's main words—you or the client?

_____

_____

_____

_____

_____

_____

_____

_____

**3. Mastery of eliciting and reflecting meaning skills.** What specific competencies have you mastered in this area? Give evidence in the space provided, in transcripts, or with audio- or videotapes.

**Identification.**   You will be able to differentiate this skill from the closely related paraphrasing and reflection of feeling. You will be able to identify questioning sequences that facilitate client talk about meaning. You will be able to identify client words indicative of meaning issues.

_____ Ability to identify and classify the skills.

_____

_____

_____ Ability to identify and write questions that elicit meaning from clients.

_____

_____

_____ Ability to note and record key client words indicative of meaning.

_____

_____

**Basic mastery.** You will be able to demonstrate the skills of eliciting and reflecting meaning in the interview. You will be able to demonstrate elementary skills in dereflection.

_____ Demonstration of eliciting and reflecting meaning in a role-played interview.

_____

_____

_____ Demonstration of dereflection in a role-played interview.

_____

_____

**Active mastery.** You will be able to use questioning skill sequences and encouragers to bring out meaning issues and then reflect meaning accurately. You will be able to use the client's main words and constructs to define meaning rather than reframing in your own words (interpretation). You will not interpret, but facilitate the client's interpretation of experience.

_____ Are you able to use questions and minimal encouragers to bring out meaning issues?

_____ When you reflect meaning, are you able to use the client's main words and constructs rather than your own?

_____ Clients do not always provide clear polar constructs. Are you able to generate possible polar constructs and test them out in the interview, intentionally changing constructs as necessary? (The check-out will be useful in testing out possible constructs you generate.)

_____ Are you able to reflect meaning in such a fashion that the client starts exploring meaning and value issues in more depth?

_____ As necessary in the interview, are you able to switch the focus in the conversation from meaning to feeling (reflection of feeling or question oriented to feeling) or content (paraphrase or question oriented to content)?

———— When a client is hyperreflecting on the negative meaning of an event or person, are you able to find something positive in that event or person and enable the client to dereflect by focusing on the positive?

**Teaching mastery.**   Ability to teach eliciting and reflecting meaning to others. The impact of your teaching is measured by the achievement of your students on the above criteria.

**4. What place do you give this skill in your repertoire of helping skills?** Is this a skill you will want to use? In what way?

_____

_____

_____

_____

_____

# REFERENCES

Beck, A. *Cognitive therapy and emotional disorders.* New York: International Universities Press, 1976.

Frankl, V. *Man's search for meaning.* New York: Simon and Schuster, 1959.

Gendlin, E. Experiential psychotherapy. In R. Corsini, *Current psychotherapies.* Itasca, Ill.: Peacock, 1979.

Kelly, G. *The psychology of personal constructs* (Vols. I and II). New York: Norton, 1955.

Lazarus, A. *Multimodal behavior therapy.* New York: Springer-Verlag, 1976.

Lukas, E. Modification of attitudes. *International Forum for Logotherapy,* 1980, *3,* 25–24.

Meichenbaum, D. *Cognitive-behavior modification.* New York: Plenum, 1977.

Rogers, C. *On becoming a person.* Boston: Houghton-Mifflin, 1961.

**8**

# Focusing: Tuning In with Clients and Directing Conversational Flow

---

**How can focusing help you and your clients?**

*Major Function*

Focusing is a skill that enables you to direct client conversational flow toward the areas you want. For those who seek not to impede or direct client talk, awareness of focusing and its power will enable you to reduce your direction of client conversation.

*Secondary Functions*

Knowledge and skill in focusing results in:

▲ Broadening your and the client's perspective on a problem through examining the issue from alternative points of view. Focusing often results in increased cognitive complexity and understanding that many of life's decisions are more difficult than at first supposed.

▲ Increased ability to observe client use of focus dimensions—specifically, where the client focuses perceptions of a person or situation.

▲ Increased ability to open or close a client according to the needs of a specific interview.

---

## INTRODUCTION

Focusing is perhaps best described through an example.

*Client:* I just had a terrible argument with the manager. She thinks I don't know what I am doing. My sales record has been good, at least as good as other people's around here.

This client statement could occur in a therapy session, a vocational counseling interview, a management performance appraisal, or a variety of interpersonal situations. The question is how the counselor can best respond.

The answer we have offered so far is that the interviewer has a virtually infinite set of ways to respond to this person. You could attend or not attend; you could ask a variety of questions; you could reflect feelings, meaning, or content. Any of these responses might be helpful. Each leads the client in a different direction.

Focusing is a skill that is *added* to the microskills discussed thus far. Focusing adds precision to client observation and microskills through selective attention to certain aspects of client talk. People tend to talk about what others will listen to or reinforce. There are many possible ways of focusing clients; the following examples illustrate two alternatives. In response to the client above, it would be possible to:

Focus on the *client: Sandy, you* sound upset. Could *you* tell me more about *your* feelings? (Reflection of feeling, open question)

Focus on the *main theme or problem: Terrible argument?* (Encourager) *or* Could you tell me about your *sales record?* (Open question)

You can see that focusing on the person may lead Sandy to talk more about personal issues, whereas focus on the main theme or problem encourages client talk about what happened and the facts of the situation. In both cases listening skills have been combined with focusing to lead the client in very different directions. Which of the two alternatives is correct? Both may be useful in obtaining a complete summary of the situation; at the same time, either could be overused.

Four additional areas of focus analysis will be presented in this chapter:

Focus on *others:* manager, other salespeople.

Focus on *mutual issues or group:* The interviewer and client relationship or the entire management team.

Focus on *interviewer:* through a self-disclosure or "I statement."

Focus on *cultural/environmental/contextual issues:* broader issues often not readily apparent, such as racial or sexual issues, company policy, economic trends, and the like.

The chapter emphasizes focus analysis as a way to ensure a complete assessment of the problem presented by a client and to understand conversational flow in the interview.

Counselors can facilitate client awareness through focusing. Many clients tend to see their situations rather simplistically and repetitively, constantly talking about other people and failing to note their own involvement in the problem or the broader contextual issues. Some counselors would even argue that a goal of successful interviewing and counseling is to facilitate client awareness of the complexity of the world. In other cases, clients are fully aware, even painfully aware, of the complexity that surrounds them, and they are unable to focus on any single issue. In both cases the interviewer's ability to enable the client to focus is critical.

The following transcript illustrates how the focusing skill is used in practice.

## EXAMPLE INTERVIEW

*Gilbert:* Well, Paul, could you tell me what you have on your mind this morning?

*Paul:* Yeah, Gilbert, I'm really pleased that Ann is accepted to college. But I think, oh my gosh, that is a terrible amount of tuition I have to come up with.

*Gilbert:* Uh-huh . . . how are you feeling about that?
(Open question, oriented to feeling. The focus is on the *client*.)

*Paul:* Well, like I say, I'm really pleased. But, gosh, that is really some responsibility there. I want to do as much as I can. With the economy not doing so well, I'm not sure I can get it all together.

*Gilbert:* Is Ann aware of the problem of the cost of going to school?
(Closed question. The focus is on *others*.)

*Paul:* Well, she's earned a fair amount of money. But I don't think she really understands how much money it is that we have to put together. We've always had enough. She just sort of seems to sit there and expect me to come up with it. That's a little troubling.

*Gilbert:* Uh-huh . . . well, are there any loans available through some of the area's federal agencies, some private foundations?
(Closed question. The focus is on the *environmental context*, larger issues that may surround the problem.)

*Paul:* I hadn't thought about that. I think I could write the university and ask. I read in the paper that there is some kind of loan program. But isn't it true that there is a possibility of the government cutting back on those programs and maybe even eliminating those things?

*Gilbert:* Well, I tell you, I had an experience with sending my own kid to school recently and I understand that, ah, that Jamie's financial support, ah . . . was going to be down assuming she stayed another year. So that could be a problem. But this financial thing seems to have you in a bit of a quandary.
(The focus in this self-disclosure is on the *interviewer*. The paraphrase and reflection of feeling at the end of the self-disclosure wisely focuses on the *main theme or problem*—that is, finances. Self-disclosures are often helpful, but for the most part they should be kept brief.)

*Paul:* Yeah, I'm concerned about how I'm going to meet all those needs. It kind of scares me.

*Gilbert:* In what way, Paul?

(Open question, focus on client.)

*Paul:* Well, I just feel a great need to solve the problem, and I'm just sitting here looking at the books and I don't see any extra money. I suspect what I'm going to have to do is cut back.

*Gilbert:* Tell me a bit more about the finances as you see them.

(Open question. Focus is on the main theme or problem.)

*Paul:* Well, I've got $1500 in the savings bank. I don't see how I can save much between now and September. Tuition and room and board are $4500 and Ann has about $750. That leaves us a bit short.

*Gilbert:* Before we go any further, Paul, let me summarize some of the factors we've been talking about. *You're* concerned and worried and feel quite responsible for *Ann's* education. A loan might help, but the *economic situation* is such that it is a question mark. *I* feel that, myself, helping a daughter through college. *Finances* really are bugging you. Now the question seems to be, what can *we* do together to help solve the problem. Is there anything that *we* have done so far that impresses you as helpful or stands out?

(In this summarization Gilbert goes through the several focus dimensions and adds the critical dimension "we," or *mutual* focus, to the problem.)

*Paul:* One thing that stands out for me is your mentioning that I feel "responsible." I know from past counseling I've been in that I tend to take more responsibility for an issue than I need to. I sometimes may make decisions for other people without listening to them. I may be making part of the problem myself.

*Gilbert:* Paul, I sense you taking the responsibility for taking responsibility. You are not alone. There is me, who is interested in helping you work things through; Ann, who undoubtedly, as I have heard you talk about her, wants to do her full share; and the college and government will want to meet their responsibilities too.

(Interpretation focusing first on the *client*, then moving again to a multiple *we* focus in an effort to enable the client to understand that he is not as alone in this matter as he thinks he is.)

*Paul:* Maybe we can work this through. I appreciate your reminding me. Sometimes I make myself alone when I don't need to be. I need to think through the possibility of working with others. Your listening to me and sharing makes me feel less alone and by myself. I don't feel as alone as I did.

Comment: The concepts of focusing here are used to illustrate that many problems are simultaneously more complex and less complex than we often think (see Box 8-1). In the individualistic Western society we often place responsibility on the individual. The individual accepts this responsibility for problem solving and fails to realize that an entire system of interrelationships is involved in solving any problem or issue.

A "we" focus as a core concept, as opposed to an "I" focus, may help individuals accept themselves as part of a system in addition to taking individual initiative and responsibility.

---

**Box 8-1    Focus analysis for interview with Paul**

MAIN ISSUE AS PRESENTED:  Large tuition bill to be paid.[1]

*Client focus*
Paul and pronoun *you*

*Main theme/problem focus*
Tuition bill and finances

*Others focus*
Ann

*Mutual group, "we" focus*
Client-interviewer relationship—"we"

*Interviewer focus*
Gilbert

*Cultural/environmental/contextual focus*
A variety of issues, some of which are outlined below

Federal agencies/private foundations

Government cutbacks/general economic conditions

Financial background and resources

Timing and preparation of application forms

College desired

Ethnic or religious background

Family experience with college (for instance, first family member to attend)

---

[1] Note that the interviewer can focus on all of these issues plus many others, or focus simply on the main theme or problem or just the individual's feelings and attitudes. Focus analysis provides a map of possible issues that need to be considered in any important decision.

## INSTRUCTIONAL READING

Six areas of focus analysis have been identified. Within each more complexity can be found. Beginning counselors and interviewers should generally start responding to the individual client before them. Research and experience have shown that simply learning to respond to the individual and her or his perceptions of the world is perhaps most basic. When responding to the client, using personal pronouns (*you, your*) and *names* is of critical consideration.

To begin this section, we will present a case concerning the heavily loaded emotional and moral issue of abortion. Your task is to practice differentiating between individual and problem/main theme focus using a variety of microskills.

*Client:* I just had an abortion.

Client focus: _____

Problem/main theme focus: _____

This is an easy example. Too many beginners focus on the main theme or problem ("Tell me more about the abortion."), which may result in a voyeuristic interview in which many facts are obtained, but little is learned about the client. An extremely important task is finding out how the client felt about the abortion and now feels about herself. ("Could you share some of your personal experiences with this?")

*Client:* I just had an abortion and I feel pretty awful. They treated me terribly, and I felt just like a piece of meat. Bob won't have anything to do with me. My parents don't know.

Client focus: _____

Problem/main theme focus: _____

_____

Focusing on the feelings and thoughts of the woman would be a clear individual or client focus. However, the woman exists in relationship to a problem (the abortion), and a main theme focus ("You feel a lot of things about the abortion . . . let's sort them out.") opens the issue even further.

At this point it becomes apparent that significant others (Bob, parents, the physician and nurses) are important in the problem. Another focus area is on others. Use the space below to make three alternative focus responses:

Focus on others (Bob): _____

Focus on others (parents): _____

Focus on others (physician and nurses): _____

_____

If you focus on Bob solely, issues around parents or feelings toward the physicians and nurses are temporarily lost. It is important to keep all significant others in mind in the process of problem resolution and problem examination, perhaps saving questions or other listening skills for a later point. For a full understanding of the abortion experience, all these people (and probably others) need to be explored. In turn, the client will likely have personal feelings and thoughts toward each of these people, and so it may be necessary to again focus on the client.

The client may continue her discussion as follows:

*Client:* I feel everyone is just judging me. They all seem to be condemning me. I even feel a little frightened of you.

A mutual focus often emphasizes the "we" in a relationship. Use the following space for a mutual focus statement.

Focus on mutual issues: _____

_____

_____

One possibility here is: "Right now, *we* have an issue. Can *we* work together to help you? What are some of your thoughts and feelings toward how we are doing?" The emphasis here is on the relationship between the counselor and the client. Two people are working on an issue, and the client accepts partial ownership of the problem. Some counseling theories would argue against this relational approach. Among most people in Western cultures emphasis on the distinction between "I" (client focus) and "me" (interviewer focus) would perhaps be more common. Among some Asian and Southern European peoples, the "we" focus may be especially appropriate: *"We* are going to solve this problem." The "we" focus provides a balance of responsibility, often reassuring to the client regardless of her or his background.

Another type of mutual focus is on the group. In this case, "we" could be extended to include the client, the counselor, Bob, the parents, and perhaps even the physician and nurses for, as long as the client has a problem, all the significant others have a problem as well. A typical approach in counseling and management problem solving in this country is to fix blame, or "put the monkey on someone's back." A relational "we" approach assumes that the group or the dyad takes responsibility for the problem, responsibility is shared, and common efforts are made toward resolution. A smoothly working encounter or therapy group often emphasizes "we" in this manner, as does the effective management or production team in industry. The well-known Japanese quality work-manship stems from a basic "we" orientation in that society. Family therapy and systems thinking often operate from a "we" concept.

Another type of focus is for the interviewer to focus on himself or herself. For our example, what would a focus on the interviewer be?

Interviewer focus: _____

An interviewer focus could be a self-disclosure about feelings and thoughts about the client or situation—for example, "*I* feel concerned and sad over what happened; *I* want to help," or "*I* too had an abortion . . . my experience was . . . ," or perhaps even some personal advice. Opinions vary as to the appropriateness of interviewer or counselor involvement. Increasingly, however, the value and power of such statements are being recognized. They must not be overused, or the client may end up doing therapy with the counselor.

Perhaps the most complex and confusing focus dimension is that of cultural/environmental/contextual issues. Some topics relating to these broad areas are listed below, along with possible responses to the client.

Moral/religious issues: "What is your church's position on abortion?"

Legal issues: "Abortion is illegal in this state. How have you dealt with this issue?"

Women's issues: "A support group for women concerning abortion is just starting. Would you like to attend?"

Economic issues: "You were saying you didn't know how to pay for the operation . . ."

Health issues: "How have you been eating and sleeping lately? Are there after-effects you feel?"

Educational issues: "Will you be able to finish the academic term?"

Work issues: "How long were you out of work?"

Ethnic/racial issues: "What is the meaning of abortion among people of your background?"

Any one of these issues, plus many others, could be important for any client. With some clients all of these areas might need to be explored for a satisfactory problem resolution. The counselor or interviewer who is able to conceptualize a client problem broadly can introduce many valuable aspects of the problem or situation. Note that much of cultural/environmental/contextual focusing depends on the interviewer bringing in concepts from her or his knowledge and not simply following ideas presented by the client.

It now would be useful for you to write responses to the following individual using a variety of focus analysis possibilities. Note that cultural/environmental/contextual has been presented first. It is helpful for the counselor or interviewer to be aware of many of these issues before responding, and while responding, to the client at other levels.

*Client:* I am having a terrible time with Sam. He's fouling up the whole department. Like last week, he got confused over budgets and cost us plenty! Now, I know he's the boss's favorite and had a good record before he came here. But he's no hot shot. He just gives me a pain. I wish I were rid of him.

Brainstorm the many possible cultural/environmental/contextual issues that might be related to this problem:

_____

_____

_____

_____

_____

_____

_____

_____

_____

_____

_____

Now write several alternative focus responses:

Client: _____

_____

Problem/main theme: _____

_____

Others: _____

_____

Mutual or group: _____

_____

Interviewer: _____

_____

Cultural/environmental/contextual: _____

_____

### Box 8-2  Key points

*Why?*

Client problems and issues have many dimensions. It is tempting to accept problems as presented and oversimplify the complexity of life. Focusing helps both interviewer and client develop awareness of the many factors relating to an issue and to organize thinking. Focusing can help a confused client zero in on important dimensions. Thus, focusing can be used to open or tighten discussion.

*What?*

There are six dimensions of focusing. The dimension you select determines what the client is likely to talk about next. Each dimension within itself offers considerable room for further examination of client issues. As a counselor or interviewer, you may:

Focus on the *client: Bill, you* were saying last time that *you* are concerned about *your* future . . .

Focus on the *main theme or problem:* Tell me more about your *getting fired.* What happened?

Focus on *others:* So, *Howard Jones* and you didn't get along. I'd like to know a little more about Howard . . .

Focus on *mutual issues or group: We* will work on this. How can *you and I* work together most effectively. (In group work "we" expands to "our group.")

Focus on *interviewer: My* experience with Howard was . . .

Focus on *cultural/environmental context:* It's a time of *high unemployment.* Given that, what types of jobs in the *economy* appeal to you?

*How?*

Focusing is consciously added to the basic microskills of attending, questioning, paraphrasing, and so on. Careful observation of clients will lead to the most appropriate focus. In assessment and problem definition it is often helpful to consciously and deliberately assist the client to explore issues by focusing on all dimensions one at a time.

*With whom?*

Focusing will be used with all clients. With most North American clients the goal is often to help them focus on themselves (client focus), but with many other people, particularly those of a Southern European or Asian background, the "we" focus may be more appropriate. The goal of much North American counseling and therapy

**Box 8-2 continued**

is individual self-actualization, whereas among other cultures it may be development of harmony with others.

Deliberate focusing is especially helpful in problem definition and assessment, where clients are assisted to see the full complexity of their problem. Moving from focus to focus can help increase client cognitive complexity and the many interconnecting issues in important decisions. With some clients who may be scattered in their thinking, a unitary focus on single dimensions may be wise.

*And?*　　　　Focus is most often multiple. It is helpful to look at an individual, the problem, and the main theme. The culture may undergird the resolution. Thus, counseling leads with multiple foci are often appropriate.

## PRACTICE EXERCISES AND SELF-ASSESSMENT

This chapter has presented several practice exercises along with the basic ideas of focusing. As such, the number of practice exercises in this section will be reduced to two, followed by the usual self-assessment and follow-up summary.

*INDIVIDUAL PRACTICE*

### Exercise 1. Writing alternative focus statements.

A 35-year-old male client comes to you to talk about an impending divorce hearing. He says:

> "I'm really lost right now. I can't get along without Eleanor. I miss the kids terribly. My lawyer is demanding an arm and a leg for his fee, and I don't really feel I can trust him. I resent what has happened over the years, and my work with a men's consciousness-raising group has clarified things for me, but only partially. How can I get through the next two weeks?"

First, use the chart on page 163 to fill in the client's main issue as you see it. Then complete the blanks for the several alternative focus categories. Be sure to brainstorm a number of cultural/contextual/environmental situations; refer to page 159 to help you develop that list.

MAIN ISSUE AS PRESENTED:

_____

| | |
|---|---|
| *Client focus* | |
| *Main theme/problem focus* | |
| *Others focus* | |
| *Mutual, group, "we" focus* | |
| *Interviewer focus* <br> *Cultural/contextual/environmental focus* | |
| Outline important issues below | |

After you have completed the chart, write below alternative focus statements as indicated:

1. Reflection of feeling focusing on the client: _____

   _____

2. Open question focusing on the main theme/problem: _____

   _____

3. Closed question focusing on others: _____

   _____

4. Reassurance statement focusing on "we": _____

   _____

5. Self-disclosure statement focusing on yourself, the interviewer:

   _____

   _____

6. Paraphrase focusing on cultural/environmental/contextual issue:

   _____

   _____

7. An imaginary summary (assuming a longer interview) in which you demonstrate mixed focus with all six dimensions in one summary:

_____

_____

_____

_____

_____

_____

## SYSTEMATIC GROUP PRACTICE

**Step 1.  Divide into groups.**

**Step 2.  Select a group leader.**

**Step 3.  Assign roles for the first practice session.**

Role-played client

Interviewer

Observer I, who will give special attention to focus of the client

Observer II, who will give special attention to focus of the interviewer

**Step 4.  Planning.**   The task of the interviewer in this case is to go through all six aspects of focus analysis, systematically outlining the client's issue. If the task is completed successfully, a broader outline of issues surrounding the client's concern should be available. The function of the skill of focusing is generally to broaden issues. However, as mentioned earlier, focusing may also be used to tighten issues and provide clarity when the client is engaged in overly diffuse and confused thinking. See mastery levels for specific guidelines for setting your personal objectives.

A most useful topic for this role-play is a decision you have to make. This could range from a vocational decision to a problem on the job to a family decision such as a vacation or large purchase. At this point in group practice real personal issues may be discussed. However, it is still possible to role-play a friend or some other situation that you know well.

Observers should examine their feedback sheet and plan their own interviews.

**Step 5. Conduct a five-minute practice session using the skill.**

**Step 6. Review the practice session and provide feedback for ten minutes.** Give special attention to interviewer achievement of goals and determine mastery competencies demonstrated.

**Step 7. Rotate roles.**

**Some general reminders.** Be sure to cover all areas of focus analysis. Many practice sessions explore only the first three dimensions. In some practice sessions interviewers talk with the same client, and each interviewer takes a different focus dimension.

*SELF-ASSESSMENT AND FOLLOW-UP*

**1. The ability of the interviewer to focus the session on many different areas offers you considerable possibility for controlling and managing the session.** This control can be used to help clients be sure they explore many broad issues relating to their concerns. At the same time, the question of control raises important professional and ethical issues in interviewing practice. Important among these is who should be responsible for direction of the interview. Some argue that focusing makes an implicit issue explicit and frees the interviewer to help the client even more. Others argue that any form of control in the interview should be avoided. What is your position on this important issue?

_____

_____

_____

## FOCUS FEEDBACK SHEET

_____ (Date)

| | |
|---|---|
| _____ | _____ |
| (Name of Interviewer) | (Name of Person Completing Form) |

_Instructions:_ Observer I will give special attention to the client and Observer II to the interviewer. Note the correspondence between interviewer and client statements.

| Statement —Record main words —Classify each statement | Client | | | | | | Interviewer | | | | | |
|---|---|---|---|---|---|---|---|---|---|---|---|---|
| | Client (self) | Main theme/ problem | Others | Mutual/group/"we" | Interviewer | Cultural/environmental/ contextual | Client | Main theme/ problem | Others | Mutual/group/"we" | Interviewer (self) | Cultural/environmental/ contextual |
| 1. _____ | | | | | | | | | | | | |
| 2. _____ | | | | | | | | | | | | |
| 3. _____ | | | | | | | | | | | | |
| 4. _____ | | | | | | | | | | | | |
| 5. _____ | | | | | | | | | | | | |
| 6. _____ | | | | | | | | | | | | |
| 7. _____ | | | | | | | | | | | | |
| 8. _____ | | | | | | | | | | | | |
| 9. _____ | | | | | | | | | | | | |
| 10. _____ | | | | | | | | | | | | |
| 11. _____ | | | | | | | | | | | | |
| 12. _____ | | | | | | | | | | | | |
| 13. _____ | | | | | | | | | | | | |
| 14. _____ | | | | | | | | | | | | |

Observations about client verbal and nonverbal behavior:

_____

_____

Observations about interviewer verbal and nonverbal behavior:

_____

_____

**2. Mastery of focusing skills.** What specific competencies have you mastered with focusing? At what level? Use the following space to assess your understanding and skills. Give evidence of your mastery level in the space provided or via supplementary materials such as videotapes and audiotapes.

**Identification.** You will be able to identify six classes of focus as they are demonstrated by interviewers and clients. You will note their impact on the conversational flow of the interview.

_____ Ability to classify focus statements by the interviewer.

_____

_____

_____ Ability to note the impact of focus statements in terms of client conversational flow.

_____

_____

_____ Ability to write alternative focus statements for a single client statement.

_____

_____

**Basic mastery.** You will be able to use the six focus dimensions in a role-played interview and in your daily life.

_____ Demonstration of focus dimensions in a role-played interview.

_____

_____

_____ Demonstration and ability to use focusing in daily life situations.

_____

_____

**Active Mastery.** You will be able to use the six focus dimensions in the interview, and clients will change the focus of their conversation as you change focus. You will also be able to maintain the same focus as your client if you choose (that is, no topic jumping). You will be able to combine this skill with earlier skills in this program (such as reflection of feeling, questioning) and use each skill with alternative focus dimensions.

Check below those skills you have mastered and provide evidence via actual interview documentation (transcripts, tapes, and so on).

_____ My clients change the focus of their conversation as I change my focus.
_____ I maintain the same focus as my clients.
_____ During the interview I can observe focus changes in the client's conversation and change the focus back to the original dimension if it is beneficial to the client.
_____ I can combine this skill area with skills presented earlier.
_____ I am able to use multiple focus dimensions with complex issues facing a client.

**Teaching mastery.** I am able to teach focusing to clients and other persons. The impact of teaching is measured by the achievement of students on the above criteria.

_____

_____

**3. Given the many possibilities for further mastery of this skill as outlined above, what single goal might you set for yourself at this point?**

_____

_____

_____

_____

# CHAPTER 9

# The Influencing Skills and the Combination Skill of Confrontation

---

**How can influencing skills help you and your clients?**

Eight skills of interpersonal influence are summarized in this chapter. A working definition of each skill, along with its major function in the interview, is given below.

| SKILL | WORKING DEFINITION | MAJOR FUNCTION |
|---|---|---|
| *Directives* | Indicate clearly to a client what action(s) the interviewer wishes the client to take. | To assist a client in understanding a task and helping to ensure action. |
| *Logical Consequences* | Indicate the likely results of a client action, which may be negative or positive. | To make clients aware of the impact of their actions and to facilitate their making a choice for the future. |
| *Self-Disclosure* | Indicates your thoughts and feelings to the client. | To facilitate client self-disclosure and provide useful models for behavior change. |
| *Feedback* | Provides accurate data on how the counselor or others view the client. | To facilitate self-exploration and self-examination using data on how others view the client. |

| SKILL | WORKING DEFINITION | MAJOR FUNCTION |
|-------|-------------------|----------------|
| *Interpretation* | Provides the client with an alternative frame of reference to view life situations. | To facilitate the client's ability to reframe life situations and view them from alternative perspectives. |
| *Influencing Summary* | Provides the client with a brief summary of what the interviewer has said or thought during a session. | To enable the client to pull together, remember, and understand the interviewer's influencing statements. |
| *Information/ Advice/ Instruction/ Opinion/ Suggestion* | Pass on information and ideas of the interviewer to the client. | To bring new points of view and information to the client's attention. |
| *Confrontation* | Points out incongruity, discrepancies, or mixed messages in behavior, thoughts, feelings, or meanings. (May involve either attending or influencing skills in combination.) | To promote client talk with a view to explanation and/ or resolution of discrepancies. |

## INTRODUCTION

The most basic dimension of effective counseling and interviewing involves hearing clients out, seeing their point of view, feeling their world.

The interviewing skills discussed so far, used effectively, may be all that are needed to produce growth and change. The several skills of attending provide the base for all interviewing in this culture.

Listening and attending are not always sufficient, however. This chapter summarizes the influencing skills and their place in the interview. It is not the function of this book to treat them in detail; this requires a book in itself (see Ivey & Gluckstern, 1976). If one is competent in the earlier skills, it may be possible to add some of the influencing skills to interviewing practice.

Counseling and interviewing may be described as a process of interpersonal influence. Whether you use elementary attending skills, questions, or directives telling clients what to do, you are always influencing the client. The earlier skills of this book influence clients indirectly through systematic patterns of questioning and listening. *The influencing skills attempt to influence the client directly.*

Recognizing our influence on clients, of course, carries with it important ethical and value issues. It is possible to use the tools of the interview in a manipulative fashion. The position of intentional interviewing is that all counseling skills, be they attending or influencing in nature, should be focused on client needs and wishes. Ethics demand respect for the client and awareness of the power relationships inherent in the interview. Interviewers and counselors, by their position, have power over their clients, and they need to use this power responsibly for the client's benefit, not their own.

Seven influencing skills or skill areas, as well as the combination skill of confrontation, are presented here. With so many skills covered in a single chapter, it is not possible to expect as complete a mastery of these skills as you may have developed with attending skills. If you truly master the attending and focusing skills, the influencing skills discussed here will develop over time.

You will note that elements common to virtually all the influencing skills are specificity and concreteness, and involving the client. Whether you are offering a client a directive, a self-disclosure, or an interpretation, the influencing skill needs to be clear and specific. To involve the client, the influencing skill needs to be relevant to her or his situation; the check-out, or perception check, is strongly suggested. A check-out, as defined earlier in the attending portion of the book, involves asking

the client for reactions to the interviewer's statement. A check-out may be explicit—for instance, "How do you react?" (to what was just said)—or it may be implicit—a questioning tone of voice at the end of the directive, self-disclosure, or other influencing skill.

In sum, a model is proposed in which you: (1) attend to the client and be sure you understand where he or she is coming from; (2) use influencing skill behavior; and (3) observe the consequence of your interviewing lead and move from that observation to your next step. Many will recognize this as a variation of the antecedent-behavior-consequent model common in some forms of helping. The antecedent in this case is the client, the behavior is that of the interviewer, and the consequent is a result of your action on the client. This is an interactive "1-2-3" that will be stressed throughout this chapter (see Box 9-1).

---

**Box 9-1  The "1-2-3" pattern of attend, influence, and observe client reaction**

*1. Attend*

In any interaction with clients it is critical that you use attending skills to determine their definition and view of the world. How do they see, hear, feel, and represent the world through "I statements" and key descriptive words for content (paraphrasing), feelings (reflection of feeling), and meaning (encouragers and reflection of meaning)?

*2. Influence*

An influencing skill is best used after you understand clients' impressions and representations of their experience. An interpretation, self-disclosure, feedback statement, or other influencing skill provides a new frame of reference or informational base on which clients may act.

*3. Check-out and observe consequences*

Following an influencing skill, use a check-out ("How does that seem?") and observe the consequences of your action. If either client verbal or nonverbal behavior, or both, becomes discrepant and you sense an increasing distance from you as interviewer, return to the use of attending skills. Influencing skills, of necessity, remove you from close observation of clients. Consequently, you must pay additional attention to client observation skills when you attempt to use influencing skills.

---

The degree of interpersonal influence desired in the interview varies from theory to theory. The word *influence* can be most upsetting to a nondirective counselor, whereas many proponents of behavior modification aim deliberately to change the client as much as possible. Most theories now seem to agree on extensive client involvement. Each skill of attending and influencing can be used for greater or lesser interpersonal influence, depending on how the skill is used. Even paraphrasing can greatly influence the client and interview process. Generally, it is possible to place the skills on a rough continuum of interpersonal influence.

Figure 9-1 rates the attending skills and several of the influencing skills in terms of their influence in the interview. The task of the counselor is often to open the client discussion on a topic and then to close when appropriate. When a client is overly talkative and becoming upset, it may be useful to change the focus and ask a closed question and then change focus and ask an open question in another area, depending on the goal of the interview. When an interview is moving slowly, an interpretation or directive may add content and flow.

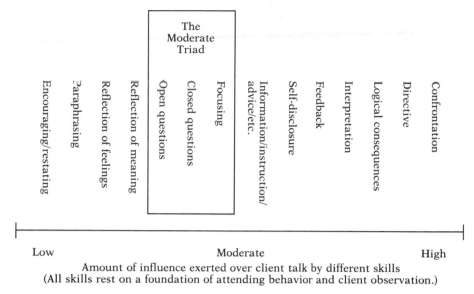

Amount of influence exerted over client talk by different skills
(All skills rest on a foundation of attending behavior and client observation.)

**FIGURE 9–1.** The interpersonal influence continuum

Basic to flow of the interview and facilitating client growth is quality attending behavior and client observation skills. The interviewer must establish contact and note the impact of that contact. These two areas provide the essential information about what skill may be appropriate at what time. Attending behavior can encourage or discourage client talk for client benefit. Client observation tells you when to change skills and focus.

The influencing skills are those where the interviewer talks most and most strongly directs the session. The attending skills allow the client to talk in more depth and determine direction. This, of course, is an oversimplification. While the continuum is generally accurate, an effective reflection of meaning or other attending skill may sometimes be more influential than a directive or confrontation. It is the timing and *how* you use the skill that are ultimately most important.

Nonetheless, you may find it helpful to think of the interpersonal influence continuum from time to time during your interviews. If you feel that you are coming across too strong and the client is resisting, it may be wise to move to lower levels of influence. Similarly, if the client is bogged down, the careful use of an influencing skill may help organize things and move the interview along more smoothly.

Most important for the beginning interviewer are the *moderate triad* of skills—open and closed questions and focusing. Experience has shown that mastery of these skills is almost as important as attending behavior and client observation. If you can ask questions effectively and focus on varying topics, you have the ability to open and close almost any topic or issue your client presents. If a client has difficulty in talking, an open question coupled with a slight change of focus may give the client space to open up. If the topic seems inappropriate, a change of focus coupled with some closed questions will usually slow the pace down. This is particularly true when the client is emotional and the interviewer isn't quite sure what to do. An open question may then be used to switch to another, less difficult, topic. Later you can return to the difficult issue. You can achieve the same effects with the other skills, but the moderate triad are "swing" skills in terms of their influence and do not seem to disrupt the interview flow as much as either side of the continuum. You will find it helpful to master the moderate triad for use in many situations.

As this chapter presents eight skills, the following presentation is different from preceding chapters. It is suggested that you read this chapter slowly, digesting each separate skill and practicing it briefly before moving to the next skill. Following the discussion of each skill are individual practice exercises. When you complete these exercises, you may want to engage in systematic group practice before moving on and reading the next skill area. You will find a sample transcript illustrative of the several influencing skills just before the Systematic Group Practice exercises and the Self-Assessment and Follow-Up suggestions.

## SUGGESTED INSTRUCTIONAL READINGS

Seven influencing skills and confrontation are discussed in the following pages; each will be covered only briefly. For further study of each skill, you can read Ivey and Gluckstern's *Basic Influencing Skills* (1976), Ivey and Authier's *Microcounseling* (1978), and Ivey and Simek-Downing's *Counseling and Psychotherapy* (1980).

## DIRECTIVES

When giving a directive, you simply tell the client what to do, what action to take, or what to say or think about next. Many texts which take the position that interviewers should not direct their clients fail to deal with the fact that an interviewer often tells the client to take a test, to free associate a dream, to try a new behavior with a spouse or colleague,

or to engage in some productive homework. Research has found that some effective interviewers offer as many as half of their leads as some form of directive. Rational-emotive therapists suggest homework assignments, behavior modifiers direct through assertion training, and even humanistically oriented counselors may at times tell their clients what to do (for instance, the Gestalt "hot-seat" exercise). Competent managers, physicians and nurses, and social workers do not hesitate to give directions to their clients. Box 9-2 on pages 176–177 gives example directives for counselors to use.

What is crucial is giving an *effective* directive. To give a directive that is likely to work, the following dimensions seem crucial:

**1. Use appropriate body language, vocal tone, and eye contact.** Demonstrate effective attending. When you use influencing skills, attending behaviors tend to be more assertive than when you are listening (for example, more direct eye contact, stronger vocal tone, forward, but not aggressive, trunk lean).

**2. Be clear and concrete in your verbal expression.** Know what you are going to say and say it clearly and explicitly. Compare the following:

*Vague:* "Go out and arrange for a test."
*Concrete:* "After you leave today, contact the testing office to take the Strong-Campbell Interest Blank. Complete it today, and they will have the results for us to discuss in our meeting next week."
*Vague:* "Straighten out your problem with Bob."
*Concrete:* "You've been having trouble with Bob for a long time. Next week, I want you to sit down for ten minutes with him and just ask him questions about how he sees the problem on the production line. Don't say anything, just ask him what he thinks and listen to him carefully. Then come back next week and we'll talk about it."
*Vague:* "Relax."
*Concrete:* "Sit quietly . . . feel the back of the chair on your shoulders . . . tighten your right hand . . . hold it tight . . . now let it relax slowly . . ."
*Vague:* "Imagine you are talking to your mother. What would you say?"
*Concrete:* "Imagine your mother is sitting in that empty chair. Say to her what you just said to me. Use the same words. Now say it again . . . again . . ."

These examples all illustrate the importance of indicating clearly to your client what you want to have happen. Directives need to be authoritative and clear, but also stated in such a way that they are in tune with the needs of the client.

**3. Check-out if your directive was heard and comprehended.** Just because you think you are clear doesn't mean the client understands what you said. Explicitly or implicitly check-out to make sure your  directive is understood. This is particularly important when a series of directives have been given. For example, "Could you repeat back to me what I have just asked you to do?" Or "I suggested three things for you to do for homework this coming week. Would you summarize them to me to

---

**Box 9-2 Example directives used by counselors of differing theoretical orientations**

| | |
|---|---|
| *1. Specific suggestions/ instructions for action* | "I suggest you try . . ." |
| *2. Paradoxical instructions* | "Continue what you are doing . . ."<br>"Do the problem behavior/thinking/action at least three times." |
| *3. Imagery* | "Imagine you are back in the situation. Close your eyes and describe it precisely. What do you see, hear, feel?"<br>"Describe your ideal day, job, life partner."<br>"Imagine you are going on a trip into your body . . ." |
| *4. Role-play enactment* | "Now, return to that situation and let's play it out."<br>"Let's role it out again, only change the one piece of behavior we agreed to." |
| *5. Gestalt hot seat* | "Talk to your parent as if he or she were sitting in that chair. Now go to that chair and answer as your parent would." |
| *6. Gestalt nonverbal* | "I note that one of your hands is in a fist, your other is open. Have the two hands talk to each other." |
| *7. Free association psychodynamic transactional analysis* | "Take that feeling and free associate back to an early childhood experience . . ."<br>" . . . to what is occurring *now* in your daily life."<br>"Stay with that feeling, magnify it. Now what flashed into your mind first?" |
| *8. Reframing/ Gendlin focusing/ dereflection* | "Identify a negative experience, thought, feeling. Now identify something positive in that experience and focus on that dimension. Synthesize it with the problem." |

---

make sure I've been clear?" Undergirding directives has an important pattern of:
1. Understanding where the client is coming from (usually gained through attending skills such as questioning and reflection of feeling).
2. Stating your position and directive clearly and concisely.
3. Checking-out to see if the directive was understood.

This "1-2-3" pattern will repeat itself in each of the influencing skills.

**Box 9-2 continued**

| | |
|---|---|
| 9. *Relaxation* | "Close your eyes and drift."<br>"Tighten your forearm, very tight. Now let it go." |
| 10. *Systematic desensitiz-ation* | a. Deep muscle relaxation.<br>b. Construction of anxiety hierarchy.<br>c. Matching objects of anxiety with relaxation. (Note similarity to dereflection process.) |
| 11. *Language change* | "Change 'should' to 'want to.' "<br>"Change 'can't' to 'won't.' "<br>Any new word/construct addition. |
| 12. *Staying with feeling/ emotional flooding* | "Go back to that feeling, get with it, make it totally you." |
| 13. *Meditation* | "Be still. Focus on one point. Relax. Concentrate on breathing. Let all thoughts slip from your mind." |
| 14. *Hypnotic trance* | "Fixate on that point. Relax. Note your breathing. Focus your awareness . . ." |
| 15. *Group work* | "Now I want you to do this . . ." |
| 16. *Teaching/ homework* | "Practice this exercise next week and report on it in the next interview."<br>"Turn to page . . ."<br>"Take out a sheet of paper . . ."<br>"Take this vocational test . . ." |
| 17. *Family therapy com-munications* | "Don't talk to me . . . talk to him *now*."<br>"Change chairs with your wife and sit closer to your daughter . . ." |

*PRACTICE EXERCISES*

**Exercise 1. What are the three major points suggested by the text for giving directives?**

_____

_____

_____

**Exercise 2. Which of the following directives are vague, and which are concrete?**

Vague    Concrete

_____ _____ "I want you to imagine you are talking to your mother."

_____ _____ "Imagine your mother is sitting in that chair. Now, talk to her just as if she were really sitting there."

_____ _____ "Talk to the secretary and take some tests."

_____ _____ "I'll introduce you to Joan, our secretary, and she will arrange for you to take the aptitude test we agreed on."

_____ _____ "Try out that idea next week."

_____ _____ "Here is some homework for you to do. Next week you are to ask five people how they spend their leisure time. This may give you some ideas for your own life and will also give you something specific to talk to people about. We'll talk about the results next week."

**Exercise 3. Write below vague and specific directives for the following situations.** Be sure to include a check-out with your directives.

Tell a client to obtain information about vocations during the coming week.

Vague: _____

_____

Concrete: _____

_____

Direct a client to engage in relaxation training during the coming week.

Vague: _____

_____

Concrete: _____

_____

Direct a subordinate to write a memo for you.

Vague: _____

_____

Concrete: _____

_____

**Exercise 4.  In a role-play, first use attending skills to clarify a problem, then test out the alternatives for directions and rate their effect and value here.**

_____

_____

_____

_____

_____

_____

_____

_____

## LOGICAL CONSEQUENCES[1]

The process of learning in this culture is heavily based on the consequences of actions. Client actions planned for the future are likely to have consequences in the client's life. For example, an individual may want to change a job simply because it offers more pay. However, the change may disrupt family life through a move, which in turn may cause other problems. Alternatively, the same move may bring unforeseen positive consequences. Explaining to others the likely consequences of their behaviors, if done sparingly and carefully, may at times be helpful in the interview or counseling session.

*Warnings* are forms of logical consequences. They inform the other person of the negative possibilities involved in a decision or action and the consequences that may result. These types of logical consequences tend to reduce risk taking and produce conformity. They often center on *anticipation of punishment*. A teacher in a disciplinary situation wants and needs a certain minimum of conformity, as does a prison guard. In interviews some clients plan very risky actions without considering the full range of possible consequences. A client considering a divorce, dropping out of school, or "telling the boss off" may profit from being informed about the consequences of the action.

[1] This skill was developed in consultation with Mary Ivey of the Amherst, Massachusetts, Public Schools. It is a variation on some basic Adlerian constructs, but it often appears in behavioral and rational-emotive counseling as well.

*Encouraging risk taking and attempting new tasks* is a more positive form of logical consequences. In the school room some children conform too much and demonstrate little creativity. They have been so conditioned by threats and warnings and bad outcomes that they are afraid to move. In such situations the goal may be to encourage risk-taking by pointing out positive outcomes of a decision or possible action. *Anticipation of rewards* is a form of logical consequences where the individual may be asked to imagine the positive consequences and rewards of new behavior or actions. In interviews you may wish to encourage clients to be more assertive or to try some new action; anticipating positive outcomes may be helpful in this process.

Logical consequences may at first seem to be a type of coercion or moralizing. Yet it is a rare human behavior that does not have costs and benefits, and it is the counselor's task to help the client sort these out while working toward a decision. You may do this through attending skills of questioning or directly through sharing logical consequences. In providing a logical consequence response, consider the following suggestions:

1. Through attending skills, make sure that you understand the situation and the way the client understands it.
2. As a client moves toward a decision, encourage thinking about positive and negative possibilities in the decision. This is often done by questioning.
3. Provide the client with data on both positive and negative consequences of the decision or action. If he or she thinks only in negative terms, help the client think of positives. If he or she is thinking only in positives, prompt thinking of negatives.
4. As appropriate to the situation, provide the client with a summary of positive and negative consequences in a *nonjudgmental* manner. With many people this step is not needed; they will have made their own judgment and decision already.
5. Let the client decide what action to take in counseling situations. In teaching or management, you may have to decide at times and actually enforce the consequences.

In counseling, logical consequences tends to be a gentle skill used to help people sort through issues more completely. It also may be used in ranking alternatives when a complex decision is at hand. In management and teaching situations the same generally holds true. In disciplinary and reward issues, however, it is important to note that the *power* rests with the manager and the teacher: they decide the consequences. In interviewing, the task is simply to assist the client in foreseeing consequences. In both management and teaching situations, letting the employee or the student decide still remains critical. People who hold power over others need to *follow through with the consequence* they warned about earlier, or their power will be lost.

*PRACTICE EXERCISES*

**Exercise 1. Define the logical consequences skill briefly in your own words.**

_____

_____

_____

_____

**Exercise 2.  Logical consequences involves the use of attending skills to understand the client's situation. Through questioning skills you can encourage the client to think through the possible consequences of actions.** ("What result might you anticipate if you did that?" "What results are you obtaining right now when you continue to engage in that behavior?") However, questioning and paraphrasing the situation may not always be enough to make the client fully aware of the logical consequences of actions. Write below, for the various types of clients and situations, logical consequence statements that might help the client understand the situation more fully.

A student who is contemplating taking drugs for the first time:

_____

_____

_____

A young woman contemplating an abortion:

_____

_____

_____

A student considering taking out a loan for college:

_____

_____

_____

An executive who has just been fired because of poor interpersonal relationships:

_____

_____

_____

A client who comes to you consistently late and who is often uncooperative:

_____

_____

_____

## SELF-DISCLOSURE

Should you share your own personal observations, experiences, and ideas with the client? Self-disclosure on the part of the counselor or interviewer has been highly controversial. Many theorists argue against sharing oneself openly and honestly, preferring a more distant, objective point of view. However, more recently, humanistically oriented counselors have demonstrated the value of appropriate self-disclosure. It appears that self-disclosure can encourage client talk, create additional trust between counselor and client, and help provide a more equal relationship in the interview. Nonetheless, not everyone agrees that this is a wise skill to include among the counselor's techniques. They express valid concern about the counselor's monopolizing the interview or abusing the client's rights by encouraging openness too early, and point out that counseling and interviewing can operate successfully without any interviewer self-disclosure at all.

Self-disclosure is a combination skill consisting of the microskills of expression of content and feeling plus focusing. Self-disclosures consist of the following aspects:

1. *Personal pronouns.* A counselor or interviewer self-disclosure inevitably involves "I statements" or self-reference, using the pronouns *I*, *me*, and *my*.
2. *Verb for content or feeling or both.* "I think . . . ," "I feel . . . ," "I have experienced . . . " all indicate some action on the part of the counselor.
3. *Object coupled with adverb and adjective descriptors.* "I feel happy about your being able to assert yourself more directly with your parents." "My experience of divorce was something like yours. I felt and still feel . . . "

Feeling words and expression of feeling are particularly important in self-disclosure. In essence, the structure of a self-disclosure is simple: it is "self-talk" by the counselor. Making self-talk *relevant* to the client is a more complex task involving the following issues, among others:

1. *Genuineness.* This is a vague term, but it can be made more concrete by emphasizing that the counselor must truly and honestly have had the experience and idea. This could be termed "genuineness in relation to self," an important beginning. But the self-disclosure must also be genuine in relation to the client. For example, a client may have performance anxiety about a part in a school play. The counselor may genuinely feel anxiety before giving a lecture to 50 people. The feelings may be the same or at least similar, but true genuineness demands a synchronicity of feeling. The counselor's experience in this case is likely too distant from the client. Self-disclosure should be fairly close to client experience; for instance, the counselor might relate a situation where he or she felt similar performance anxiety in a parallel situation at the same age.
2. *Timeliness.* If a client is talking smoothly about something, counselor self-disclosure is not necessary. However, if the client seems to want to talk about a topic but is having trouble, a slight leading self-disclosure by the counselor may be helpful. Too deep and involved a self-disclosure may frighten or distance the client.
3. *Tense.* The most powerful self-disclosures are usually made in the present tense ("Right now I feel _____.") However, variations in tense can be used to strengthen or soften the power of a self-disclosure. Consider the following:

*Client:* I am feeling really angry about the way my husband sulks when I go out to work. He really ticks me off.

*Counselor: (Present tense)* Right now, I like the way you are fighting. It makes me feel good to see you fighting for your rights.

*(Past tense)* I can see that you felt angry. I've always liked that. I've felt that way toward my husband too.

*(Future tense)* I know you're going to make it in the future. I think anger is a good motivator.

Clearly, effective self-disclosure can be a complex task, yet it can open the interview to new dimensions of sharing and helpfulness. Whether you wish to use this skill and how often are important decisions.

## PRACTICE EXERCISES

The structure of a self-disclosure consists of "I statements" made up of three dimensions: (1) the personal pronoun "I" in some form; (2) a verb such as *feel, think, have experienced;* and (3) a sentence object describing what you think or what happened.

Imagine that a client comes to you with each of the problems below. In each case write one effective and one ineffective self-disclosure. Before you write your statements, assume that you have already attended to the client carefully and that a self-disclosure indeed might be appropriate at this moment. Nonetheless, include a check-out with each statement.

"I just can't get along with men. They bug me terribly. They seem so macho and self-assured. I feel they are always looking down on me. How do you feel toward them?"

Effective: _____

_____

_____

Ineffective: _____

_____

_____

"I find myself afraid and insecure in large groups. It just doesn't feel right. What should I do?"

Effective: _____

_____

_____

Ineffective: _____

_____

_____

"I'm concerned about how you feel toward me. You remind me of my parents. Just how do you feel toward me?"

Effective: _____

_____

_____

Ineffective: _____

_____

_____

## FEEDBACK

Feedback is concerned with providing clients with clear data on their performance and/or how others may view them. It may even involve self-disclosures on your part.[2] As indicated earlier in the Guidelines for Effective Feedback (Box 2-2 in Chapter 2), feedback is centrally concerned with the following:

To see ourselves as others see us,
To hear how others hear us,
And to be touched as we touch others . . .
These are the goals of effective feedback.

Feedback to one another is important in the process of developing skills in counseling and interviewing. The guidelines given earlier for practicing effective feedback in small group sessions are equally critical in counseling and interviewing. To paraphrase the guidelines suggested earlier:

1. The client receiving feedback should be in charge. Feedback is likely to be most successful if the client solicits it. However, at times you as interviewer will have to determine if the client is ready and able to hear accurate feedback. Only give as much feedback as the client can use now.
2. Feedback should focus on strengths and/or something the client can do something about. It does little good to tell a client to change many things that are wrong. It is more effective to give feedback on positive dimensions and build on strength. When you talk about negatives, they should be areas the client can do something to change or adapt to.
3. Feedback should be concrete and specific. Just as with directives, it does little good to offer vague feedback. For example, "You aren't able to get along with the group" is not as helpful as "You had two arguments with Ginny that upset both of you, and now you are disagreeing strongly with Lois. What does this mean to you?"
4. Feedback should be relatively nonjudgmental. Critical to being nonjudgmental is accepting vocal tone and body language. Too often feedback turns into evaluation—"You did that exercise very well," compared to "I saw you relax and heard your joy as you went through that exercise." Stick to the facts and specifics. Facts are friendly; judgments may or may not be.

---

[2] Once you as an interviewer have established good rapport with your clients, your feedback about your impressions of them is one of the most powerful influencing skills. This type of feedback probably should not be used in the early stages of interviewing, but rather saved until you have more experience and practice.

5. Feedback should be lean and precise. Most people have many areas that could profit from change. However, most of us can change only one thing at a time and can hear only so much. Don't overwhelm the client. Select one or two things for providing feedback and save the rest for later.

6. Check-out to see how your feedback was received. Just as in an effective directive, check to see how the other person reacts to feedback. "How do you react to that?" "Does that sound close?" "What does that mean to you?" are three examples that involve the client in feedback and will indicate whether or not you were heard and how useful your feedback was.

Again, note the "1-2-3" pattern: (1) attend to the client; (2) use the influencing skill; (3) check-out to determine how well the skill was received and how useful it was.

Note also that clarity and concreteness are just as important in effective feedback as they are in effective direction-giving. Good advice and instruction both require the "1-2-3" pattern and concreteness and clarity if they are to be meaningful to the client. These same principles apply to all the influencing skills.

Another type of feedback is more judgmental. *Praise* and certain types of *supportive statements* provide your positive judgment of the client. Negative judgments may be shown through *reprimands* and certain types of punishments. In judgmental feedback the interviewer takes a more active role.

Judgmental feedback is often considered inappropriate in counseling situations. However, management settings, correctional institutions, schools and universities, and other face-to-face settings often require judgmental feedback. Most often judgmental feedback involves an interviewer who has some *power* over the life of the client or other person. (Some would argue, in fact, that nonjudgmental feedback is impossible if the interviewer has any power over the client. Thus, all feedback, to some extent, could be considered judgmental.)

The suggestions for judgmental types of feedback such as praise, support, reprimands, and punishments follow the same guidelines as those proposed earlier in this section. Such feedback tends to be most effective when the client is in charge as much as possible, and when the feedback includes some emphasis on strengths as well as weaknesses, is concrete and specific, and is lean and precise. Judgmental feedback can be delivered in a tone of voice that is nonjudgmental and factual, removing some of the sting. The check-out is particularly important in judgmental feedback. It provides the client with an opportunity to react, and the interviewer has some idea of how the feedback, positive or negative, was received.

A special type of feedback relates closely to self-disclosure. Here you, as the interviewer, share your direct, immediate feelings about the client. This type of self-disclosure feedback can be very helpful to the client if used well. Used poorly it can be destructive.

*PRACTICE EXERCISES*

**Exercise 1.   What are the six main points of effective feedback?** Summarize them below in your own words.

1. _____

2. _____

3. _____

4. _____

5. _____

6. _____

7.  What else would you add? _____

_____

**Exercise 2.   In business a manager may give an employee periodic feedback about work performance.** In an encounter group you may give someone else in the group your impressions of his or her behavior. (Note how similar feedback and self-disclosure are in this case. However, feedback provides specific concrete data about behavior, whereas a self-disclosure may consist more of subjective impressions.) In correctional institutions, schools, and other teaching situations, feedback may be used to praise or reprimand others.

Select three situations and summarize your perceptions of effective and ineffective feedback you have observed in the past.

_____

_____

_____

_____

**Exercise 3.   Self-disclosure types of feedback can be particularly powerful.** Share some of your positive and negative life experiences around this form of feedback. How does this feedback compare with the criteria suggested in this section (that is, non-judgmental, concrete, and so on)?

_____

_____

_____

_____

_____

_____

_____

_____

## INTERPRETATION[3]

 Though interpretations may vary in content, depending on the theoretical orientation from which they are drawn, they all have one element in common: the interviewer presenting the client with a new frame of reference through which to view the problem or concern and, hopefully, better understand and deal with the situation. Interpretation should be contrasted with reflection of meaning, where the interviewer assists the client to find new meanings and interpretations.

Reflection of meaning may be necessary and helpful *before* you attempt an interpretation. Reflections of meaning often lead clients to their own new frames of reference as they examine their own world, making an interpretation unnecessary. However, examining meaning may also loosen your clients' constructs and thinking and help prepare them for your alternative frame of reference, your interpretation.

[3]Much of the description of interpretation is taken from Ivey, *Microcounseling* (Springfield, Ill.: Charles C Thomas, 1971, pp. 174–176) and is used by permission. The concepts outlined in this skill were developed jointly with John Moreland of Ohio State University.

A client may be worried and upset over a troubling dream. Different theories of helping would interpret the dream differently, but each provides a new frame of reference for understanding the dream. For example:

*Client:* I dreamed I was walking along cliffs with the sea raging below. I felt terribly frightened; I couldn't find my parents.
*Counselor:* (Psychodynamic) You'd really like to get rid of your parents, but the thought is terrifying.

(Transactional analysis) I note you are looking to find or take care of your parents. This is very similar to what is going on in your life right now. They've just moved in with you, and you've said earlier they were like children and you were like the parent.

(Trait-and-factor) You've just entered college and it feels as if you might fall off the cliffs. You wish your parents were here to help you.

Which is the "correct" interpretation? Depending on the situation and context, any of these interpretations could be helpful or harmful. The value of the interpretation depends on the client's reaction to it. Each provides the client with a new, alternative way to consider the situation. In short, interpretation renames or redefines "reality" from a new point of view. By contrast, a reflection of meaning would use the meaning questioning sequence and then ask the client what sense or meaning he or she obtains from the data.

Interpretation may be compared to reflection of feeling, reflection of meaning, and the paraphrase. In those three skills the interviewer remains in the client's *own* frame of reference. In interpretation the frame of reference comes from the counselor's personal and/or theoretical constructs. The following are examples of interpretation compared with other skills:

*Client (who has a record of absenteeism):* I really feel badly about missing so much work.
*Interviewer:* (Reflection of feeling) You're really troubled and worried.
(Paraphrase/restatement) You've been missing a lot of work.
(Interpretation) You've missed a lot of work and you are aware of your boss's view of absenteeism. This gives you concern as to whether or not you'll be able to keep the job.
*Client (with agitation):* My wife and I had a fight last night after watching this sexy movie. I tried to make love, and she rejected me again.
*Counselor:* (Reflection of feeling) You're upset and troubled.
(Paraphrase) You had a fight after the movie and were rejected again sexually.
(Interpretation) Sounds like your fear of rejection caused you to be rejected by your wife.

*(Interpretation)* Your wife only turns you on enough for sex with some outside stimulus such as a movie.

*(Interpretation)* The feelings of rejection trouble you. Are these feelings similar to the dream you had last week?

In each of the above interpretations, the interviewer or counselor adds something beyond what the client has said. There are a multitude of responses that may be made to any client utterance.

Interpretation has traditionally been viewed as a mystical activity in which the interviewer reaches into the depths of the client's personality and provides new insights. However, if we consider interpretation as merely a new frame of reference, the concept becomes less formidable. Viewed in this light, the depth of a given interpretation refers to the magnitude of the discrepancy between the frame of reference from which the client is operating and the frame of reference supplied by the interviewer. For example, a client may report feeling overly upset when the boss makes a minor criticism. The interviewer, counselor, or therapist may have noted this as a constant pattern. Several interpretations could be made, with varying depth:

"You seem to react very strongly to virtually any criticism from your boss."

"You appear to have a pattern of difficulty with authority."

"You feel very unsure of yourself and need approval to validate your worth."

"Your boss represents your father, and you are repeating the same patterns with him that you experienced with your father's criticism."

Interpretations will vary with the theoretical orientation of the interviewer. You may wish to examine the situations in this section and interpret them from varying theoretical perspectives with your supervisor or a colleague. The successful interviewer has many alternative interpretations available and selects them according to the long-term and immediate needs of the client.

Interpretations are best given in the "1-2-3" pattern of attending carefully to the client, providing the interpretation, and then checking-out the client's reactions to the new frame of reference (for instance, "How does that idea come across to you?"). If an interpretation is unsuccessful, the interviewer can use data obtained from the check-out to develop another, more meaningful, response.

Finally, it should be mentioned that reflection of meaning used in combination with questioning skills often enables clients to make their own interpretations and generate their own new frames of reference. A client working effectively with an interviewer using the skill of reflection of meaning is often better able to make interpretations than a skilled counselor.

*PRACTICE EXERCISES*

Interpretations provide alternative frames of reference or meanings for events in a client's life. In the examples below provide an attending response (question, reflection of feeling, or the like) and then write an interpretation. Include a check-out in your written interpretation.

**Exercise 1.** "I just can't get along with men. They bug me terribly. They seem so macho and self-assured. I feel they are always looking down on me. How do you feel toward them?"

Attending response: _____

_____

Interpretation from a feminist frame of reference: _____

_____

_____

Interpretation from a Freudian frame of reference: _____

_____

_____

Interpretation from your frame of reference: _____

_____

_____


**Exercise 2.** "I'm thinking of trying some pot. Yeah, I'm 'only 13,' but I've been around a lot. My parents really object to it. I can't see why they do. My friends are all into it and seem to be doing fine."

Attending response: _____

_____

Interpretation from a conservative frame of reference: _____

_____

_____

_____

Interpretation from an occasional user's frame of reference: _____

_____

_____

Interpretation from your own frame of reference: _____

_____

_____

## INFLUENCING SUMMARY

This skill needs to be mentioned only briefly. It is similar to the attending summary except that the counselor or interviewer summarizes the interview from her or his point of view. Special attention is often given to what the interviewer has suggested and commented on during the session. One brief example can illustrate this skill:

*Counselor:* Bill, so far in this session we've talked about your need to control or own what happens in your relations with others. I've suggested that this need stems from your relationship with your father, who behaved in much the same fashion. You learned your behavior through his model. I've suggested several alternative things for you to try during the week. One of them was to sit quietly in a meeting and simply observe what goes on between people. Another was to deliberately seek to control your relationship with your wife—do what you've always been doing and note what happens before and what happens after you seek to control her behavior. Finally, I've suggested you consider joining an assertion training group getting organized in the community. Does that sum it up? What are your reactions and plans?

An influencing summary of this type integrates the several strands of thought involved in an interviewer's intervention and provides an opportunity to obtain client feedback. No practice exercises are suggested for this skill. This is not to deny its importance. It is suggested you practice this skill in conjunction with other practice sessions in the influencing series.

## INFORMATION/ADVICE/INSTRUCTION/OPINION/SUGGESTION

Influencing skills can be divided into an almost infinite array of specialized topics. Excessive emphasis in this area may lead you to forget attending.

All the above skills, in one form or another, are concerned with imparting information to the client. The task is to be clear, specific, and relevant to the client's world. This is not to negate the importance of these skills, for most forms of interviewing, counseling, and even therapy rely on imparting information to clients. An important part of both transactional analysis and rational-emotive therapy, for example, is directly instructing clients in the content of their theories. Relaxation trainers often teach their clients how to relax at home. Instructional procedures in management, medicine, and other interviewing situations are equally or more important.

Providing helpful information consists of steps closely related to those already discussed under influencing skills:

1. Attend to the client and be sure that he or she is ready for the information or advice.
2. Be clear, specific, concrete, and timely in your instructional procedures. The concepts already discussed under feedback, directives, and logical consequences may be especially helpful in preparing more complex programs of instruction.
3. Check-out with the client to make sure that your ideas have been understood.

Psychological education—the direct instruction of clients in the skills of living—often uses these skills. Again no practice exercises are suggested with this skill. However, as you teach the skills of interviewing to clients and others, you will be needing and using effective information giving and instruction.

## CONFRONTATION

The most powerful of the attending and influencing skills, resting near the top of the microskills hierarchy, is confrontation. A blend of attending, influence, and focus dimensions, confrontation is a complex of skills that often results in client examination of core issues. When client discrepancies, mixed messages, and conflicts are confronted skillfully and nonjudgmentally, clients are encouraged to talk in more detail and to resolve their problems and issues.

Confrontation involves two major steps. The first, identifying mixed messages, conflict, and incongruity, has been discussed under client observation. The second step is pointing these issues out clearly to clients and helping them work through to conclusion. As such, the skills of questioning, client observation, reflective listening, and feedback loom large in effective confrontation.

**Step 1: Identify incongruities and mixed messages.**  When a person gives a clear, unambiguous message, he or she may be said to be congruent, integrated, and whole. You know where that person "is at." By contrast, when a person offers a double message or says one thing verbally and something else nonverbally, the person may be said to be incon-

gruent, contradictory, and conveying mixed messages (Ivey & Litterer, 1979, p. 99).

The question is how to identify incongruity. This is best done through client observation, questioning, and reflective listening. For example:

*Client:* I think I should get a raise.

*Counselor:* Could you tell me the reasons you think you deserve more money?

*Client:* I've been here a long time, and lots of people make more than I do. It doesn't seem fair, especially with the rise in the cost of living.

*Counselor:* Earlier, you said you like to take it easy on the job whenever you can. You try to come in late when you feel you can get away with it. How does that square with your desire for a raise?

*Client:* Well, from that point of view, perhaps I'll have to work a little harder if I am going to get what I deserve, or think I deserve.

Needless to say, it isn't always that easy. The interviewer asked the client a question to elaborate on wishes and followed with a paraphrase of past discussion that contradicted the client's wishes. The final question ("How does that square with your desire for a raise?") prompts the confrontation.

A confrontation is actually a process or series of steps leading toward identification and discussion of discrepancies. When the discrepancy is specifically identified by pointing out the incongruity or mixed message, the client often sees the issue and resolves the matter there and then. More likely, however, more extensive discussion involving reflective listening and influencing skills may be required to resolve the incongruity fully.

Several types of incongruity and mixed messages can be identified. Important among them are inconsistencies:

1. *Between two statements.* An example might be when a client says at one point that she cares very much for her husband, but later in the interview directly contradicts that statement. Feelings, thoughts, and meanings may also conflict (see Figure 7-1, Chapter 7).
2. *Between what one says and what one does.* A client may express sincere interest in taking vocational tests to clarify future plans but fail to show up for the testing time and time again.
3. *Between statements and nonverbal behavior.* A client may say he enjoys coming for counseling or for a job interview, but his face may be tight and tense and his hands shaking.
4. *Between two nonverbal behaviors.* Teeth may be clenched while the client smiles.
5. *Between statements and the context.* A client may say he is going to resolve a family problem when it is clear that he has neither the power nor the money to bring about the resolution. An individual

may say she is at fault for not finding a job when the economy has a high rate of unemployment.

6. *Between two or more people.* The incongruity may exist between a husband and wife or between a counselor and a client.

**Step 2: Work toward resolution of incongruity and mixed messages.**
As noted earlier, simply labeling the incongruity through a nonjudg-mental confrontation may be enough to resolve a situation. More likely, however, incongruity will remain as a problem to be resolved. It is central to focus on elements of the incongruity rather than on the person as the problem. Confrontation is too often thought of as blaming a person for her or his faults; rather, the issue is facing the incongruity squarely through steps such as the following:

1. Identify the incongruity clearly. Using reflective listening skills, summarize it for the client. Often the simple question "How do you put those two together?" will lead a client to self-confrontation and resolution.
2. Through the use of questioning and other listening skills, draw out the specifics of the conflict or mixed messages. *One at a time*, give attention to each part of the mixed message, contradiction, or conflict. If two people are involved, attempt to have the client examine both points of view. It is important at this stage to be nonjudgmental and nonevaluative. Aim for facts.
3. Periodically summarize the several dimensions of the incongruity. The model confrontation statement, "On the one hand . . . , but on the other hand . . ." appears to be particularly useful in summarizing incongruity. Follow this with a check-out (for example, "How does that sound to you?"). Try to include new incongruities that appear in your summary.
4. If necessary, provide feedback with your opinions and observations about the discrepancies. One of the 17 directives suggested earlier may help you break through the incongruity. Other influencing skills such as interpretation and self-disclosure may be used as well. Remember the "1-2-3" pattern of attend, influence, and check-out.

If the incongruity is not resolved by this process, it may be necessary to say, "You see it that way, I see it this way . . . we'll have to go at it again." Don't give up on positions you believe are correct, but allow your point of view to be modified by input from the client. Many clients are unaware of their mixed messages and discrepancies. Pointing out these issues gently but firmly can be extremely beneficial to clients. Finally, a wide variety of attending and influencing skills may be used to follow-up and elaborate on confrontations.

*PRACTICE EXERCISES*

### Exercise 1. Observation in identification of incongruity.

The six types of client discrepancies pointed out in the chapter on client observation skills are repeated again as the first phase of the confrontation skill. If you have not completed the observation exercise for discrepancies (Exercise 7 of Chapter 4), complete that exercise now before you go further. The ability to identify client discrepancies through client observation skills is central to the use of confrontation.

### Exercise 2.  Practicing confrontation of incongruity.

An employee comes in late for the fifth day in a row and says:

> "Boss, I'm sorry, but there just isn't anything I can do. Usually, I can make it, but not today."

A confrontation statement from the boss in this case might be:

> "Bob, on the one hand you say you aren't usually late. On the other hand, we both know you've been late all this week. How do you put those two together?"

Critical in such statements is a nonjudgmental tone of voice and body language. Perhaps the most difficult aspect of a successful confrontation is not showing judgment through nonverbal displays of anger or frustration.

The model sentence, "On the one hand. . . , and on the other hand . . ." provides a standard and useful format for the actual confrontation. Variations include "You say . . . but you do . . . ," "I see . . . at one time, and at another time I see . . . ," and "Your words say . . . , but your actions say . . ." In each of these examples the client is being "pinned to the wall" with specific facts. The importance of being nonjudgmental and including the check-out as a final part of the confrontation cannot be overstressed.

Write confrontation statements for the following situations. Remember to include a check-out with the confrontation.

> A client breaks eye contact, speaks slowly, and slumps in the chair while saying, "Yes, I really like the idea of getting out into the library and getting the vocational information you suggest. Ah . . . I know it would be helpful for me."

_____

_____

_____

_____

_____

"Yes, my family is really important to me. I like to spend a lot of time with them. When I get this big project done, I'll stop working so much and start doing what I should. Not to worry."

_____

_____

_____

"I really want to go to _____University, but I fear I don't have the money or grades to get there."

_____

_____

_____

"My daughter and I don't get along well. I feel that I am really trying, but she doesn't respond. Only last week I bought her a present, but she just ignored it."

_____

_____

_____

## EXAMPLE INTERVIEW

In the following excerpt the client has just completed a role-played assertion training exercise in which she has practiced being more assertive and direct with her mother. The counselor is reviewing the process. Several different influencing skills are used at the end of the interview.

_Karen:_ So, Priscilla, we've just been going over the assertion training exercise, and . . . uh . . . to sum it up, it seems like it began with your saying you could never face up to your mother and it was really something that scares you. And now, all of a sudden, we see you in a role-play meeting her more directly, standing up straighter, talking more firmly . . . What kind of sense do you make of this?
[This is a confrontation summarizing two distinct aspects of Priscilla: (1) the shy and frightened daughter overpowered by the mother; and (2) the newly assertive woman defining her own space. The confrontation points out these two dimensions. In response to confrontation the client is usually expected to talk in more detail and begin a synthesis of the discrepancies.]

_Priscilla:_ Well, ah . . . I guess because of this training I've finally realized that my mother's expectations for me are to live out my life the way she did . . . you know . . . to be a housewife, and, while I've always appreciated the way she's cared for me . . . ah . . . I'm a lot more concerned about having a career as well as marriage and having more independence than she does. I think in the role-plays I was finally able to tell her in a very direct way that, while I appreciated her wishes for me that . . . ah . . . I really wanted her to respect the role I want to play in my own life.

*Karen:* I have to admire what you've done, Priscilla. You realize the result of living up to expectations isn't good for you. Ah . . . you've shown you can really do it. It must feel good to do what you've done. (This is an example of feedback that is somewhat judgmental and that encourages the client to realize she indeed *can* do it. Supportive or praising elements are included.)

*Priscilla:* Well, I'll tell you, Karen—at the end it feels good when I'm trying to confront my mother and tell her that I am going to pursue a career, that I am going to do the best I can with myself. I see how uncomfortable she gets with that . . . ah . . . It's very difficult to deal with her in a fairly direct manner and tell her this is the way I want it to be and I want her to accept me and give me support. It usually turns out pretty well when I face up to what I believe.

*Karen:* I think you've got it figured out pretty well. And, then, I've got to give you a caution or warning that this is just a beginning role-play, and you'll have to give it more practice and more thinking. In a moment we can get into how it might really work. But unless we start planning to take what we did here into real life, we're going to find that it doesn't happen easily. Ah . . . in continuing, I have to tell you I went through assertion training myself . . . a couple years ago. I had trouble asserting myself with my husband and . . . ah . . . he . . . uh . . . I did the same as you in a group role-play and everything went fine. Yet when I went back to him, I couldn't do anything. What seemed to help was talking a little bit further with some friends. Then doing a few more role-plays. How does that sound to you?

(Karen begins with a discussion of the logical consequences of practice or nonpractice of the learning. This is to ensure that newly learned behavior actually can be transferred to real life. The possible logical consequences are followed by a self-disclosure in which Karen talks about some of her own experiences with assertion training.)

*Priscilla:* It definitely makes sense. It's very similar to that, the kind of thing that I'm feeling, and, frankly, I appreciate your sharing your personal thoughts because I just couldn't imagine somebody like you ever having trouble dealing directly with anyone.

*Karen:* What are some of your fantasies, Priscilla, about some of the difficulties you might have in taking some of these assertion training exercises out and using them with your mother?

(This is an open question leading to the important question of skills transfer. Concepts, behaviors, and learnings from the interview often do not transfer to real life without careful planning.)

*Priscilla:* Well, I think the major . . . the fantasy that hits me most powerfully is that I don't want my mother to reject me. And yet, I don't want to give up living my life the way I want to . . .

*Karen:* Um-hum . . .

*Priscilla:* I have this fear, sort of in the pit of my stomach, that by going out and doing this career thing that I've always wanted to, and can do pretty well at, that I'm going to somehow . . . somehow she's not going to love me any more. That makes it so hard.

*Karen:* So, from . . . ah . . . that kind of ties in with that dream you had a while back. Doesn't it? Where you had this feeling your mother was rejecting you by not coming to your graduation.

*Priscilla:* Uh-huh.

*Karen:* And, it sounds like you're replaying that again, that same fear of rejection. How does that sound?

(Karen here puts together present anxieties with those expressed earlier in a dream. This putting together of two elements is a mild interpretation.)

*Priscilla:* Ah . . . yeah, it's almost like I don't have any control of that. I really want to please her because she's such a good person. Those ideas kind of pop up when I'm asleep and when I'm awake at some level.

*Karen:* Now, Priscilla, we've got some possibilities with that . . . The interview is ending, but we can explore that in the new session with something called cognitive behavior modification, where we go about such things as thought stopping and learning to deal with our thoughts. Another possibility is psychodynamic dream analysis.

(This is an example of information or explanation.)

*Priscilla:* Yeah, I'd like to do that.

*Karen:* Our time is up now, Priscilla. We've gone through the issues with your mother. I've role played your mother. We talked about possibilities and tested where you might assert yourself more effectively. We've also talked about the need for more practice as I've found in my own experience. Ah . . . now, it looks like you may need to examine some of your feelings and thoughts and what they mean. We can look into that in the next session.

During the coming week, I'd like you to try once going out and deliberately interacting with your mother in a way in which you consciously do *not* assert yourself. Simply do what you have in the past and notice what happens in response. Don't use the skills at all. And, during the week, I'd like you to try just one situation where you test out tentatively the skills we practiced today. Is that clear?

[Karen begins her final comment with an influencing summary, which includes some aspects of the attending summary as well. She then moves to a directive, where she goes over a homework assignment for Priscilla during the coming week. The directive is fairly specific and concrete and ends with a check-out ("Is that clear?").]

Comment: A review of the visual, kinesthetic, and auditory words used by the two women is interesting. Karen uses primarily visual words,  with some auditory as well. Priscilla uses primarily a kinesthetic vocabulary. It would be important that Karen make more of an attempt to match systems in the future. On the other hand, the key constructs and descriptors used by Priscilla are matched fairly well, probably giving the interview the glue to be successful. Yet Karen would do well to match her language system and style even more with that of the client. Matching language is one clear way to show you understand the client's point of view and feelings. As you move to influencing skills, you naturally tend to fall back to your own way of representing the world. In using attending skills, matching client language systems and style is easier. The several skills are demonstrated here only briefly, but the example does illustrate how they might be used in a typical interview.

---

## Box 9-3  Key points

| | |
|---|---|
| *1. "1-2-3" pattern* | In any interaction with a client first attend and obtain the client's frame of reference, then use your influencing skill, and add a check-out to obtain the reaction to your use of the skill. |
| *2. Interpersonal influence continuum* | The influencing and attending skills may be arranged from low to high degrees of influence. Encouragers and paraphrasing are considered relatively low in influence, whereas confrontation and directives are high in influence. |
| *3. Moderate triad* | The "swing skills" of the interpersonal influence continuum are focusing and open and closed questions. They provide a framework for determining the topic of conversation while keeping a balance between influencing and attending skills. |
| *4. Directives* | Indicating clearly to a client what action to take. Central to an effective directive is: (1) appropriate body language, vocal tone, and eye contact; (2) clear and concrete verbal expression; (3) checking-out to make sure the directive was heard. |
| *5. Logical consequences* | Indicating the likely results of a client action. (1) Use attending skills to make sure you understand the |

**Box 9-3 continued**

|  |  |
|---|---|
|  | situation and how it is understood by the client. (2) Encourage thinking about positive and negative consequences of a decision. (3) Provide the client with your data on the positive and negative consequences of a decision. (4) Summarize the positives and negatives. (5) Let the client decide what action to take. |
| 6. *Self-disclosure* | Indicating your thoughts and feelings to a client. (1) Use personal pronouns ("I statements"), (2) verb for content or feeling ("I feel . . ." "I think . . ."), and (3) object coupled with adverb and adjective descriptors ("I feel happy about your being able to assert yourself . . ."). Self-disclosure tends to be most effective if it is genuine, timely, and in the present tense. |
| 7. *Feedback* | Providing accurate data on how the counselor or others view the client. (1) The client should be in charge. (2) Focus on strengths. (3) Be concrete and specific. (4) Be nonjudgmental. (5) Keep feedback lean and precise. (6) Check-out to see how your feedback was received. |
| 8. *Interpretation* | Providing the client with an alternative frame of reference. (1) Attempt to use a reflection of meaning first to see if the client can make his or her own interpretation. (2) Provide your interpretation or reframing of the situation. (3) Check-out to determine how the interpretation was received. |
| 9. *Influencing summary* | Providing the client with a brief summary of what you have been saying or thinking over a session. Like other skills, this should be timely, should be in words the client can understand, and should include a check-out to determine how the summary was received. |
| 10. *Information/ advice/ instruction/ opinion/ suggestion* | Passing on information and ideas of the interviewer to the client. The "1-2-3" pattern is again critical, and the information should be clear, concrete, and timely. |
| 11. *Confrontation* | Pointing out incongruities, discrepancies, and mixed messages in behavior, thoughts, feelings, or meanings. (1) Identify incongruities through the six categories identified in client observation skills. (2) Through questioning and other skills, draw out the specifics of the |

**Box 9-3 continued**

conflict or mixed message. (3) Periodically summarize the several dimensions of the incongruities and include a check-out. (4) As necessary, provide your own opinions, suggestions, and interpretations to facilitate client self-discovery.

## PRACTICE EXERCISES AND SELF-ASSESSMENT

There are too many skills mentioned in this chapter to expect early mastery. However, a few activities can increase your understanding of these concepts.

### INDIVIDUAL PRACTICE

During the next week observe conversations and meetings and note the frequency and the effectiveness of influencing skills used by your friends and colleagues. Record your observations below:

_____

_____

_____

_____

_____

_____

_____

_____

_____

_____

### SYSTEMATIC GROUP PRACTICE

Small group practice with the influencing skills requires practice with each skill. The general model of small group work is suggested, but only one skill should be used at a time.

**Step 1. Divide into practice groups.**

**Step 2. Select a leader of the group.**

**Step 3. Assign roles for each practice session.**

Role-played client

Interviewer

Observer I

Observer II

**Step 4. Planning.**   In using influencing skills, the acid test of mastery is whether the client actually does what is expected (for example, does the client follow the direction given?) or uses the feedback, self-disclosure, and so on, in a positive way. For each skill different topics are likely to be most useful. Some ideas follow:

*Directives.* The interviewer may give homework in the rational-emotive style of behavioral suggestions from an assertion training model. The Gestalt "hot seat" operates with directives, as does the trait-and-factor style when indicating to a client how to engage in a vocational search.

*Logical Consequences.* A member of the group may present a decision he or she is about to make. The counselor can explore the negative and positive consequences of this decision.

*Self-disclosure.* A member of the group may present any personal issue. The task of the counselor is to share something personal that relates to the client. Again, the check-out is important to obtain client feedback.

*Feedback.* Most useful is for the interviewer to give direct feedback to another member of the small group about his or her performance in the training sessions. Alternatively, the role-played client may talk about an issue and the counselor provide feedback sharing perceptions of the situation as factually as possible. A check-out should be included.

*Interpretation.* A client role-play may present an issue of interpersonal conflict. After using questions and reflective listening skills, the counselor may interpret from either a personal point of view or from some theoretical orientation. The check-out is again crucial.

*Influencing summary.* This skill may be best practiced in conjunction with other skills. At the end of the practice session the counselor may summarize what he or she has been doing.

*Information/advice/and so on.* The interviewer may give information about a particular theory or set of facts to the group. The group gives feedback on specificity and the ability of the information-giver to be clear, interesting, and helpful. Psychological education may be used. Interviewing skills may be taught.

*Confrontation.* The client may present a situation of interpersonal conflict, indecision, or situational confusion. The task of the counselor is to identify the discrepancies and to feed them back to the client. Some effort to work through the conflict may be included in the practice session.

**Step 5. Conduct a three- to five-minute practice session using the skill.**  You will find it difficult to use each influencing skill frequently as these skills must be interspersed with attending skills to keep the interview going. Attempt to use the skill in question at least twice during the practice session.

**Step 6. Review the practice session and provide feedback for 10 to 12 minutes.**  Remember to stop the tape and provide adequate feedback for the counselor.

**Step 7. Rotate roles.**

**Some general reminders.**  With advanced groups well versed in attending skills, considerable progress can be made with the influencing skills. Each skill will be learned most effectively if it is practiced separately. Once again, accurate feedback to the counselor will be most helpful in facilitating personal growth and development.

### SELF-ASSESSMENT AND FOLLOW-UP

Eight skill areas are identified in this chapter. They are listed on page 206 with each level of mastery. Check off those areas for which you have demonstrated mastery. Demonstrated mastery, again, means provision of evidence in written or taped form. Verification by an external observer

## INFLUENCING SKILLS FEEDBACK SHEET

_____ (Date)

_____     _____
(Name of Interviewer)                 (Name of Person Completing Form)

_____

_Instructions:_ Observer I will attempt to write down as much of each skill as possible and classify it. Observer II will give special attention to concreteness and clarity and the implicit or explicit use of the perception check.

| 1. List the wording of the influencing skill as closely as possible. Do not record attending skills. | Concreteness and clarity | | | Perception check included? | |
|---|---|---|---|---|---|
| | Lo | Med | Hi | Yes | No |
| a. _____ _____ | | | | | |
| b. _____ _____ | | | | | |
| c. _____ _____ | | | | | |
| d. _____ _____ | | | | | |
| e. _____ _____ | | | | | |
| f. _____ _____ | | | | | |

2. Did the interviewer follow the "1-2-3" pattern of attend, use the influence skill, and check-out?

3. General impressions of the interview.

competent in the skill is another form of validating mastery of a skill area. Remember that the requirements for each level of mastery are:

**Identification:** Ability to write statements representing the skill in question and to identify and/or classify the skill when seen in an interview.

**Basic mastery:** Demonstration of your ability to use the skill in a role-played interview.

**Active mastery:** Demonstration of your ability to use the skill in interviews with specific impact and effects on clients. (Note functions of each skill at the beginning of the chapter.)

**Teaching mastery:** Ability to teach the skill to others. In turn, the effectiveness of your teaching is demonstrated by their mastery level as above.

| SKILL AREA | Mastery Levels | | | | Brief Evidence of Achieving Mastery Level |
| | Identification | Basic | Active | Teaching | |
|---|---|---|---|---|---|
| Directives | | | | | |
| Logical consequences | | | | | |
| Self-disclosure | | | | | |
| Feedback | | | | | |
| Interpretation | | | | | |
| Influencing summary | | | | | |
| Information/ advice/ instruction/ opinion/ suggestion | | | | | |
| Confrontation | | | | | |

Given the complexity of this chapter and the many possible goals you might set for yourself, list below three specific goals you would like to attain in the use of influencing skills within the next month.

1. _____

2. _____

3. _____

## REFERENCES

Ivey, A., and Authier, J. *Microcounseling.* Springfield, Ill.: Charles C Thomas, 1978.

Ivey, A., and Gluckstern, N. *Basic influencing skills.* No. Amherst, Mass.: Microtraining, 1976.

Ivey, A., and Litterer, J. *Face to face.* No. Amherst, Mass.: Amherst Consulting Group, 1979.

Ivey, A., and Simek-Downing, L. *Counseling and psychotherapy.* Englewood Cliffs, N.J.: Prentice-Hall, 1980.

CHAPTER **10**

# Achieving Specific Goals in the Interview: Selecting and Structuring Skills

---

**How can the concepts of this chapter be used to help you and your clients?**

This chapter deals with six basic concepts. Brief definitions and the function of each concept now follow:

| CONCEPT | DEFINITION | FUNCTION |
|---|---|---|
| *Basic Listening Sequence (BLS)*   | The skills of questioning, encouraging, paraphrasing, reflection of feeling, and summarizing make up the BLS. The BLS appears in similar form in varying fields such as counseling, management, medicine, and social work. | To assist in defining a client's problem and/or outcome desired from the interview. Emphasis is on the client's frame of reference. The BLS helps ensure that the interviewer understands the problem as the client experiences it. It is also useful in assessing client developmental level. |
| *Positive Asset Search* | The positive asset search uses the BLS to draw out specific client positive assets which may be brought to bear on a problem. | To identify and emphasize client strengths. Too often counseling and interviewing turns on weakness and difficulty. The positive asset search provides the client with a solid base for personal growth. |

| CONCEPT | DEFINITION | FUNCTION |
|---|---|---|
| *Client Developmental Level* | Four levels of client development are suggested. Clients at low developmental levels are more in need of influencing skills, whereas clients at high levels of development may profit from attending skills. | To provide a rough guide to client functioning in a particular area, thus suggesting whether or not an attending or influencing approach is most effective. Clients may vary in developmental level depending on the area discussed. |
| *Interviewer Style* | Different interviewers use different proportions of attending and influencing skills. For example, a Rogerian interviewer uses mainly attending skills, whereas a manager with an inexperienced new employee uses mainly influencing skills. | To provide awareness that different counseling and interviewing styles may differ in effectiveness depending on the "match" between interviewer style and client developmental level. |
| *Empathy* | Viewing the world from the client's frame of reference requires skilled use of attending. Empathy can be divided into specific dimensions, such as concreteness, immediacy, and a nonjudgmental attitude. | To improve the quality of the interview and the helpfulness of attending and influencing skills used. |
| *Structuring the Interview* | An interview has five stages: (1) establishing rapport and structuring; (2) gathering information; (3) defining outcomes; (4) confronting client incongruity and generating alternatives; and (5) generalizing and transferring learning. | To ensure purpose and direction in the interview, and to help define and achieve specific outcomes. Different theories of interviewing give varying attention to each phase. |

## INTRODUCTION

To recapitulate the definition in Chapter 1, *intentionality* means determining your goals and aims and then deciding among a range of alternative actions. The intentional interviewer knows what he or she wishes to see happen in the session. The intentional interviewer has more than one action, thought, or behavior available for use in the continually changing atmosphere of the interview. The intentional interviewer can generate alternative possibilities in a given interview situation and select from many different theories using a variety of skills and qualities. The intentional interviewer can act decisively, note feedback in response to that action, and then act in accord with the new data, adapting styles to suit different cultural groups.

If something doesn't work, don't try more of the same . . . try something different! Each client you face in the interview is unique and will respond individually to the skills you present. What works with one person at one time may not work five minutes later. Yet, it is possible to have skills, skill sequences and structures, and techniques with which you can achieve specific objectives in your sessions.

Once you have mastered the several skills of attending and influencing, it is important to put them together in a smoothly flowing, integrated interview. This chapter provides a framework for integrating the skills into the interview and presents six basic concepts that are helpful in becoming a skilled interviewer. The practice exercises at the conclusion of the chapter will assist in the process of skill integration.

## THE BASIC LISTENING SEQUENCE

Observations of interviews in counseling, therapy, management, medicine, and other settings have revealed a common thread of skill usage. As we saw in Chapter 1, many successful interviewers begin their sessions with an open question, following this with closed questions for diagnosis and clarification. The paraphrase checks out the content of what the client is saying, and the reflection of feeling (usually brief in the early stages) examines key emotions. These skills are followed by a summary of the concern expressed by the client. Encouragers may be used throughout the interview to enrich and help bring in details.

Though the above set of skills appears in many different situations, it is not a rigid sequence. Each counselor or interviewer adapts skill usage to meet the needs of the client and the situation. The effective interviewer uses client observation skills to note client reactions and intentionally *flexes* in the moment to provide the skill and support the client needs. It may be appropriate to begin some interviews with a self-disclosure or even a directive. Gestalt therapists (see Perls, 1969) observe client nonverbal and verbal discrepancies and may start by telling clients specific actions to follow. The basic listening sequence, though common, is used in many variations and styles.

For the beginning counselor or interviewer mastery of the basic listening sequence can be most beneficial. Table 10-1 gives examples of the basic listening sequence in counseling, management, and medical interviewing. A special advantage of mastering this sequence is that, once a basic set of skills is defined, it can be used in many different situations. It is not unusual for a person skilled in the concepts of intentional interviewing to be conducting vocational counseling at a college in the morning, training parents in communication skills in the afternoon, consulting with a physician about diagnostic interviewing over dinner, and then working as a management consultant around group meeting skills in the evening. The microskills approach can be applied in many settings. In each case the BLS has the objective of bringing out client data—facts and feelings—for later interviewer and client action.

An additional important point should be made. Not only are listening skills and the BLS useful in many situations, the other influencing skills also have parallel applications in many different fields. For example, clear directives may be even more important in management and medicine than they are in counseling. A major problem arises in all fields when people have a responsibility to tell others what to do but don't

**TABLE 10–1.** Three examples of the Basic Listening Sequence

| Skill | Counseling | Management | Medicine |
|---|---|---|---|
| Open question | "Could you tell me what you'd like to talk to me about . . ." | | |
| Closed questions | "Did you graduate from high school?" "What specific careers have you looked at?" | "Who was involved with the production line problem?" "Did you check the main belt?" | "Is the headache on the left side or on the right? How long have you had it?" |
| Encouragers | Repetition of key words and restatement of longer phrases. | | |
| Paraphrases | "So you're considering returning to college." | "Sounds like you've consulted with almost everyone." | "It looks like you feel it's on the left side and may be a result of the car accident." |
| Reflection of feeling | "You feel confident of your ability but worry about getting in." | "I sense you're upset and troubled by Hank's reaction." | "It appears you've been feeling very anxious and tense lately." |
| Summarization | In each case the effective counselor, manager, or physician summarizes the problem from the client's point of view *before* diagnosing from the interviewer's point of view. | | |

transmit their directions and information clearly and concretely. Feedback, information, and all the influencing skills are useful in many fields related to interviewing. Parents, teachers, social workers, community hot-line volunteers, and people in general can profit from improvement in their basic communication skills.

## THE POSITIVE ASSET SEARCH

Counseling, interviewing, and psychotherapy can be a difficult experience for some clients. People come to discuss problems and resolve conflicts. The focus of the session can rapidly become a depressing litany of failures and fears.

People grow from their strengths, not from their weaknesses. The positive asset search is a useful method to assure a more optimistic and directed interview. Rather than just ask about problems, the effective interviewer seeks constantly to find positive assets upon which the client can focus. Even with very complex issues, it is possible to find good things about the client and things that the client does right. Emphasizing positive assets gives the client some personal power in the interview.

To conduct a positive asset search the interviewer simply uses the BLS to draw out the client's positive aspects and then reflects them back. This may be done systematically as a separate part of the interview or used constantly throughout the session.

Specifically, the positive asset search appears in the interview in the following ways:

1. The interviewer may begin a session by asking what has happened recently that the client feels good about. Or, the interviewer may comment about some positive strength in the client, noted in reading a file.
2. In the problem definition phase of the interview, the interviewer may use the BLS to bring out positive client assets in detail. For example, in response to a client who has just lost a job and feels depressed and worried: "You say you're worried and feel lost. At the same time, I know you held that job for four years. Could you tell me one thing you liked about the job or felt you did well?"
3. A client may constantly repeat negative self-statements. These may be paraphrased and then followed by feedback from a more positive viewpoint. For example: "Yes, losing a job is traumatic and really hurts. At the same time, I see that you have several strengths—a good sense of humor, some valuable skills, and a history of perseverance in the face of difficulty. All this will help you work through this."

Frankl's dereflection and Gendlin's focusing discussed in Chapter 7 provide two additional examples of the positive asset search. To highlight specific concrete assets of the client in context with real problems is a very helpful way of promoting positive change, and is central to any intelligent approach to human problems.

The positive asset search should be related to the empathic concept of positive regard discussed later in this chapter. Positive regard stresses the importance of attending to positive client assets whereas the positive asset search is more "results" oriented. Does the client actually produce a positive asset? Positive regard may be considered a basic mastery concept whereas the positive asset search demands active mastery.

The positive asset search is a new term in the helping field. Theoretically, it may be described as a psycho-educational intervention that emphasizes human development rather than the "medical model" that emphasizes remediation of problems. At the same time, it is a "meta-construct" found under different titles in many different forms of interviewing, counseling, and therapy. At times, the positive asset search may negate the need for traditional problem solving in the session. Client strengths will overcome weaknesses.

## CLIENT DEVELOPMENTAL LEVEL AND INTENTIONALITY

Intentionality is not only a goal for interviewers, it is also a goal for clients. A client comes to an interview *stuck*—having either no alternatives for solving a problem or a limited range of possibilities. The task of the interviewer is to eliminate stuckness and substitute intentionality. *Stuckness* is an inelegant, but highly descriptive, term to describe the opposite of intentionality (see Perls, 1969). Other words that represent the same condition include *immobility, blocks, repetition compulsion, inability to achieve goals, lack of understanding, limited behavioral repertoire, limited life script, impasse, lack of motivation,* and many other terms. *Stuckness* may also be defined as an inability to reconcile discrepancies and incongruity. In short, clients often come to the interview because they are stuck for a variety of reasons and seek intentionality.

The general concept of intentionality is helpful as we think about the clients we serve in the interview. However, intentionality is complex and needs more amplification since each client has different needs. Hersey and Blanchard (1979) have suggested four basic levels of client development, ranging from low to high. It is important to match interviewing style with the client's developmental level. The four developmental levels as they relate to intentionality are as follows:

**Level D-1.**  Intentionality is lacking. The client is stuck with no alternatives or, at best, a limited range of possibilities. The client lacks skills and may need to be told what to do. The client may have a major discrepancy of which he or she is unaware. Examples of clients at this developmental level include:

▲ A new employee on the job with extremely limited experience.
▲ A highly disturbed psychiatric inpatient.
▲ Students learning a new subject field.
▲ A client who may be at a higher developmental level in other areas but who is constantly repeating old, stuck behavior or thought patterns in the area of concern.

**Level D-2.**  Some degree of intentionality is present. The client may understand some incongruities but be unaware of others. The client is often stuck on several issues. The client has skills but is not always able to use them. Examples include:

▲ An employee who has been promoted to a new job, part of which he or she understands and has experienced before.
▲ Most neurotic patients or clients.
▲ Most clients who come in for counseling. They may function well in general, but have certain areas of their lives where they are stuck (for example, lack of vocational information, inability to conduct a job search, lack of communication with a spouse).

**Level D-3.** The client has intentionality but has not developed as fully as possible. The client requires assistance in finding his or her own way but needs only limited help from others. Examples of clients at this developmental level include:

▲ The employee who generally is a self-starter and does satisfactory work but is stuck on a particular issue.
▲ Clients who seek to better already solid performance and can present their problems and concerns quite clearly. Such clients often present the "YAVIS" syndrome (young, attractive, verbal, intelligent, successful) and are particularly amenable to counseling.

**Level D-4.**  The client operates with intentionality and is able to generate a wide range of alternatives and choose wisely from them. If interviewing assistance is needed, it tends to be brief or focused on self-learning. Examples include:

▲ Employees who are self-starters and operate well on their own.
▲ "YAVIS" clients seeking self-development.

As a general rule, clients at the lowest developmental levels require more influencing skills than those at higher levels. For example, clients at the D-1 level often need to be told what to do (although they still require attending skills to help them draw out their hidden potential). Clients at the D-2 level are ready for more interactive interviewing; a balance of attending and influencing skills is generally most appropriate for them. At D-3, clients are self-starters and may need only a minimal number of influencing skills. Such clients often respond best to attending skills that help them form their own thoughts, feelings, and meanings. Clients at D-4 can usually solve their own problems. They may come for interviewer support and guidance only when they require assistance on a specific issue, which they usually define clearly.

It is important to remember that this is only a rough schema. Clients at all developmental levels can profit from confrontation and directives just as low developmental clients can gain from the relationship-oriented attending skills. Some counseling and therapy theories argue that all clients should be treated in the same manner. However, data are beginning to support the idea that matching your style of interviewing with client problems and personal style may be beneficial (for instance, see Berzins, 1977). Clearly, not all people are the same, so we should not expect them to respond uniformly to our interviewing behaviors. You can benefit the greatest number of clients by being flexible and having several alternatives available to them.

## ASSESSING CLIENT DEVELOPMENTAL LEVEL

How can you determine the developmental level of the client so that you can match your style with individual needs and special client problems? Critical to this assessment is your ability to attend to the client, use the basic listening sequence (BLS), and observe client verbal and nonverbal behavior.

Following are some specific suggestions for determining the developmental level of clients:

**1. Assume a new client is at the D-2 level.**   Here, a balance of attending and influencing skills is appropriate. If the client appears to be more independent and a self-starter, assume D-3 and use more attending skills. If the client appears puzzled and you note incongruities, move to D-1 assumptions and actions.

**2. Use client observation skills to note client attending behaviors.**   If you are using too many influencing skills, clients will tend to avert their eyes (perhaps even raising them to the ceiling), frown, increase their speech rate and volume, and shift their body language (for instance, sitting forward in an aggressive fashion, sitting back with arms folded, jiggling legs or drumming the chair impatiently). On the other hand, if clients find you listening too intently, their eyes will tend to be downcast (or looking directly at you, seeking information), their bodies will be slumped and discouraged, and their vocal tone lowered.

*Your client observation skills tell you when you are mismatching your counseling style or statement with the client's felt need.* Though the above rules are true perhaps only 80% of the time, they do provide useful guidelines for when to shift your style. Clients seeking more from you will tend to show the "down" pattern; that may be the time to shift to more influencing skills or to confront the client with your own desire not to influence at that time. If the client shows the "avoidance" pattern and says "but . . . ," then it is probably time to return to attending skills and the basic listening sequence.

**3. Note client incongruities.** A large number of verbal and nonverbal incongruities in the client's behavior or life is often a sign of a lower developmental level. If the client is unaware of incongruity, assume a lower developmental level. If the client has only a few incongruities and is able to state these clearly, assume a higher developmental level and a need for more attending skills.

**4. Use the basic listening sequence to draw out client problems and obtain data for assessment of developmental level.**

**5. Use the newspaper sequence of who, what, where, when, how, why to obtain an overall assessment of client functioning.** Use client observation skills and focusing to note client reaction and to obtain as complete a picture of the situation as possible.

**6. Note client "I statements."** Low developmental level clients will tend to say "I can't . . . ," "I won't . . . ," "I'm not able . . . ," "I'm not interested . . . ," "I'm out of control . . ." Higher developmental level clients tend to say "I can . . . ," "I will . . . ," and "I am able . . ." One goal of effective interviewing is to change client "I statements" from low developmental levels to higher levels.

**7. Note client feelings and adjective descriptors.** Lower developmental level client feelings tend to be ambivalent and confused, or clients may avoid feelings completely. They may also act inappropriately (for example, laughing while talking about a sad event) and/or show a preponderance of negative feelings about self and others. Higher developmental level clients will be able to describe their feelings accurately, and the feelings will be relevant to the situation.

Lower level development may be shown by adjective descriptors and feelings that indicate passivity, negative evaluation, and impotency (*hopeless, bad, discouraged, and the like*) as opposed to higher level activity, positive evaluation, and potency (such as *glad, satisfied, making a difference*).

**8. Other assessment possibilities.** Lower developmental levels in middle-class culture tend to have an external locus of control ("They are responsible for my problems") versus an internal locus ("I am responsible for my behavior"). Lower developmental level clients may have an exclusively one-dimensional time perspective (for instance, only thinking in the past), whereas higher level clients will use past, present, and future time dimensions. Lower developmental levels tend to be represented by dependent personalities; higher developmental levels may demonstrate more independence.

**9. Culture and developmental level.** What makes for a high developmental level in one group may be considered low in another. For example, Westerners generally value independence, activity, and a strongly assertive personality. Among many Eastern people, the opposite may represent a highly developed individual. Japanese, for example, often value dependence over independence and even may consider the overly independent individual rude and uncouth. Value and personality differences among different peoples must be considered in assessing developmental level.

All these assessment possibilities are rough guidelines. However, if you find a client operating on a demonstrated lower level in several of the areas defined here, you may expect that your diagnosis is relatively correct.

The developmental level concept can help you think about how counseling styles might change as a person grows in understanding. A deeply disturbed psychiatric patient, for example, is low in virtually all developmental skills and needs to be told what to do. At this stage listening doesn't work; highly directive intervention such as medication may be most appropriate. However, as the client develops, it may be possible to institute assertion training or a combination of techniques all leading to sufficient intentionality so that release from the hospital is possible.

A new employee in industry may require direction and teaching in the early stages (D-1). If all goes well, the participative, "coaching" style (Style 2) may be most appropriate. If the employee develops well and shows creativity (D-3), the best approach may be the supportive attending skills and minimal use of influencing skills. If the employee becomes truly self-sufficient (D-4), the manager needs to intervene only occasionally by maintaining contact (attending behavior) and client observation skills.

One goal of interviewing and counseling, then, could be defined as moving the client to a higher-developmental level of intentionality. A successful interviewing or counseling series should ideally lead in the following directions:

| *From* | *To* |
|---|---|
| Low developmental level and intentionality. | High developmental level and greater intentionality. |
| Incongruous verbal and nonverbal behavior. | Congruent and genuine verbal and nonverbal behavior. |
| Negative "I statements" ("I can't"). | Positive "I statements" ("I can"). |
| Negative or mixed, confused, and inappropriate emotions. | Positive emotions appropriate to the context. Acceptance of necessary "negative" feelings as real (such as sadness after a major loss). |
| Passive, impotent, and negative evaluative adjective descriptors. | Active, potent, and positive evaluative descriptors. |
| External locus of control. | Internal locus of control. |
| Narrow time dimension. | Ability to live in the past, present, and future. |
| Dependence. | Independence. |

These interviewing and counseling goals are culturally dependent and typical of white, middle-class, North American values. It has been demonstrated, for example, that dependency and an external locus of control is often characteristic of a healthy Asian personality (Sue, 1981). Earlier, it was mentioned that different cultural groups may have vastly different patterns of verbal and nonverbal communication. All the suggestions here for developing intentionality are culture-specific and would need adaptation when applied to people of varying cultures and backgrounds.

Further, it should again be noted that clients present different developmental levels as they talk about different topics or issues. The interviewer must use client observation skills to note gradual and/or sudden changes in client development level and move to a new style as necessary. For example, you may be working with a client who shows little understanding of the vocational world (D-2) and readily accepts your advice and suggestions of the coaching style. The topic may shift to feelings and values around religion, where the client is operating at D-3. A change in counselor or interviewing style to Style 3 (client-directed) is appropriate.

Effective helping and matching of style with developmental level can also be informed by an understanding of empathy, a way to examine quality of relationships in interviewing.

In any case, you will find that noting client attending behavior patterns will be the most helpful indicator of how the client is responding to you. If you have not matched the client's developmental level satisfactorily, you will note discrepancies in the client's eye contact, body language, and verbal following patterns.

*It is critical to remember that developmental level is task-specific.* That is, a client may be at D-3 in terms of work and community leadership, but operating at D-1 or D-2 in terms of personal satisfaction or family relationships. Effective diagnosis and assessment of developmental level must always be changing with the topic or area of discussion. Virtually every client is a mixture of developmental levels.

The following paragraphs describe a conceptual model for matching interviewer style with client needs.

## A CONCEPTUAL MODEL FOR INTERVIEWER STYLE USAGE

Figure 10-1 illustrates the use of attending and influencing skills (interviewer style) in relation to client developmental level. Here we see four basic styles:

**Style 1: Telling.**   The interviewer directs the session, using influencing skills extensively. This is most appropriate for clients at developmental level D-1. Examples of Style 1 interviewing are medical inpatient psychiatry, traditional one-to-one instruction or teaching, and working with a new inexperienced employee.

**Style 2: Coaching.**   The interviewer balances attending and influencing skills and works with the client in a participative manner. The interviewer knows things that the client doesn't and is willing to share them. This style is most appropriate for developmental level D-2. Examples are vocational counseling, assertion training, cognitive behavior modification, and reality therapy.

**Style 3: Client-directed.**   The interviewer supports the client's search through primary use of the attending skills. Nondirective and modern Rogerian counseling styles are typical of this approach.

**Style 4: Low involvement.**   The interviewer tends to let self-starters alone to develop their own goals and methods. The manager who leaves

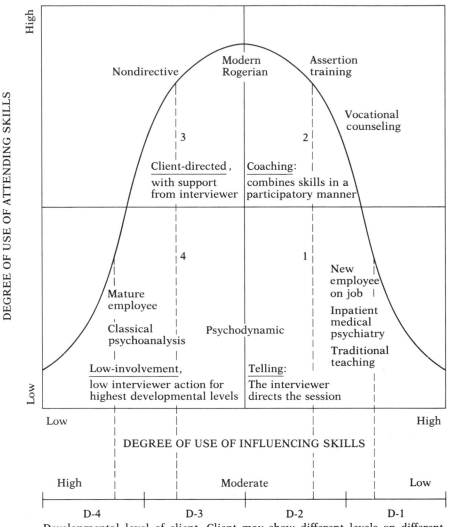

**FIGURE 10–1.** Interviewer style, client development, and expected frequency of skill usage. (Developed in consultation with Ken Blanchard, Blanchard Training and Development. This is an adaptation of his situational leadership model.)

a mature employee alone is one example of this style. The classical psychoanalyst who works with patients "on the couch" also leaves the direction of the session to the client.

The model in Figure 10-1 points out the need to match interviewer style with client developmental level. At the same time, this is a *general framework.* In this culture it is almost always wise to start work with clients assuming a D-2 level and use a blend of attending and influencing skills to assess where the client is developmentally. Key to that assessment is use of attending skills. As we have emphasized throughout this book, first attend, then influence, and then check-out where the client seems to be.

Almost invariably, clients will present several levels of development in one interview. An older woman entering the job market for the first time may be operating at a low level (D-1) vocationally and not have even the most elementary job-seeking skills. At the same time, she may have had wide experience in volunteer work and be a successful home-maker and counselor to her children and neighborhood families. In these areas of her life, she may be at level D-3 or D-4. Thus, in a single interview it may be necessary to move through several different interviewing styles depending on the issue discussed. For the purposes of vocational counseling it may be best to begin with a coaching/consulting style for a D-2 client. On specific vocational issues a telling style may be needed.

As the client develops more confidence, knowledge, and experience, successful counseling will help her or him move in vocational expertise from D-1 to D-2 and higher levels. You'll find you can change your counseling style as the client grows. The cycle suggested here starts with attending to find out where the client is developmentally, then moves to a telling style, and continues to change from that point in response to the client's reaction and movement.

In the process of vocational counseling, the client may talk about difficulties with her children. In this area she may present a different level of development (such as D-3), and a basically client-directed attending approach on this problem may be more appropriate.

Together, the concepts of interviewer style, client development, and differential use of attending and influencing skills form a "roadmap" that suggests which skill may be most useful to a client in a given situation.

As indicated in Figure 10-1, different counseling and interviewing theories have general patterns that appear to be in accord with different client needs. It is suggested that the modern Rogerian and listening approaches to counseling are best suited for higher developmental level clients. Most clients, however, come to counseling for information and to solve problems for which they don't have the answers inside themselves (D-2). Thus, in most practical, day-to-day situations, Style 2 coaching—interviewing and counseling—is common. Examples of Style 2 interviewing include vocational trait-and-factor, rational-emotive therapy, assertion training, reality therapy, transactional analysis, Gestalt therapy, and many other approaches.

Remember: interviewing and counseling are for the client, not for the interviewer or counselor. Quality use of attending skills and influencing skills requires matching interviewing style with the client's developmental level. Another approach to developing quality helping relationships entails empathy, which we will consider in the following section.

## QUALITATIVE ASPECTS OF INTERVIEWING SKILLS: EMPATHY

The skills of attending and influencing are not always sufficient in themselves to provide quality relationships with clients. Most basic is the quality of empathy—experiencing the client's world as if *you* were the client. This means moving into the client's frame of reference. The attending skills—particularly paraphrasing, reflection of feeling, and reflection of meaning—are deeply involved in developing basic empathy. Empathy manifests itself in the interview behaviorally when the interviewer or counselor truly understands the client and is able to paraphrase the client's main ideas accurately. In such cases the counselor will often be found using the *important words* of the client, but distilling and shortening the main ideas.

In *basic empathy*, as described above, counselor responses are roughly interchangeable with those of the client. In *additive empathy* the counselor or interviewer uses influencing skills and *adds* congruent ideas and feelings from another frame of reference to facilitate client exploration. Attending skills, used well, can themselves be additive. Reflection of meaning, especially, operates from the client's frame of reference and adds depth beyond the mere reflection of feeling and paraphrasing.

Empathy, then, is a major goal of both attending and influencing skills. If the skills are used ineffectively, however, they may subtract from client experience. Lack of empathy *subtracts* from the helping process. Subtractive responses are those that take something away from the client and usually indicate poor listening skills, although inappropriate influencing skills are often subtractive as well.

It is possible to rate empathy on a rough five-point scale, and you may wish to examine each of your responses for the degree to which it manifests empathy. (See also Carkhuff, 1969, for further discussion of these concepts.) Here are examples of five levels of empathy in response to a client:

*Client:* I don't know what to do. I've gone over this problem again and again. My husband just doesn't seem to understand that I don't really care anymore. He just keeps trying, but it doesn't seem worth bothering with him anymore.

*Level 1 Counselor (subtractive):* That's not a very good way to talk. I think you ought to consider his feelings, too.

*Level 2 Counselor (slightly subtractive):* Seems like you've just about given up on him. You don't want to try anymore.

*Level 3 Counselor (basic empathy or interchangeable response):* You're discouraged and confused. You've worked over the issues with your husband, but he just doesn't seem to understand. At the moment, you feel he's not worth bothering with. You don't really *care*.

*Level 4 Counselor (slightly additive):* You've gone over the problem with him again and again to the point you don't really *care* right now. You've tried hard. What does all this mean to you?

*Level 5 Counselor (additive):* I sense your hurt and confusion and that right now you really don't care anymore. Given what you've told me, your thoughts and feelings make a lot of sense to me. At the same time, you've had a reason for trying so hard. You've talked about some deep feelings of caring for him in the past. How do you put that together right now with what you are feeling?

To be empathic means to take risks, and higher level responses are not always well received by clients. As the counselor attempts to move toward additive responses, the risk goes up. Risk, in this case, means "risk of error." You may have excellent listening skills, but when you seek to add your own perceptions you may be out of synchrony with client needs.

A Level 3 interchangeable response is fairly safe and direct. When the counselor strives for higher level additive responses, they may sometimes be completely off the mark, and the client will respond negatively. This does not mean the counselor response was necessarily bad; it may be simply that the client wasn't quite ready at that moment, or the client's developmental level on that topic was too low.

In any case, how the client responds to your interviewing lead is more important than some external rating of the response. No interviewer can always predict client responses to leads. It is here that client observation skills and the ability of the interviewer to *flex* and change the next lead to fit the needs of the client are most important. Flexing requires the interviewer to note client response to interventions and intentionally provide another response more in synchrony with client needs of the moment. The following A-B-C pattern illustrates the flow necessary in flexing and true empathic responding.

A. The interviewer observes the client's verbal and nonverbal behavior and consciously or unconsciously selects a verbal lead (skill) with the potential for facilitating client development. (The counselor in the example above may select the level 5 response as likely to facilitate talk and deeper exploration.)

B. The client reacts to the counselor's statement with verbal and non-verbal behavior. (In this case the client may say angrily, "I don't put that together. What I want at the moment is to get away. Are you pushing me back toward him?")

C. The interviewer again observes the client's verbal and nonverbal behavior and selects another verbal lead (skill) with the possibility of facilitating client development. (After the client's angry response the counselor may try a Level 3 response: "What I just said made you feel angry. You want very much to get away from him right now.")

The A is the antecedent, the B is the behavior of the client, and the C is the consequent behavior of the counselor in response to the client. True empathy requires the interviewer constantly to flex and be ready to change and adapt to each unique client.

A number of authorities have given extensive attention to empathy (for example, Carkhuff, 1969; Egan, 1975; Ivey & Authier, 1978; Rogers, 1957, 1975). Carkhuff and Rogers are considered the basic authorities on this topic. To produce quality helping relationships, it is often useful to consider positive regard, respect and warmth, concreteness, immediacy, nonjudgmental attitudes and authenticity or congruence as foundations of empathy. We have referred to these dimensions explicitly and implicitly throughout this book; we will summarize them briefly now, with suggestions for noting them in the interview.

**1. Positive regard** may be defined as selecting positive aspects of client experience and selectively attending to positive aspects of client statements. There is a tendency in much of interviewing and counseling to work solely on problems and omit reference to strengths and capabilities. A five-point scale may be developed for positive regard (and for the other qualities discussed in this section), with the same five anchor points as for empathy. For example:

| Level | 1 | 2 | 3 | 4 | 5 |
|---|---|---|---|---|---|
| Subtractive | | Interchangeable | | | Additive |

A subtractive response is one in which the counselor finds something wrong with the client. An interchangeable response is one in which the counselor notes or reflects accurately what the client has talked about. In an additive response the counselor points out to the client how, even in the most difficult situation, the client is doing something positive. For example, the counselor may tell a client suffering from depression and talking about many problems: "John, I respect your ability to describe your problems so clearly. You've got your reasons for feeling so depressed. Tell me a bit more about your ability to define problems in the present and past." Carl Rogers was particularly good at delving into the most complex problem or person and finding positive qualities. Positive regard is perhaps the most basic aspect of true empathy.

**2. Respect and warmth** may be most easily rated if considered kinesthetic and nonverbal. You show respect and warmth by your posture, your smile, and your vocal tone. Your ability to be congruent with your body language and your willingness to touch (in appropriate situations) are indicators of respect and warmth.

**3. Concreteness** has been stressed throughout this book. A concrete counselor statement aims toward specifics rather than vague generali-ties. As interviewers, we are most often interested in specific feelings, specific thoughts, and specific examples of actions. As has been stressed many times, one of the most useful of all open questions is "Could you give me a specific example of . . . ?" Concreteness makes the interview live and real. The directive, the feedback skill, and interpretation all need to be highly specific or they may become lost in the busy world of the client.

Nevertheless, there are times when concreteness is not the most appropriate response. Some problems are best discussed in more general terms, and some cultural groups prefer to be less specific. Cultural differences of expression in empathy, respect and warmth, and concreteness must always be kept in mind.

**4. Immediacy** is a useful concept to give the interview timeliness. It is most easily described in terms of language. You may respond to a client who is angry in three tenses: "You *were* angry . . . you *are* angry . . . you *will be* angry." We tend to respond to others in the same tense in which they are speaking. You will find some clients who always talk in the past tense, and they may profit from present-tense discussion. Others are always in the future, and some are constantly in the present. The most useful response is generally in the present. A change of tense may be used to speed up or slow down the interview. We have found that, in counseling styles of many types, responses that include all three tenses tend to be the most powerful of all.

Another way to view immediacy is in terms of the relationship between the counselor and client. The more personal that relationship is, the more immediate it is. As issues of closeness between interviewer and client become manifest, this type of immediacy may be very powerful. A relationship is made immediate in this sense by a focus on the counselor and client ("we" focus) and by being in the present tense.

**5. A nonjudgmental attitude** is difficult to describe. Closely related to positive regard and respect, a nonjudgmental attitude requires you to

suspend your own opinions and attitudes and assume a value neutrality in relation to your client. Many clients come with issues and concerns that may be counter to your beliefs and values. If you listen to your clients carefully, you will come to an understanding of how they might have taken that position or action. People who are working through difficulties and issues do not need to be judged or evaluated; they need acceptance for themselves and their actions as they are.

A nonjudgmental attitude is expressed through vocal tone and body language and by statements indicating neither approval nor disapproval. However, as in all qualities and skills, there are times when judgment may facilitate client exploration. There are no absolutes in counseling and interviewing.

**6. Authenticity and congruence** are the reverse of discrepancies and mixed messages, which we discussed under confrontation. The hope is that the counselor or interviewer can be congruent and genuine and not have many discrepancies. Needless to say, life is full of discrepancies and paradoxes, and your ability to flex in response to the client may be the most basic dimension of authenticity.

## A SIMPLE STRUCTURE FOR THE INTERVIEW[1]

Not only do basic skills cut across different areas of interpersonal relationships and professions; these skills also have different parts to play throughout an interview. This section summarizes one simple structure for the interview and illustrates how different skills play different parts in the several segments. This interviewing structure is one that can be used in many different settings with appropriate adaptations for the situation and person. *It is not the only interviewing structure*, but will provide a rationale and organization that can produce results.

The interview can be organized into five basic stages (see Table 10–2):

---

[1] The concepts here were originated by the author in a conversation with William Matthews, University of Massachusetts. This should be considered a jointly developed conceptual frame.

**Table 10–2.** A simple five-stage structure for the interview

| Definition of stage | Function and purpose of stage | Commonly used skills |
| --- | --- | --- |
| 1. *Rapport and structuring.* "Hello." | To build a working alliance with the client and to enable the client to feel comfortable with the interviewer. Structuring may be needed to explain the purpose of the interview. Structuring functions to help keep the session on task and to inform the client what the counselor can and cannot do. | Attending behavior to establish contact with the client, and client observation skills to determine appropriate method to build rapport. Structuring most often involves the influencing skill of information giving and instructions. |
| 2. *Gathering information, defining the problem, and identifying assets.* "What's the problem?" | To find out why the client has come to the interview and how he or she views the problem. Skillful problem definition will help avoid aimless topic jumping and give the interview purpose and direction. Also to identify clearly positive strengths of the client. | Most common are the attending skills, especially the basic listening sequence. Other skills may be used as necessary. If problems aren't clear, you may need more influencing skills. The positive asset search often reveals capabilities in the client that are useful in finding problem resolution. |
| 3. *Determining outcomes. Where does the client want to go?* "What do you want to have happen?" | To find out the ideal world of the client. How would the client like to be? How would things be if the problem were solved? This stage is important in that it enables the interviewer to know what the client wants. The desired direction of the client and counselor should be reasonably harmonious. With some clients, skip phase 2 and define goals first. | Most common are the attending skills, especially the basic listening sequence. Other skills used as necessary. If outcome is still unclear, more influencing skills may be helpful. With clients from other cultures and those who are less verbal, this phase should often precede phase 2. |
| 4. *Exploring alternatives and confronting client incongruities.* "What are we going to do about it?" | To work toward resolution of the client's issue. This may involve the creative problem-solving model of generating alternatives (to remove stuckness) and deciding among those alternatives. It also may involve lengthy exploration of personal dynamics. This phase of the interview may be the longest. | May begin with a summary of the major discrepancies. Depending on the issue and theory of the interviewer, a heavy use of influencing skills may be expected. Attending skills still used for balance. |
| 5. *Generalization and transfer of learning.* "Will you do it?" | To enable changes in thoughts, feelings, and behaviors in the client's daily life. Many clients go through an interview and then do nothing to change their behavior, remaining in the same world they came from. | Influencing skills, such as directives and information/explanation, are particularly important. Attending skills used to check-out client understanding of importance of the stage. |

**Stage 1. Rapport and structuring.** "Hello." Some interviewers give extensive attention to this stage, whereas others simply assume it and start immediately. Introducing the interview and building rapport obviously are most important in the first interview with a client. In some cases rapport building may be quite lengthy and blend into treatment. An example is reality therapy with a delinquent youth, where playing ping pong and getting to know the client on a personal basis may be part of the treatment. In most counseling and interviewing, however, this stage is quite short. After a brief "hello" the interviewer immediately moves to some discussion of what the client wants.

Some clients need to have the interview explained and structured for them. This may be their first interview and they do not know how to behave. Setting the stage for this type of client can be extremely important. In such cases the interviewer explains the purpose of the interview and what he or she can and cannot do. Welfare interviewers, for example, find that they can assist clients more if they indicate very early in the session what their powers are. If the client has a different need, immediate referral is possible, with minimum frustration for both client and interviewer.

Many psychiatric and psychoanalytic treatment interview series begin with extensive structuring and diagnostic work before regular interviews begin. The client and therapist may decide not to continue at this stage.

The most important microskills for rapport building are basic attending behavior and client observation skills. Basic attending is used to demonstrate that you understand the client and are interested.

Client observation is critical at this stage of the interview. Is the client comfortable and relaxed? What major nonverbal behaviors do you observe? Is this client primarily auditory, visual, or kinesthetic? All observations are helpful in the process of rapport development. Self-disclosure on your part may be helpful with some clients. In a continuing series of sessions, summarization may be used so that past interviews are integrated with the current session.

Clarity and concreteness in influencing skills is central to structuring the interview. You may need to provide information about what is going to happen, directions for client action, and feedback and advice.

The positive asset search may be an important part of rapport building. With a nervous or insecure client, taking time to outline specific and concrete client assets provides the client with a secure base from which to confront difficult problems. What is most important is that the interviewer be open, authentic, and congruent with the client, and flexibly meet the needs expressed by that client.

Nevertheless, you should remember that many—perhaps most—interviews begin with some variation of "Could you tell me how I might be of help?" In much of interviewing rapport can be assumed, but when it is necessary, it is the most important issue in the entire interview. Unless the client has some liking and trust for you, you won't go far. Again, your ability to observe clients will tell you when it is appropriate to move to Stage 2.

**Stage 2. Gathering information, defining the problem, and identifying assets.** "What's the problem?" The first task of the interviewer is

to find out why the client is there and what the problem is. Coupled with that is gathering necessary information about the client and the problem. Clients often confuse interviewers with a long list of issues and concerns. One simple rule is that the *last* item a client presents in a "laundry list" of problems is often the one of central concern—watch for it, but be prepared to redefine the problem as you listen further.

The basic listening sequence is crucial in defining problems and gathering information. Open and closed questions will help define the issue as the client views it. Encouragers and paraphrases will provide additional clarity and provide an opportunity for you to check-out if you have heard correctly. Acknowledgment of emotions through reflection of feeling will provide an important beginning understanding of the emotional underpinnings. Summarization provides a good way to put the several ideas the client has presented in an orderly form. In some cases reflection of meaning may supplement this process by broadening conceptual frames.

The central task at this point is defining the problem as the client feels it. This can be supplemented by gathering information and data about the client and the client's perceptions. The basic *who, what, where, when, how,* and *why* series of questions provide one short and often useful frame to make sure you have covered the most important aspects of information gathering and problem definition.

The function of this phase of the interview is to define central client concerns. What is the real world of the client? What problem seeks resolution, or what opportunity needs to be actualized? Failure to develop clarity about these issues often results in an interview that wanders and lacks purpose.

At the same time, it is important to give attention to client strengths. The positive asset search should be part of this segment of the interview or systematically included later in the session. Always remember a very central point of this text—*clients grow from strength.*

**Stage 3. Determining outcomes. Where does the client want to go?** "What do you want to have happen?" The third stage focuses on where the

client wants to go. Many counselors and interviewers will summarize the problem of the client and then ask a question such as "What would you imagine the ideal solution to be?" "Where do you want to go with this?" "Could you take a moment, draw back, and develop a fantasy of what you would like to have happen?" or some variation on this theme. After the client proposes some solution, you may use the basic listening sequence, and more details about the client's thoughts and feelings about ideal solutions will be generated. Often clients can solve their own problems in this stage of the interview.

Some clients prefer to have this stage of the interview early in the session, even before problem definition. With high school discipline problems, less verbal clients, and those of some cultural groups, moving quickly to defining a clear outcome may help rapport development. Some clients dislike lengthy analysis of the problem and want action *now*. If you adapt your interviewing style to meet this simple, but obvious need, you will be able to achieve counseling success with many clients that more traditional problem-focused methods cannot reach.

Another type of client who may profit from exploring this phase of the interview first is the client experiencing vocational indecision. The problem is often vague, confused and ambiguous. Sorting out a clear goal first may later result in better problem definition and asset identifications.

A maxim for the confused interview, be it discipline, vocational, or even marital counseling, is "define a goal, make the goal explicit, search for assets to help facilitate goal attainment, and only then examine the nature of the problem." At times clear goal definition and a solid asset search may make problem identification unneeded.

The phrase *determining outcomes* adds weight to idealized client direction. Whether you are conducting long-term therapy or meeting briefly with a client in an employment service, asking what the client wants to come out of the interaction is critical in reaching an outcome. Too often the client and counselor assume they are working toward the same outcome when actually each of them wants the client to head in a different direction. A client may be satisfied with sleeping better at night, but the counselor wants complete personality reconstruction. The client may want brief advice about how to find a new job, whereas the counselor wants to give extensive vocational testing and suggest a new career. Of course, clients often expect and want more than the interviewer can deliver. Clarifying this issue early in the session through the questions above can save immense time and effort.

The question of determining outcomes is of interest from a theoretical as well as a practical perspective. Rogers talks about many clients having incongruence between the real self and the ideal self. Behavioral psychologists often talk about present behavior as compared to desired behavioral goals. Reality therapists talk about fulfilling unmet needs, and trait-and-factor counselors speak of facilitating a client's decision to act. Many theoretical orientations ask: "Where is the client, and where does she or he want to go?" "What is the difference between the real world and the desired world?" Blanchard and Johnson, in their primer of effective management, *The One-Minute Manager*, summarize the issue succinctly:

> If you can't tell me what you'd like to be happening, . . . you don't have a problem yet. You're just complaining. A problem only exists if there is a difference between what is actually happening and what you desire to be happening [1981, p. 3].

Once the discrepancies—between the real self and ideal self, between the real situation and the desired situation, between the nature of the relationship now and the desired relationship, and so on—are clear, it is possible to confront issues clearly and precisely. A wide variety of skills, techniques, and theories are available to explore and confront the conflict faced by the client.

The confrontations may be used to summarize the discrepancy or incongruity between the problem and the desired outcome. In addition, the positive asset search may be used to support the idea that the client can do something about his or her problem. For example, consider the following model sentences:

| | |
|---|---|
| Trait and factor decision-making | "On the one hand the problem may be summarized as . . . and on the other hand your desired outcome is . . . and you have the following assets and strengths to help you reach your goal(s) . . ." |
| Rogerian | "Your real self, as you describe yourself, is . . . Yet you see your ideal self as . . . and you have several positive qualities such as . . . which may help you become more what you want to be." |
| Behavioral | "Your present behavior is . . . but you would like to behave differently. For example, you would ideally like to . . . and you note the following positive behaviors and actions from the past . . ." |
| Psychodynamic | "The dream was . . . and it troubled you. You'd like to understand the dream and its implications for action. You've been able to use free association and dream techniques in the past successfully. Can you use them now?" |

Marital counseling

"Your present relationship is described as . . . but you would like to see it change as follows . . . As a couple you seem to have several strengths such as . . . which will be helpful in resolving the conflict."

Vocational counseling (confused client)

"You are searching for a college major (or life career) and aren't really sure of your possibilities. Yet you've described your short and long-term goals rather clearly . . . You've had several positive work experiences in the past . . . How do you put that together?"

Note that all these model confrontation sentences bring together the problem definition and the desired outcome. The positive asset summary is used to help the client realize that he or she is personally capable of problem resolution.

Many clients of a high developmental level (that is, D-3) can use such a summary as a springboard to action. They will resolve the discrepancy on their own with your support. Clients at a D-2 or lower level will require more influencing skills and active direction on your part. Observing your client's verbal and nonverbal reaction to this summary will help you determine your style of interview in Stage 4 following.

**Stage 4. Exploring alternatives and confronting client incongruity.** "What are we going to do about it?" The purpose of this stage of

the interview is problem solving and relief for the client. The problem may be deciding between two positive alternatives, discovering unconscious interpersonal dynamics, making a vocational choice, or resolving any of a wide variety of issues the client may face. The client at this stage is stuck and unable to come up with productive alternatives. The task of the counselor or interviewer is to explore possibilities and to assist the client in finding new ways to act more intentionally in the world.

How does the interviewer confront and explore incongruity? Two major routes appear to be available: (1) Summarizing the client conflict and frame of reference and using attending skills plus confrontation to facilitate client problem resolution. (2) Summarizing the client conflict and frame of reference and *adding* the interviewer's frame of reference through influencing skills (such as feedback, self-disclosure, instruction, directives, interpretation) and/or applying alternative helping theories (such as Gestalt, psychodynamic, behavioral).

Let us consider a business manager talking with an employee about a conflict between the purchasing department and the production department. With the interview structure suggested here, the first task of the manager is to establish rapport with the employee. This is followed by gathering information and defining the problem. Here many discrepancies may be identified. Next, the ideal resolution can be determined. Where does the employee (and the manager in this case) want to go? What outcome is desired? Having defined the real world and the ideal world, the manager can then assist the employee to confront these discrepancies. The manager may self-disclose how he or she solved similar problems in the past. The manager may give the employee advice or a simple directive to solve the problem.

Alternatively, the problem may turn out to be more complex than was originally believed. Then a combination of attending and influencing skills may be required to explore other possibilities and generate new alternatives. The manager needs to be aware that development of intentionality is a major goal of the interview. If a manager provides all the answers for the employee, the employee will not develop and grow and may become excessively dependent on the manager—or perhaps resist the manager's good advice and sabotage the effort. On the other hand, if the manager doesn't provide enough data from his or her background and experience, the employee may flounder. Some reasonable balance is needed.

Counseling works in a similar fashion. The counselor needs to establish rapport, define the problem, and establish desired client outcomes. The distinction between the problem and the desired outcome is the major incongruity the interviewer seeks to resolve. This incongruity or discrepancy may be resolved in three basic ways: (1) The counselor can use attending skills to clarify the client's frame of reference and then feed back via a confrontation what the client has said. Often the client will generate her or his own new synthesis and resolve the problem there. (2) If the first alternative is not successful, the interviewer can add interpretation, self-disclosure, and other influencing skills in an attempt to resolve the discrepancy. In this case, the counselor will be working from a personal frame of reference or theory. (3) In systematic problem solving the counselor and the client together generate or brainstorm alternatives for action and set priorities for the most effective possibilities.

To determine your own style of interviewing, it may be best in the early stages of work to operate from your own theoretical frame of reference. Take time and explore the client's issue from his or her frame of reference and add your own as you feel appropriate, keeping in mind the goal of intentionality and the generation of new alternatives for the client. Common sense provides ways to explore and seek outcomes. Experience with alternative theories of helping can later suggest additions to your own point of view. Used with sensitivity and caring, your own past experience will often be helpful to the client.

It is good to keep the basic problem-solving model in mind throughout the interview, particularly in this phase:

1. Define the problem (keeping in mind the goal or desired outcome)
2. Generate alternatives
3. Decide on action

During this phase of the interview, it is particularly important to keep the problem in mind while generating alternatives for solution (whether they are practical and commonsensical or theoretical systems of interviewing) and an eventual decision for action. However, decision for action is not enough. You must also plan to make sure that feelings, thoughts, and behaviors generalize beyond the interview itself. Stage 5 of the interview speaks to this issue.

**Stage 5.  Generalization and transfer of learning.**  "Will you do it?" The information conveyed, the concepts learned in the interview, the new behaviors suggested may all be for naught if systematic thought is not given to the transfer and generalization of the interview to daily life. The complexities of the world are such that taking a new behavior back to the home setting is difficult.

Consider the management and counseling situations again. The manager may give good advice about solving the problem between the production and purchasing departments, but if the employee reverts to the older, inefficient, *stuck* behavior, the problem will continue. The counselor and client may work through an excellent vocational plan or method of resolving family conflict. But if the client returns to the same work setting or the same family complex, transfer of what has been learned may be extremely difficult or impossible.

Many therapies, both traditional and modern, work on the assumption that behavior change will come out of new unconscious learning; they "trust" that clients will change spontaneously. Change does not come easily, and maintaining any change in thoughts, feelings, or behavior is even more difficult. Behavioral psychology has given considerable thought to transfer of training and has developed an array of techniques for transfer; even so, clients still revert to earlier, less intentional behaviors. Below are some specific methods different theoretical schools have used to facilitate transfer of learning from the interview.

1. Role-playing. Just as in the practice sessions of this book, the client can practice the new behavior in a role-play with the counselor or interviewer. This emphasizes the specifics of learning and increases the likelihood that the client will recognize the need for the new behavior after the session is over.
2. Imagery. Having a client imagine what the disturbing event will be like and what he or she will need to do may be helpful.

3. Behavioral charting and progress notes. The client may keep a record of the number of times certain behaviors occur and report back to the counselor. With some clients an informal diary of personal subjective reactions may be more helpful.

4. Homework. The interviewer may suggest specific tasks for the client to try during the week to follow up on the interview. This is an increasingly common practice in counseling.

5. Paradoxical instructions. Through the pioneering work of Victor Frankl it has been found that directing clients to continue stuck behavior during the next week may be helpful. For example, if a client has difficulty with frequent arguments with a spouse, the counselor may suggest that the client *deliberately* start several arguments during the week. Out of paradoxical directives such as this, clients often learn to manage their stuck or out-of-control behavior.

6. Family or group counseling. Sometimes individual problems are deeply merged with difficult marriage, family, or work-group arrangements. Transfer of individual counseling or interviewing information and skills is extremely difficult given the difficulty of behavior change in a system. An increasing number of counselors now seek to involve spouses and families in the counseling process. In work settings managers and personnel people increasingly see organizational development and team building as critical to improving individual skills and transfer of behavior.

7. Follow-up and support. It may be helpful to ask the client to return periodically to check on maintenance of behavior. At this time the counselor can also provide social and emotional support through difficult periods.

8. Do-use-teach. *Intentional Interviewing and Counseling* emphasizes immediate practice or *doing* the skill or concept being taught. The most popular and effective part of teaching is immediate practice in the training session—*do it!* In counseling the same principle appears to be true. Clients learn new ideas most effectively if they practice them in role-plays with the counselor or interviewer. Next, behavioral contracts to *use* the skill in an outside situation are helpful. The more specific the context and the behavior, the more likely it is that the training will be generalized. Finally, *teaching* what you have learned to others is a deeper level of mastery. In this program we emphasize learning how to teach interviewing skills to others—your clients and your colleagues. Similarly, it can be helpful to have clients teach what they have learned. Teaching requires the highest competence and can help ensure generalization and transfer.

These are but a few of the many possibilities to help develop and maintain client change. Each individual will respond differently to these techniques, and client observation skills are called for to determine which technique or set of techniques is most likely to be helpful to a particular person. For maximal impact and behavior transfer, a combination of several techniques is suggested. Evidence is clear that behavior learned in the interview does not necessarily appear in daily life without careful planning.

Finally, it should be mentioned that different theories of interviewing give different emphasis to various parts of the interview. Table 10-3 summarizes the amounts of time various approaches devote to the different stages. A reality therapist may spend several days in an informal setting just getting to know a delinquent youth, while the behavioral change procedures may be implemented over a relatively short time and extensive attention may be given to behavioral transfer. In Haley's problem solving therapy, and in much of the strategic/structural school, definition of problem may take 90 percent of the time. This school believes that if the problem is defined carefully and precisely, the resolution often will be a natural and logical consequence of the process. Gestalt and psychodynamic counselors pay relatively little attention to problem definition, preferring to work primarily at Stage 4 in which they apply their varying theories to the client. Similarly, they give little attention to maintenance of change.

Given the wide variety of models and theories, it is difficult to prescribe the most effective balance of time and effort to be spent in each phase of the interview. Rather, it seems most effective to use careful client observation to determine the appropriate moment to move from stage to stage. Nevertheless, it is possible to make some generalizations.

For most interviews a relatively short time is required for rapport building. Problem definition will vary with the complexity of the issue and should not be overlooked. Stage 3, the ideal world of the client, may sometimes be skipped if problem definition is clear, but it usually is helpful to give some time to this stage for it can open new alternatives

 you and the client may have overlooked. The bulk of most interviews takes place in the fourth stage—alternative exploration and confrontation of incongruity. It is here the differing styles and theories of the interview vary the most. Many theories of counseling pay no attention to the fifth stage, generalization, with the result that change produced in the interview often doesn't last very long. Current thinking is that this stage is of importance equal to, if not greater than, the other four stages.

As you work through your first interviews, checking off in your mind whether or not you have used the concepts of each stage will supply a roadmap. Later, as you find your own style and become comfortable with alternative theories, you will want to develop your own structure for the interview, changing and balancing the stages in your own way to meet the needs of unique clients.

**TABLE 10–3.** Expected amount of time spent in stages of the interview in different settings and situations

| | Vocational Counseling Interview | Psychoanalytic/ Psychotherapy | Assertion Training | Medical Diagnostic Interview | New Product Sales Interview[3] | Manager Helping Subordinate Problem Solve | Ineffective Welfare Interviewer |
|---|---|---|---|---|---|---|---|
| 1. Rapport/structuring "Hello!" | Some | Little or none | Some | Little | Great | Some | Little or none |
| 2. Gathering information/defining the problem and identifying assets "What's the problem?" "What are your strengths?" | Medium | Little or none | Great | Great | Some | Great | Some |
| 3. Determining outcomes "What do you want to have happen?" | Medium | Little or none | Medium | Little or none | Some | Great | Little |
| 4. Exploring alternatives/ confronting incongruities "What are we going to do about it?" | Medium | Great[1] | Medium | Some | Great | Medium | Great[4] |
| 5. Generalization and transfer of learning "Will you do it?" | Some | Little or none | Medium | Little[2] | Some | Some | Some |

[1]Psychoanalysis spends the bulk of its time exploring client issues. [2]Most medical interviews are diagnostic and problem defining, with the physician telling the client what to do. Most physician directives are vague at stage 5, which is a partial cause of low patient compliance with prescriptions. [3]A sales interview needs a relationship and emphasis on the product (stage 4, explaining the product), but it is also important to know the client's needs and dreams (stages 2 and 3). Closing the sale is stage 5, which differentiates good salespeople from poor. [4]The ineffective welfare interviewer spends most of the time giving answers, with little attention to what the larger issues are.

237

**Box 10-1  Key points**

*1. Basic listening sequence*
The skills of questioning, encouraging, paraphrasing, reflection of feeling, and summarizing make up the BLS. The basic listening sequence is useful in many different interviewing settings and in defining problems and outcomes in the interview.

*2. Positive asset search*
Clients grow from strengths. Time in every interview should be given to identify positive assets and capabilities that may be used to solve problems and generate future development.

*3. Client developmental level*
D-1  Intentionality is lacking, with no, or at most a few, alternatives for action. Example: inexperienced new employee.

D-2  Some degree of intentionality. The client may understand some incongruities but be unaware of others. Client has skills, but is not always able to use them. Example: most counseling clients.

D-3  Client has intentionality but has not developed as fully as might be desired. Requires assistance in finding own way. Example: person who is generally a self-starter and with listening from another can find own direction.

D-4  Client operates with full intentionality and is not likely to need help. Example: "YAVIS" client seeking further self-development.

*4. Assessing client developmental level*
Suggestions for determining client developmental level include: (1) Assume client starts at the D-2 level. (2) Use client observation skills and note client attending behaviors (two client styles may be generally observed—clients who avoid or challenge you because you are using too many influencing skills, and clients who seek more from you because you use too few influencing skills). (3) Note client incongruities. (4) Use BLS to draw out client concerns. (5) Use newspaper question sequence to obtain problem assessment. (6) Note client "I statements." (7) Note client feelings and adjective descriptors. (8) Note locus of control (internal/external), time perspective, dependence/independence.

*5. Interviewer style*
Style 1—Telling. Interviewer directs the session and uses extensive influencing skills.

Style 2—Coaching. Interviewer works with the client and uses a balance of attending and influencing skills.

**Box 10-1 continued**

|  | Style 3—Client-directed. Interviewer uses primarily attending skills and helps the client search for his or her own resolution. |
|  | Style 4—Low-involvement. Interviewer has minimal actions with higher level development clients. |
| 6. *Empathy* | Experiencing the client's world as if *you* were the client. Requires attending skills and using the *important words* of the client, but distilling and shortening the main ideas. |
| 7. *Additive empathy* | Interviewer *adds* meaning and feelings beyond those originally expressed by the client. If done ineffectively, may *subtract* from the client's experience. Empathy is best assessed by the client's reaction to a statement, not by simple rating of interviewer's comments. |
| 8. *Positive regard* | Selecting positive aspects of client experience and selectively attending to positive aspects of client statements. |
| 9. *Respect and warmth* | Attitudinal dimensions usually shown through nonverbal means such as smiling, touching, and a respectful tone of voice, even when differences are apparent. |
| 10. *Concreteness* | Being specific rather than vague in interviewing statements. |
| 11. *Immediacy* | An interviewer statement may be in the present, past, or future tense. Present-tense statements tend to be the most powerful. Immediacy is also viewed at the immediate "we" relationship between interviewer and client. |
| 12. *Nonjudgmental attitude* | Suspending your own opinions and attitudes and assuming a value neutrality in regard to clients. |
| 13. *Authenticity and congruence* | The opposite of incongruity and discrepancies. The interviewer is congruent with the client and authentically him- or herself in their relationship. |
| 14. *Five stages of the interview (Also see Table 10-2)* | Stage 1—Rapport and structuring ("Hello"). Stage 2—Gathering information and defining the problem ("What's the problem?"). Stage 3—Determining outcomes ("What do you want to have happen?"). Stage 4—Exploring alternatives and client incongruities ("What are we going to do about it?"). Stage 5—Generalization and transfer of learning ("Will you do it?"). |

## PRACTICE EXERCISES AND SELF-ASSESSMENT

Mastery of the skills of this chapter is a complex process you will want to work on over an extended period of time. Some basic exercises for individual and systematic group practice in each skill area follow.

*BASIC LISTENING SEQUENCE*

### Exercise 1. Illustrating how the BLS functions in different settings.

Imagine that you are role-playing a counseling interview and are serving as a counselor. Write counseling leads as they might be used to help a client solve the problem "I don't have a job for the summer." In this case you will have to imagine that the client has responded. Write responses that represent the BLS.

Open question: _____

_____

Closed question: _____

Encourager: _____

Paraphrase: _____

_____

Reflection of feeling: _____

_____

Summary: _____

_____

_____

Now imagine you are a manager talking with an employee who has been late with a critical assignment. Your task is to use the BLS to find out what the employee's explanation is before you take action.

Open question: _____

_____

Closed question: _____

Encourager: _____

Paraphrase: _____

_____

Reflection of feeling: _____

_____

Summary: _____

_____

_____

Finally, imagine yourself as a physician. You have a patient who comes in with a severe headache. Your first task in diagnosis is to find out the patient's view of the illness. Again, write BLS interviewing leads that might be helpful in obtaining that diagnosis.

Open question: _____

_____

Closed question: _____

Encourager: _____

Paraphrase: _____

_____

Reflection of feeling: _____

_____

Summary: _____

_____

_____

**Exercise 2.  Systematic group practice in the BLS.**

**Step 1.  Divide into groups.**

**Step 2.  Select a group leader.**

**Step 3.  Assign roles for the first practice session.**

Role-played client
Interviewer
Observer I
Observer II

**Step 4.  Planning.**   The task of the interviewer is to draw out the problem using the BLS, and to summarize the problem at the end. You should note that this is the second stage of the interview structure (defining the problem and gathering data).

The suggested topics for practicing the BLS are:

▲ A problem in vocational choice, past or present.
▲ Difficulty in making a major decision such as purchasing a car, moving, changing jobs.
▲ Role-playing a manager determining why an employee failed to complete an assignment correctly.
▲ Role-playing a social worker doing a home visit.
▲ Consulting with a teacher about a child who has gotten into discipline difficulties.

**Step 5.  Conduct a five-minute practice session using the BLS.**

**Step 6.  Review the practice session and provide feedback for ten minutes.**

**Step 7.  Rotate roles.**

*POSITIVE ASSET SEARCH*

**Exercise 1.  The positive asset search as manifested in two types of interview.**

You are role-playing a counseling interview. Write counseling leads using the BLS to draw out client positive assets and strengths.

In a vocational counseling interview, the client says: "Yes, I am really confused about my future. One side of me wants to continue a major in psychology, the other—thinking about the future—wants to change to business." Use the BLS to draw out client positive assets. In some cases below and on page 245, you will have to imagine client responses to your first open question.

Open question: _____

_____

Closed question: _____

Encourager: _____

Paraphrase: _____

_____

# BASIC LISTENING SEQUENCE FEEDBACK SHEET[2]

_____ (Date)

_____          _____
(Name of Interviewer)                                    (Name of Person Completing Form

_____

_Instructions:_ Observers I and II will attempt to record the statements of the interviewer as accurately as possible. They will then record the skill category and focus of the interviewer's statements.

| Statement of Interviewer | SKILLS | | | | | | FOCUS | | | | | |
| --- | --- | --- | --- | --- | --- | --- | --- | --- | --- | --- | --- | --- |
| | Open question | Closed question | Encourager | Paraphrase | Reflection of feeling | Summary | Client | Main theme/ problem | Others | Mutual/group/"we' | Interviewer (self) | Cultural/contextual/ environmental |
| 1. _____ | | | | | | | | | | | | |
| 2. _____ | | | | | | | | | | | | |
| 3. _____ | | | | | | | | | | | | |
| 4. _____ | | | | | | | | | | | | |
| 5. _____ | | | | | | | | | | | | |
| 6. _____ | | | | | | | | | | | | |
| 7. _____ | | | | | | | | | | | | |
| 8. _____ | | | | | | | | | | | | |
| 9. _____ | | | | | | | | | | | | |
| 10. _____ | | | | | | | | | | | | |
| 11. _____ | | | | | | | | | | | | |
| 12. _____ | | | | | | | | | | | | |
| 13. _____ | | | | | | | | | | | | |
| 14. _____ | | | | | | | | | | | | |
| 15. _____ | | | | | | | | | | | | |

[2]The structure of this form was suggested by Robert Marx.

## BASIC LISTENING SEQUENCE FEEDBACK SHEET continued

Did the interviewer draw out the client via the BLS? With what impact on the interview?

_____

_____

_____

_____

_____

_____

_____

_____

_____

_____

_____

_____

_____

_____

_____

_____

_____

Reflection of feeling: _____

_____

Summary: _____

_____

_____

    You are counseling a couple considering divorce. The husband says: "Somehow the magic seems to be lost. I still care for Jo, but we still argue and argue—even over small things." Use the positive asset search to bring out strengths and resources in the couple that they may draw on to find a more positive resolution to their problems. In marriage counseling, in particular, many counselors err by failing to note the strengths and positives that originally brought the couple together.

Open question: _____

_____

Closed question: _____

Encourager: _____

Paraphrase: _____

_____

Reflection of feeling: _____

_____

Summary: _____

_____

_____

## Exercise 2.  The positive asset search in daily life.

Use the BLS to draw out a positive asset of a friend or family member. This can be particularly helpful to them when they face a troubling issue or concern. Reminding people they have strengths helps them solve problems on their own. Report your results here and on page 246.

_____

_____

_____

_____

_____

_____

_____

_____

_____

_____

_____

_____

_____

_____

**Exercise 3.   Systematic group practice in the positive asset search.**

**Step 1.   Divide into groups.**

**Step 2.   Select a group leader.**

**Step 3.   Assign roles for first practice session.**

Role-played client
Interviewer
Observer I
Observer II

**Step 4. Planning.**   The task of the interviewer is to draw out positive assets or strengths of the clients by using the BLS and to summarize them accurately at the end of the practice session. Special attention should be given to the feelings and emotions of the client about the positive assets.

The client can plan to talk about a positive life experience or success. This may be a skill, a special interest, a successful handling of a difficult personal issue.

Observers should note the skills of the interviewer and the reactions of the clients—both verbally and non-verbally.

**Step 5.   Conduct a five-minute practice session using the BLS.**

**Step 6.   Review the practice session and provide feedback for ten minutes.**

**Step 7.   Rotate roles.**

## POSITIVE ASSET FEEDBACK SHEET

_____ (Date)

_____     _____
(Name of Interviewer)          (Name of Person Completing Form)

_____

*Instructions:* Observer I will record the statements of the interviewer as accurately as possible so that an ongoing log of the session is available to facilitate discussion. Observer II will rate key nonverbal and verbal reactions of the clients.

_____

Statements of the Interviewer:

1. _____
2. _____
3. _____
4. _____
5. _____
6. _____
7. _____
8. _____
9. _____
10. _____
11. _____
12. _____
13. _____
14. _____
15. _____
16. _____
17. _____
18. _____
19. _____
20. _____
21. _____

**POSITIVE ASSET FEEDBACK SHEET continued**

22. _____

23. _____

24. _____

25. _____

26. _____

27. _____

28. _____

29. _____

Observation of client's verbal and nonverbal reactions here.

1. _____

2. _____

3. _____

4. _____

5. _____

6. _____

7. _____

8. _____

9. _____

10. _____

11. _____

12. _____

13. _____

14. _____

15. _____

16. _____

17. _____

18. _____

19. _____

20. _____

*IDENTIFYING AND ASSESSING CLIENT DEVELOPMENTAL LEVEL*

### Exercise 1.  Identifying client developmental level.

 A number of specific ways have been suggested in this chapter to help identify the developmental level of the client. Following are some brief client statements. Identify the likely developmental level of each client and indicate the most appropriate style of interviewing.

| Developmental Level of Client | Recommended Interviewing Style | |
|---|---|---|
| _____ | _____ | "I'm sure what you are saying is correct. You're the expert. But I've worked by myself for a long time with a lot of success, and I think I know most of the answers." (Eyes upward and looking away, arms crossed over chest, foot jiggling. You as interviewer are aware the client or subordinate's past performance has been superior.) |
| _____ | _____ | "I can't solve my problems. I just sit and mope, and I've done that now for six months. I just feel like a limp dishrag." (Eyes downcast, leaning forward as if asking for something. Your observations of this client suggest that he or she hasn't been able to do anything for a period of time.) |
| _____ | _____ | "I am really getting into this vocational plan we are developing. I think it may just get me the job I want. What do we do next?" (Direct eye contact, forward trunk lean, open posture. This behavior is congruent with the rest of the interviewing sessions you have engaged in, in a participatory, coaching fashion.) |
| _____ | _____ | "I've thought about it a lot and have some good ideas, but I need someone to listen and help me sort things through." (Direct eye contact, forward trunk lean, smooth, assured vocal tones. Your experience suggests this client has been able to work things out with minimal help.) |

_____  _____   "Always in the past I've been able to solve problems with my boss. But the techniques I've used in the past don't seem to work anymore, and I think I'm stuck. He seems to be getting after me. What do you suggest?" (Forward trunk lean, open body posture, hesitant vocal tone, eye contact variable. This is a veteran employee who has previously been virtually on his or her own.)

_____  _____   "I feel so dependent on my husband. How could he leave me alone? I thought we had a good marriage. I've never even handled the books or the income tax. I don't know what job to get. What should I do?" (Variable eye contact, slumped in chair, worried vocal tone with rapid speech. This client has a limited education, no work experience, and is new to this area of the country.)

_____  _____   "My Dad's ill. I've always been able to keep up with my work and done well. But the last few weeks, I just seem to sit and worry all the time." (Congruent, direct eye contact, body language. This client has visited you in the past for assertiveness training and has responded well.)

_____  _____   "I'd like to tackle that new job. It looks like a blast. I know I can handle it." (Direct eye contact, congruent body language. You are aware, however, that this client has a history of failing to complete assignments and overestimating ability. The client has resisted suggestions from you in the past.)

### Exercise 2. Systematic group practice in assessing developmental level (see page 252 for Feedback Sheet).

This exercise is a variation of the old parlor game of charades. Each member of the group role plays a client before the group. The group as a whole "interviews" the client, using the BLS. After the group has had three minutes to interview the client, they discuss the interview and determine the developmental level and the likely most appropriate interviewing style match. The positive asset search will be helpful in determining developmental level as well.

**Exercise 3. Systematic group practice in matching and mismatching interviewing style.**

**Steps 1, 2, and 3 are identical to Exercise 1 under BLS.**

**Step 4.  Planning.**   Exercise 1 in this section presents several brief client scenarios. Different members of the group role play these clients with accompanying verbal and nonverbal behaviors. The interviewer's task is first to match interviewing style with client developmental level and use the appropriate balance of attending and influencing skills. After completing this task successfully, change abruptly to another interviewing style and note what happens to client verbal and nonverbal behavior.

**Step 5.   Conduct a three-minute practice session with style matching and then three minutes with style mismatching.**

**Step 6.   Review the practice session and provide feedback for nine minutes.**

**Step 7.   Rotate roles.**

*EMPATHY*

**Exercise 1.  Writing helping statements representing the five levels of empathy.**

A client says to you: "I'm really anxious. I got caught by the Internal Revenue Service for not declaring all my income. I objected to paying money for causes I don't believe in, like the money spent on war. Before I always tried to be straight, but I think I may have overdone it this time!"

Write statements representing the five levels of empathy below and on page 253. These statements can be from any skill category, but paraphrasing, reflection, and interpretation are the clearest and easiest statements to write.

Level 1 (subtractive): _____

## ASSESSING DEVELOPMENTAL LEVEL FEEDBACK SHEET

_____ (Date)

_____    _____
(Name of Interviewer)              (Name of Person Completing Form)

_____

*Instructions:* Observers I and II are to complete the form below, and then their perceptions of the client developmental level and the counselor style may be compared.

_____

1. What developmental level is represented by the client? Specify evidence in terms of observable behavior in the space provided.

   _____ Attending behavior patterns.

   _____ Discrepant verbal or nonverbal behavior.

   _____ Nature of "I statements."

   _____ Nature of feeling words and emotions.

   _____ Nature of adjective descriptors (activity, potency, and evaluation).

   _____ External versus internal locus of control.

   _____ Apparent developmental level (D-1, D-2, D-3, D-4). (Cite reasons for your conclusion below.)

2. What counseling style is the interviewer using? Circle one style below and cite specific evidence for your conclusion, drawing from skill usage and techniques of the interviewer.

   Style 1        Style 2        Style 3            Style 4
   (Telling)      (Coaching)     (Client-directed)  (Low-involvement)

   Evidence in terms of interviewing behavior:

3. What happens to the client when interviewer style is deliberately mismatched?

Level 2 (slightly subtractive): _____

_____

Level 3 (interchangeable response): _____

_____

Level 4 (slightly additive): _____

_____

Level 5 (additive): _____

_____

"My boy has gone to college, and I miss him terribly. We got along just fine and did so many things together. But now he doesn't write very often. I'm glad he is doing well, but what about me?"

Again, write statements representing the five levels of empathic responding.

Level 1 (subtractive): _____

_____

Level 2 (slightly subtractive): _____

_____

Level 3 (interchangeable response): _____

_____

Level 4 (slightly additive): _____

_____

Level 5 (additive): _____

_____

## Exercise 2.  Defining empathic dimensions.

Definitions of the several empathic dimensions are presented on pages 224–226. Return to those pages and in the space below write a definition in your own words of each concept and provide at least one example from your observations of interviews.

Positive regard: _____

_____

_____

_____

Respect and warmth: _____

_____

_____

_____

_____

Concreteness: _____

_____

_____

_____

Immediacy: _____

_____

_____

_____

Nonjudgmental attitude: _____

_____

_____

_____

Authenticity and congruence: _____

_____

_____

_____

_____

## Exercise 3.  Rating interview behavior on empathic dimensions.

Any systematic group practice exercise from this chapter or the whole book may be used. Alternatively, you may wish to rate an audiotape, videotape, transcript, or live interview on empathic responding. Provide specific and behavioral evidence for your conclusions using the empathy feedback sheet.

# EMPATHY FEEDBACK SHEET

_____ (Date)

| _____ | _____ |
| --- | --- |
| (Name of Interviewer) | (Name of Person Completing Form) |

_Instructions:_ Observers are to (1) view an interview or segment of an interview and rate empathic responding on a five-point scale; and (2) provide specific behavioral evidence for their decisions.

| (Subtractive) Level 1 | Level 2 | (Interchangeable) Level 3 | Level 4 | (Additive) Level 5 | Provide specific behavioral evidence in the space provided justifying your rating |
| --- | --- | --- | --- | --- | --- |
|  |  |  |  |  | 1. Overall empathy rating |
|  |  |  |  |  | 2. Positive regard |
|  |  |  |  |  | 3. Respect and warmth |
|  |  |  |  |  | 4. Concreteness |
|  |  |  |  |  | 5. Immediacy |
|  |  |  |  |  | 6. Nonjudgmental attitude |
|  |  |  |  |  | 7. Authenticity and congruence |
|  |  |  |  |  | 8. Other observations |

*STRUCTURING THE INTERVIEW*

 Using the following model, role play a vocational interview in a practice session. The client should role play a real (current or past) vocational indecision issue or imagine a graduating high school senior who can't decide whether to work or go to college or an individual analyzing his or her career. Use the following sequence in your practice session:

1. Develop rapport in your own style with the client. Follow this with *structuring* the session by saying something like, "What we are going to do in this session is first discuss your issues of vocational choice, then we'll discuss some outcomes you'd like to see happen, followed by exploration in more detail of the alternatives you face. Finally, we'll talk about how anything you learn today can be used after you leave the interview. Is that okay?"

2. Gather information, define the problem, and identify assets. Use the basic listening sequence to define the problem from the client's point of view. Be sure to identify at least one client asset which may be helpful in solving the problem.

3. Determine outcomes. Again, use the basic listening sequence and determine where the client would like to go. Keep in mind that with some clients this phase should precede phase 2.

4. Explore alternatives. Summarize the real and the ideal world for the client and brainstorm with the client alternatives that might be helpful to resolve the problem. With the client, establish priorities for the alternatives. Discuss and *confront discrepancies* as appropriate to the situation. Use a balance of attending and influencing skills in this section.

5. Generalization. After establishing priorities, suggest specific activities the client might engage in to follow through on the alternatives generated. Note the list of possibilities to assist generalization in the chapter and add more as you feel appropriate.

Practicing the structure of the interview requires at least a half-hour per person, and an hour is preferable for developing the interview and later debriefing. As such, specific plans for meeting in pairs for a significant period of time are required. Alternatively, groups of four may meet for half a day to conduct practice sessions. In a class situation the full hour should be given to the person practicing interview structuring.

# STRUCTURING THE INTERVIEW FEEDBACK SHEET

_____ (Date)

_____          _____
(Name of Interviewer)                              (Name of Person Completing Form)

_Instructions:_ The interviewer will conduct a brief vocational counseling interview of 10–20 minutes and demonstrate each of the five steps for structuring the interview. The observers will comment on each stage and note the balance of attending and influencing skills used in each stage.

|  | Number of skills (indicate by checks) | |
|---|---|---|
|  | Attending | Influencing |
| Stage 1: Rapport and structuring. Did the interviewer establish rapport? How? Did the interviewer provide structuring? | | |
| Rapport | | |
| Structuring | | |
| Stage 2: Gathering information, defining the problem, and identifying assets. Did the interviewer use the basic listening sequence? The moderate triad? Was the problem defined clearly and summarized with a positive asset identified? | | |
| Basic listening sequence | | |
| Information gathered | | |
| Positive asset search | | |

**STRUCTURING THE INTERVIEW FEEDBACK SHEET** continued

| | Number of skills (indicate by checks) | |
|---|---|---|
| | Attending | Influencing |
| Problem defined and summarized | | |
| Stage 3: Determining outcomes. Did the client and the interviewer determine some idealized outcome of the session? Was the basic listening sequence used? | | |
| BLS | | |
| Ideal outcome | | |
| Stage 4: Exploring alternatives and confronting incongruity. What types of alternatives were generated, and how effective are they? Were specific issue(s) of incongruity identified and confronted? | | |
| Issues of incongruity identified and confronted | | |
| Alternatives generated | | |
| Stage 5: Generalization. Were specific plans for taking ideas from the interview made and explored with the client? How were they received by the client? Can the positive asset search facilitate client generalization? | | |
| Plans explored with/received by client | | |
| Positive asset search | | |

*SELF-ASSESSMENT AND FOLLOW-UP IN SELECTING SKILLS AND*
*STRUCTURING THE INTERVIEW*

Six important concepts with four sets of practice exercises have been presented in this chapter. They are listed, with each level of mastery, on the following form. Check those areas for which you have demonstrated mastery. Provide evidence in the form of tapes, transcripts, or observations that you have mastered the concepts. Space is provided for brief summaries of evidence.

**Identification:** Ability to define the concept, identify it through observation.

**Basic mastery:** Ability to use the skill in a role-played interview.

**Active mastery:** Ability to use attending skills intentionally to facilitate or discourage client talk.

**Teaching mastery:** Ability to teach others.

1. Basic listening sequence: Ability to use the BLS in a variety of interviews with a variety of problems. You can help the client define the problem and define ideal outcomes from her or his frame of reference.
2. Positive asset search: Ability to use the BLS to draw out client assets and strengths.
3. Client developmental level: Ability to assess client functioning in the interview through observation and the BLS.
4. Interviewer style: Ability to use the developmental level concept to match attending and influencing style in the interview with each individual client's changing developmental levels.
5. Empathy: Ability to rate and classify empathy in a variety of interviews and demonstrate the several concepts with clients.
6. Structuring the interview: Ability to work systematically through the interview's five suggested stages and to achieve the specific outcome desired by the client. The ultimate measure of active mastery is whether or not your client does something to achieve his or her goals and desired outcomes.

| CONCEPT AREA | MASTERY LEVELS | | | | BRIEF EVIDENCE OF ACHIEVING HIGHEST MASTERY LEVEL |
|---|---|---|---|---|---|
| | Identification | Basic | Active | Teaching | |
| Basic listening sequence | | | | | |
| Positive assets search | | | | | |
| Client developmental level | | | | | |
| Interviewer style | | | | | |
| Empathy | | | | | |
| Structuring the interview | | | | | (Active mastery: does the client do something differently as a result of your interview?) |

The concepts of this chapter are critical in your ability to integrate skills in the actual interview. Examine your mastery level summary and then define below specific goals for improving your interviewing effectiveness over the next three months.

_____

_____

_____

_____

_____

_____

_____

## REFERENCES

Berzins, J. Therapist-patient matching. In A. Gurman and A. Razin (Eds.), *Effective psychotherapy.* New York: Pergamon, 1977.

Blanchard, K., and Johnson, S. *The one-minute manager.* San Diego, Calif.: Blanchard-Johnson, 1981.

Carkhuff, R. *Helping and human relations* (Vols. 1 and 2). New York: Holt, Rinehart and Winston, 1969.

Egan, G. *The skilled helper.* Monterey, Calif.: Brooks/Cole, 1975.

Hersey, P., and Blanchard, K. *Management of organizational behavior.* Englewood Cliffs, N.J.: Prentice-Hall, 1979.

Ivey, A., and Authier, J. *Microcounseling.* Springfield, Ill.: Charles C Thomas, 1978.

Perls, F. *Gestalt therapy verbatim.* Moab, Utah: Real People Press, 1969.

Rogers, C. The necessary and sufficient conditions of therapeutic personality change. *Journal of Consulting Psychology,* 1957, *21*, 95–103.

Rogers, C. Empathic: An unappreciated way of being. *The Counseling Psychologist,* 1975, *5*, 2–10.

Sue, D. *Counseling the culturally different.* New York: Wiley, 1981.

CHAPTER **11**

# Skill Integration:
# Putting It All Together

---

## General mastery goals for interviewing

*Major Function*

The interview may be considered a vehicle for achieving client objectives. This is most true in counseling and interviews concerned with helping people—welfare and employment counseling, medical interviewing, and the like. Much management interviewing has the same objective. However, in management, teaching, corrections, and many institutional settings, the objective of the interview may be to achieve interviewer objectives. In other words, functions of the interview will vary from context to context and situation to situation. The developmental level of the client and the interviewer will partly determine the function of the interview.

*Mastery Goals*

To demonstrate competence in interviewing as a whole, the following levels of mastery may be manifested:

*Level 1* (identification): You will be able to identify skills, empathic qualities, and interview structure through observation and classification of the interview. You will note, through client observation skills, the impact of these dimensions on the client.

*Level 2* (basic mastery): You will be able to demonstrate in an interview: (1) the several skills emphasized in this book; (2) a simple interviewing structure that consists of five stages; (3) the basic listening sequence.

*Level 3* (active mastery): You will be able to use the skills, focus dimensions, and empathic qualities to produce predicted effects on the client. You will be able to meet the several basic mastery goals for each skill and skill area in this book. You will be able to conduct a basic interview with a definable structure (the five stages or some systematic alternative) with demonstrable impact on client verbal behavior and actions after the interview. The real test of basic mastery is whether the client changes. In addition, you will be able to engage in one or more theoretical approaches to the interview in addition to your own natural style.

*Level 4* (teaching mastery): You will demonstrate your ability to teach what you have learned to clients and other trainees.

## INTRODUCTION

This chapter is concerned primarily with presenting a complete interview, and a detailed analysis of it, using the concepts of this book. Skill integration at a high level is demonstrated only in real interviews with real impact and effect on a client. Your task in this chapter is to examine this demonstration interview. Then, you will be asked to present your own interview in which you demonstrate your natural style of helping and those concepts of this book that have proven meaningful to you.

This chapter has the following specific goals:

1. To provide you with a system and format for classifying your own and others' interviewing behavior.
2. To provide you with an example interview illustrating skill usage and the several stages of the interview.
3. To present information on planning for the interview and to suggest a format for interview planning over several sessions.
4. To encourage you to record a second interview and to demonstrate your own mastery of the several skills and concepts presented here. In particular, it is hoped that you will compare your natural style with any changes you have made through your contact with this book. What do you want to keep and strengthen from your natural style? What do you want to add from the suggestions in *Intentional Interviewing and Counseling?* How might you change and combine the two?

## EXAMPLE INTERVIEW

Following is a brief vocational interview that illustrates: (1) skill classification; (2) the five stages of the interview; and (3) the importance of client observation skills to modify interviewer behavior and flex with the special needs of the client (Table 11-1). Following the interview is a discussion of the session on several dimensions discussed in *Intentional Interviewing and Counseling* and an interviewing plan for a second interview.

This interview is a first interview illustrating that vocational counseling is closely related to personal counseling. Note how the relationship between job change and personal issues develops during the session.

The client is 36 years old and divorced with two children. She has worked as a physical education teacher for a number of years. She indicated in her information file completed before counseling that "I find myself bored and stymied in my present job of P.E. teacher. I think it is time to look at something new. Possibly, I should think about business. Sometimes I find myself a bit depressed with it all." The counselor is attempting to illustrate several mastery goals of the interview in one demonstration session.

The interview is presented in a structured transcript that includes: the client's and interviewer's statements; statements organized into the five stages of the interview; subjective comments and evaluations of the counselor's and client's statements; and scoring and classification of the counselor's leads.

The *A's* in the transcript represent the counselor's use of attending and influencing skills plus focusing dimensions. In addition, when a confrontation is present, it is also scored. Note that multiple skills are frequently used. *J's* represent the client's focus in her comments.

## PLANNING THE GOALS OF AN INTERVIEW

Given the systematic five-stage structure of the basic interview, it is possible to develop a plan for the interview before it takes place. If you don't know where you are heading, you are less likely to help the client. This does not mean you need to impose your view or concepts on the client; rather, you can think through what you want to do to help the client achieve his or her objectives.

You are about to read a transcript of an initial interview session. However, before the interview was held, the interviewer, Al, developed an interview plan, which is presented in Box 11-1. This interview plan was developed from a study of a client file that

**Box 11-1 Interview plan and objectives (before an interview)**

After studying the client file before the first session, or after reviewing the preceding session, indicate issues you anticipate being important in the session and how you plan to handle them. (The following plan includes Al's assessment of his forthcoming interview with Jane.)

*1. Rapport/ structuring*

*Special issues anticipated around rapport development? What structure for this interview do you have? Do you plan to use a specific theory?*
Jane appears to be a verbal and active person. I note she likes swimming and physical activity. I like to run . . . this may be a common bond. I think I'll be open as to structure but keep the five phases in mind. It looks like she may want to look into vocational choice, and she may be unhappy with her present job. I should keep in awareness her divorce, as this may also be a personal issue. I'll use the basic listening sequence to bring things out and probably work in a trait-and-factor decision-making model.

*2. Problem definition/ identification of assets*

*What are the anticipated problems? Strengths? How do you plan to define the problem with the client? Will you emphasize behavior, thoughts, feelings, meanings?*
Jane seems to be full of strengths. I tend too often to emphasize negatives. I should work on bringing out what she *can do*. I'll use the basic listening sequence to bring out issues from her point of view. I'll be most interested in her thoughts about her job and her plans for the future. However, I should be flexible and watch for other issues. Jane may well bring out several issues. I'll summarize them toward the end of this phase, and we may have to list them and set priorities if they are many.
Mainly, however, I expect an interview on vocational choice.

*3. Defining outcomes*

*What is the ideal outcome? How will you bring out the idealized self or world?*
I'll ask her what her fantasies and ideas are for an ideal resolution and then follow up with the basic listening sequence. I'll end by confronting and summarizing the real and the ideal. It's worked for me in the past and probably will work again.
As far as outcome, I'd like to see Jane defining her own direction from a range of alternatives. Even if she stays in

**Box 11-1 continued**

| | |
|---|---|
| | her present job, I hope we can find that it is the best alternative for her. |
| 4. *Exploring alternatives/ Confronting incongruity* | *What types of alternatives should be generated? What theories would you likely use here? What specific incongruities have you noted or do you anticipate in the client?*<br>I hope to begin this stage by summarizing her positive strengths. Too early to say what are the best alternatives. However, I'd like to see several new possibilities considered. Counseling and business are indicated in her pre-interview form as two possibilities. They seem good. Are there other possibilities? The main incongruity will likely be between where she is and where she wants to go. I'll be interested in her personal life as well. How are things going since the divorce? What is it like to be a woman in a changing world? I expect to ask her questions and develop some concrete alternatives even in the first session . . . hopefully she will act on some of them following our first session. I think vocational testing may be useful. |
| 5. *Generalization* | *What specific plans, if any, do you have for transfer of training? What will enable you personally to feel that the interview was worthwhile?*<br>Drawing from the above, I'll feel satisfied if we have generated some new possibilities and we can get some exploration of vocational alternatives after the first session. We can plan from there. Hopefully, we can generate at least one thing she can do for homework before our second session. |

consisted of a pre-interview questionnaire. As you will note, the interview plan is oriented to help a 36-year-old woman develop her own unique vocational plan and to make possible a discussion between client and counselor of personal issues as well. The plan is considered a structure to help the client achieve her objectives.

Although it is, of course, sketchy, the plan does illustrate that it is possible to plan a session before it happens. As it turns out, Al's objectives were roughly realized in the session. However, if Jane had had differing needs, the interview plan could have been scrapped at that time and more appropriate interventions used. Remember: an interview plan is only a plan; it is not a definitive roadmap.

**TABLE 11–1.** The Al and Jane five-stage interview

SKILL CLASSIFICATION

| Attending summary | Enc./restatement | Paraphrase | Reflect. feeling | Reflect. meaning | Open question | Closed question | Client | Main theme/prob. | Others | "We"/group/dyad | Interviewer | C-E-C situation | Feedback | Adv./info./expl. | Self-disclosure | Interpretation | Logical conseq. | Directive | Influ. summary | Confrontation | Counselor and client statements | Comment |
|---|---|---|---|---|---|---|---|---|---|---|---|---|---|---|---|---|---|---|---|---|---|---|
| | | | | | | | | | | | | | | | | | | | | | **Stage 1. Rapport/Structuring** | |
| | | | | | A | | A | | | | | | | | | | | | | | 1. *Al:* Hi Jane. How are you today? | As Jane walked in, Al saw her hesitate and sensed some awkwardness on her part. At Jane 2 it may be noted that she has two speech hesitations. Consequently, Al decides to take a little time to develop rapport and give Jane some sense of ease in the interview. Note that he took a positive aspect of Jane's past. It is often useful to build on the client's strengths even this early in the session.<br><br>The distinctions between providing information and a self-disclosure are illustrated at Al 5 and Jane 6. Al only comments that he's been getting out, whereas Jane gives information and personal feelings as well. |
| | | J | | | | | J | | | | J | | | | | | | | | | 2. *Jane:* Ah . . . just fine . . . How are you? | |
| | | | | | | | A | J | | | A | | | A | | | | | | | 3. *Al:* Good, just fine. Nice to see you. . . . Hey, I was noting in the folder that you've done a lot of swimming. | |
| | | | | | | | J | J | | | | | | | | | | | | | 4. *Jane:* Oh, yeah (smiling) . . . I like swimming, I enjoy swimming a lot. | |
| | | | | | | A | A | A | | | A | | | A | | | | | | | 5. *Al:* With this hot weather, I've been getting out. Have you been able to? | |
| | | | | | | | J | | | | | | | | | | | | | | 6. *Jane:* Yes, I enjoy the exercise. It's good relaxation. | |
| | | A | A | | | | A | | | | | | | | | | | | | | 7. *Al:* I also saw you won quite a few awards along the way. (*Jane:* Um-humm) . . . You must feel awfully good about that. | |
| | | | | | | | J | | | | | | | | | | | | | | 8. *Jane:* I do. I do feel very good about that. It's been lots of fun. | |

*(continued)*

267

# TABLE 11–1. continued

| Counselor and client statements | Comment |
|---|---|
| 9. *Al:* Before we begin, I'd like to ask if I can tape-record this talk. I'll need your written permission too. Do you mind? | Obtaining permission to tape-record interviews is essential. If the request is presented in a comfortable, easy way, most clients are glad to give permission. At times it may be useful to give the tapes to clients to take home and listen to again. |
| 10. *Jane:* No, that's OK with me. (Signs form permitting use of tape for *Intentional Interviewing and Counseling.*) | |
| **Stage 2. Gathering information and defining the problem.** 11. *Al:* Could you tell me, Jane, what you'd like to talk about today? | In this series of leads you'll find that Al uses the basic listening sequence of open question, encourager, paraphrase, reflection of feeling, and summary in order. Many interviewers in different settings will use the sequence or a variation to define the client's problem. |
| 12. *Jane:* Well . . . ah . . . I guess there's a lot of things that I'd like to talk about. You know I went through . . . ah . . . a difficult divorce and it was hard on the kids and myself and . . . ah . . . we've done pretty well. We've pulled together. The kids are doing better in school and I'm doing better. I've . . . ah . . . got a new friend (breaks eye contact). But you know, | As many clients do, Jane starts the session with a "laundry list" of issues. Though the last thing in a laundry list is often what a client wants to talk about, the eye-contact break around her "new friend" raises an issue that should be watched for in the interview. |

## SKILL CLASSIFICATION

| | Attending | | | | | | | Focus | | | | | | Influencing | | | | | | | C |
|---|---|---|---|---|---|---|---|---|---|---|---|---|---|---|---|---|---|---|---|---|---|
| Statement | Attending summary | Enc./restatement | Paraphrase | Reflect. feeling | Reflect. meaning | Open question | Closed question | Client | Main theme/prob. | Others | "We"/group/dyad | Interviewer | C-E-C situation | Feedback | Adv./info./expl. | Self-disclosure | Interpretation | Logical conseq. | Directive | Influ. summary | Confrontation |
| 9 | | | | | | | A | | A | | | | | | A | | | | | | |
| 10 | | | | | | | | J | | | | | | | | | | | | | |
| 11 | | | | | | A | | A | | | | | | | | | | | | | |
| 12 | | | | | | | | J J | J J J | J J | | | | | | | | | | | |

I've been teaching for thirteen years and really feel kind of bored with it. It's the same old thing over and over every day; you know . . . parts of it are OK, but lots of it I'm bored with.

13. *Al:* You say you're *bored* with it?

"I'm bored" is an important "I statement."

14. *Jane:* Well, I'm bored, I guess, . . . teaching field hockey and . . . ah . . . basketball and softball, certain of those team sports. There are certain things I like about it though. You know I like the dance, and you know I like swimming—I like that. Ah . . . but . . . you know . . . I get tired of the same thing all the time. I guess I'd like to do some different things with my life.

Note that Jane elaborates in more detail on the word *bored*. Al used verbal underlining and gave emphasis to that word, and Jane did as most clients would—she elaborated on the meaning of the word to her. Many times short encouragers and restatements have the effect of encouraging client exploration of meaning and elaboration on a topic. "I'd like to do some different things" is a more positive "I statement."

15. *Al:* So, Jane, if I hear you correctly, sounds like change and variety are important instead of doing the same thing all the time.

Note that this paraphrase has some dimensions of an interpretation in that Jane did not use the words *change and variety.* These words are polar constructs to boredom and doing "the same things all the time." This paraphrase takes a small risk and is slightly additive to Jane's understanding. It is an example of the positive asset search, in that it would have been possible to hear only the negative "bored." Working on the positive suggests what *can* be done. Note her response.

16. *Jane:* Yeah . . . I'd like to be able to do something different. But, you know, ah . . . teaching's a very secure field, and I have tenure. You know, I'm the sole support of these two daughters, but I think, I don't know what else I can do exactly. Do you see what I'm saying?

Jane, being heard, is able to move to a deeper discussion of her issues. She has equated "something different" with a lack of security. As the interview progresses, you will note that she associates change with risk. It is these basic constructs, already apparent in the interview, that undergird many of her issues.

*(continued)*

**TABLE 11–1. continued**

| # | Counselor and client statements | Comment | Skill Classification |
|---|---|---|---|
| 17. | *Al:* Looks like the security of teaching makes you feel good, but it's the boredom you associate with that security that makes you feel uncomfortable. Is that correct? | This reflection of feeling contains elements of a confrontation as well in that the good feelings of security are contrasted with the boredom associated with teaching. Note that Al matches Jane's visual system with "looks like . . ." | Confrontation: A; Main theme/prob.: A A; Client: A A; Reflect. feeling: A |
| 18. | *Jane:* Yeah, you know, it's that security. I feel good being . . . you know . . . having a steady income and I have a place to be, but it's boring at the same time. You know, ah . . . I wish I knew how to go about doing something else. | Note that Jane often responds with a "Yeah" to the reflections and paraphrases before going on. Here she is wrestling with the confrontation of Al 17. She adds new data as well in the last sentence. | Main theme/prob.: J J; Client: J J |
| 19. | *Al:* So, Jane, let me see if I can summarize what I've heard. Ah . . . it's been tough since the divorce, but you've gotten things together. You mentioned the kids are doing pretty well. You talked about a new relationship. *I hear you mention that.* (*Jane:* Yeah.) But the issue right now that you'd like to talk about is that . . . this feeling of boredom (*Jane:* Ummm . . .) on the job, and yet you like the security of it. But maybe you'd like to try something new. Is that the essence of it? | This summarization concludes the first attempt at problem definition in this brief interview. Al uses Jane's own words for the main things and attempts to distill what has been said thus far in a few words. The positive asset search has been used briefly in this section ("You've gotten things together . . . kids . . . doing well"). See also other leads in this section that emphasize client strength. Jane sits forward and nods with approval throughout this summary. The confrontation of the old job with "maybe you'd like to try some- | Confrontation: A; Client: A; Attending summary: A |

| Dialogue | Classification | Commentary |
|---|---|---|
| 20. *Jane:* That's right. That's it. | J  J | "thing new" concludes the summary. Note the check-out at the end of the summary to encourage Jane to react. |
| **Stage 3. Determining outcomes. Where does the client want to go?** | | |
| 21. *Al:* I think at this point it might be helpful if you could define for me what are some things that might represent a more ideal situation? | A   A | In stage 3 the goal is to find where the client might want to go in a more ideal situation. You'll note that the basic listening sequence is present in this stage, but it does not follow in order as in the preceding stage. |
| 22. *Jane:* Ummm. I'm not sure. There are some things I like about my job. I certainly like interacting with the other professional people on the staff. I enjoy working with the kids. I enjoy talking with the kids. That's kind of fun. You know, it's the stuff I have to teach I'm bored with. I have done some teaching of human sexuality and drug education. | J  J  J | Jane associates interacting with people as a positive aspect of her job. When she talks about "enjoying working with kids," her vocal tone changes, suggesting that she doesn't enjoy it that much. But the spontaneous vocal tone returns when she mentions "talking with them" and she talks about teaching subjects other than team sports. |
| 23. *Al:* So, would it be correct to say that some of the teaching where you have worked with kids on content of interest to you has been fun? What else have you enjoyed about your job? | A  A   A | The search here is for positive assets and things that Jane enjoys. |
| 24. *Jane:* Well, I must say I enjoy having summer vacations and the same vacation time that the kids have. That's a plus in the teaching field. (Pause). | J  J | |
| 25. *Al:* Yeah . . . | A | Jane found only one plus in the job. Al probes for more data via an encourager. No focus is classified on this type of encourager. |

(continued)

**TABLE 11–1.** continued

| | Attending summary | Enc./restatement | Paraphrase | Reflect. feeling | Reflect. meaning | Open question | Closed question | Client | Main theme/prob. | Others | "We"/group/dyad | Interviewer | C-E-C situation | Feedback | Adv./info./exp. | Self-disclosure | Interpretation | Logical conseq. | Directive | Influ. summary | Confrontation | Counselor and client statements | Comment |
|---|---|---|---|---|---|---|---|---|---|---|---|---|---|---|---|---|---|---|---|---|---|---|---|
| | | | | | | | | | | | | | | | | | | | | | | *(headers: Attending / Focus / Influencing / C)* | |
| 26 | | | | | | | | J | | J | | | | | | | | | | | | 26. *Jane:* You see, I like being able to . . . Oh, I know, one time I was able to do teaching of our own teachers and that was really . . . I really felt good being able to share some of my ideas with some people on the staff. I felt that was kind of neat, being able to teach other adults. | Jane brings out new data that supports her earlier comments that she liked to teach when the content was of interest to her. The "I statements" here are more positive and the adjective descriptors indicate more self-assurance. |
| 27 | | | | | | | A | A | | A | | | | | | | | | | | | 27. *Al:* Do you involve yourself in counseling with the students you have very much? | A closed question with a change of topic to explore other areas. |
| 28 | | | | | | | | J | | J | | | | | | | | | | | | 28. *Jane:* Well, the kids . . . you know, teaching for them is a nice, comfortable environment, and kids stop in before class and after class and they talk about their boyfriends and the movies they go to and so on; I find I like that part of it too . . . about their concerns. | Jane responds to the word *counseling* again with discussion of interactions with people. It seems important to Jane that she have contact with others. |
| 29 | A | | | | | | A | A A | A A | A A | | | | | | | | | | | | 29. *Al:* So, as we've been reviewing your current job, it's the training, the drug education, some of the teaching you've done with kids around different topics other than health and phys. ed. (*Jane:* That's right.) And getting out and doing training and other stuff with teachers . . . ah, sharing some of your expertise there. And the | This summary attempts to bring out the main strands of the positive aspects of Jane's job. In an ongoing interview, a closed question on a relevant topic can be as facilitating as an open question. Note, however, that the interviewer still directs the flow more with the closed question. |

*SKILL CLASSIFICATION* — Attending / Focus / Influencing / C

| Transcript | Commentary |
|---|---|
| counseling relationships. (*Jane*: Ummm.) Out of those things, are there fields you've thought of transferring to? | |
| 30. *Jane*: Well, a lot of people in physical education go into counseling. That seems like a natural second thing. Ah ... of course, that would require some more going to school. Uhmm ... I've also thought about doing some training for a business. Sometimes I think about moving into business ... entirely away from education. Or even working in a college as opposed to working here in the high school. I've thought about those things too. But I'm just not sure which one seems best for me. | Jane talks with only moderate enthusiasm about counseling. In discussing training and business, she appears more involved. Jane appears to have assets and abilities, has many positive "I statements," is aware of key incongruities in her life, and seems to be internally directed. She is most likely operating at client developmental level D-3, but vocationally for this interview may be at level D-2, where most clients are found. |
| 31. *Al*: So the counseling field, the training field. You've thought about staying in schools and perhaps in management as well. (*Jane*: Um-hum, Um-hum.) Anything else that occurs to you? | This brief paraphrase distills Jane's ideas in her own words. |
| 32. *Jane*: No, I think that seems about it | |
| 33. *Al*: Before we go further, you've talked about teaching and the security it offers. But at the same time you talk about *boredom*. You talk with excitement about business and training. How do you put this together? What does it *mean* to you? | This summary includes confrontation and catches both content and feeling. The question at the end is directed toward issues of meaning. The word *boredom* was underlined with extra vocal emphasis. |
| 34. *Jane*: Uhh ... Ah ... If I stay in the same place, it's just more of the same. I see older teachers, and I don't want to be like them. Oh, a few have fun; most seem just *tired* to me. I don't want to end up with that. | Jane elaborates on the meaning and underlying structure of *why* she might want to avoid the occasional boredom of her job. When she talks about "end up like that," we see deeper meanings. |

(continued)

**TABLE 11–1.** continued

| Counselor and client statements | Comment | Confront. | Influ. summary | Directive | Logical conseq. | Interpretation | Self-disclosure | Adv./info./expl. | Feedback | C-E-C situation | Interviewer | "We"/group/dyad | Others | Main theme/prob. | Client | Closed question | Open question | Reflect. meaning | Reflect. feeling | Paraphrase | Enc./restatement | Attending summary |
|---|---|---|---|---|---|---|---|---|---|---|---|---|---|---|---|---|---|---|---|---|---|---|
| 35. *Al:* You don't want to end up with that. | | | | | | | | | | | | | | | A | | | | | | A | |
| 36. *Jane:* Yeah, I want to do something new, more exciting. Yet, my life has been so confused in the past, and it is just settling down. I'm not sure I want to risk it. | Jane moves on to talk about what she wants, and a new element—risk—is introduced. Risk may be considered the polar construct of security. | | | | | | | | | | | | | | J | | | | | | | |
| 37. *Al:* So, Jane, risk frightens you? | This reflection of feeling is tentative and said in a questioning tone. This provides an implied check-out and gives Jane room to accept it or suggest changes as they clarify the feeling. | | | | | | | | | | | | | | A | | | | A | | | |
| 38. *Jane:* Well, not really, but it does seem scary to give up all this security and stability just when I've started putting it together. It just feels strange. Yet, I do want something new so that life doesn't seem so routine...and...ah...I think maybe I have more talent and ability than I used to think I did. | Jane uses many kinesthetic words. While visual descriptors are there as well, feeling and kinesthetic experience are more prominent. As meaning is explored, the interview moves toward deeper levels of experience. Jane maintains eye contact, but on close examination, she appears to be "in herself" and thinking inwardly rather than responding outwardly to Al. Her pupils are somewhat dilated in this internal frame of reference. | | | | | | | | | | | | | J | J | | | | | | | |
| 39. *Al:* So, you've felt the meaning in this possible job change as an opportunity to use your *talent* and take risks in something new. This may be con- | This reflection of meaning also confronts underlying issues that impinge on Jane's decision. It contains elements of the positive asset search or | A | | | | | | | | | | | | A A | A A | | | A | | | | |

*SKILL CLASSIFICATION:* C — Confrontation; Influencing (Influ. summary, Directive, Logical conseq., Interpretation, Self-disclosure, Adv./info./expl., Feedback); Focus (C-E-C situation, Interviewer, "We"/group/dyad, Others, Main theme/prob., Client); Attending (Closed question, Open question, Reflect. meaning, Reflect. feeling, Paraphrase, Enc./restatement, Attending summary)

| | | |
|---|---|---|
| positive regard as Al verbally stresses the word *talent*. He is beginning to be a little closer in terms of Jane's kinesthetic system in the check-out. | Jane is reinterpreting her situation from a more positive frame of reference. Al could have said the same thing as an interpretation, but through reflection of meaning Jane is able to come up with her own definition. As a client, she is capable of functioning at developmental level D-3, where she demonstrates the ability to solve her own problems, and the counselor only needs attending skills. For vocational search, however, Jane is functioning more at level D-2, and she needs more active participation and direction from the counselor.<br><br>At this point, Al decides to move to stage 4 of the interview. It would be possible to explore problem definition and ideal worlds in more detail. However, later interviews can take these matters up. Al decides to move on to the next stage. | Al combines feedback on positive assets with some self-disclosure here and uses this lead as a transition to explore alternative actions. The emphasis here is on the positive side of Jane's past experience. Al's vocal tone communicates warmth, and he leans toward Jane in a genuine manner. |
| trasted with the feelings of stability and certainty where you are now. But *now*, as you are, also means you may end up like some people you don't want to end up like. Am I reaching the sense of things? How does that grab you? | 40. *Jane:* Exactly! But I hadn't touched on it that way before. I do want stability and security, but not at the price of boredom and feeling down so much of the time as I have lately. Maybe I do have what it takes to risk more. | **Stage 4: Exploring alternatives and confronting client incongruity.**<br><br>41. *Al:* Jane, from listening to you, I get the sense that you do have considerable ability. Specifically, you can be together in a warm, involved way with those you work with. You can describe what is important to you. You come across to me as a thoughtful, able sensitive person. (Pause) |

A

J            A

*(continued)*

**TABLE 11–1. continued**

| SKILL CLASSIFICATION | | | | | | | | | | | | | | | | | | | | | | |
|---|---|---|---|---|---|---|---|---|---|---|---|---|---|---|---|---|---|---|---|---|---|---|
| | C | Influencing | | | | | | | Focus | | | | | | Attending | | | | | | | |
| Counselor and client statements | Confrontation | Influ. summary | Directive | Logical conseq. | Interpretation | Self-disclosure | Adv./info./expl. | Feedback | C-E-C situation | Interviewer | "We"/group/dyad | Others | Main theme/prob. | Client | Closed question | Open question | Reflect. meaning | Reflect. feeling | Paraphrase | Enc./restatement | Attending summary | Comment |
| 42. *Jane:* Ummmm . . . . | | | | | | | | | | | | | | | | | | | | | | During the feedback, Jane at first shows signs of surprise. She sits up, then relaxes a bit, smiles and sits back in her chair as if to absorb what Al is saying more completely. There are elements of praise in Al's comment. |
| 43. *Al:* Other things for job ideas may develop as we talk . . . ah . . . I think it might be appropriate at this point to explore some alternatives you've talked about. (*Jane:* Um-huh.) The first thing you talked about was that what you liked teaching was drug education and sexuality. What else have you taught kids in that general area? | | | A | | | | | | | | | | A A | A A | | A | | | A | | | At this point, Al starts exploring alternatives in a little more depth. The systematic problem-solving model of define the problem, generate alternatives, and set priorities for solutions is in his mind throughout this section. He begins with a mild directive. |
| 44. *Jane:* Let's see . . . The general areas I liked were human sexuality and drug education, and family life and family growth and those kinds of things. Ah . . . sometimes communication skills. | | | | | | | | | | | | | J | J | | | | | | | | |
| 45. *Al:* Have you attended workshops on these types of things? | | | | | | | | | | | | | A | | A | | | | | | | Closed questions can be helpful in determining specific background items important in decision making. |
| 46. *Jane:* I've attended a few. I kind of enjoyed them. I've enjoyed them . . . I really did. You know, I've gone to university and taken workshops in | | | | | | | | | | | | | J J J | J J | | | | | | | | |

276

| Dialogue | Commentary |
|---|---|
| values clarification and communication skills. I liked the people I met. | |
| 47. *Al:* One of the roles for more and more teachers and pupil personnel people is getting into psychological education and workshops . . . training in communication skills or values clarification. That's one aspect you would enjoy. Is that right? | Here, a brief piece of occupational information is being shared with Jane. It is followed by a reflection of feeling coupled with a check-out. |
| 48. *Jane:* I think I would enjoy that sort of thing. Um-hmmm . . . It sounds interesting. | |
| 49. *Al:* Sounds like you have also given a good deal of thought to . . . ah . . . extending that to training in general. How aware are you of the business field as a place to train? | Jane's background and interest in a second alternative is explored. |
| 50. *Jane:* I don't know that much about it. You know, I worked one summer in my Dad's office so I do have an exposure to business. That's about it. They all have been saying that a lot of teachers are moving into the business field. Teaching is not too lucrative, and with all the things happening with Proposition 13 here in California and all the cutbacks, business is a better possibility for teachers these days. It just seems like an intriguing possibility for me to investigate or look into. But I don't know much about it. | Jane talks in considerably more depth and with more enthusiasm when she talks about business. The important descriptive words she has used with teaching include *boring, security, interpersonal interactions*, while *interest* and *excitement* were used with training and teaching psychologically oriented subjects as opposed to physical education. Now she mentions cutbacks. Business has been described with more enthusiasm and as more lucrative. We may anticipate that she will eventually associate the potential excitement of business with the negative construct of risk and the lack of summer vacations and time to be with her children. |
| 51. *Al:* Mm-humm . . . so you've thought about it . . . looking into business, but you've not done too much about it yet. | This paraphrase is somewhat subtractive. Jane did indicate that she had summer experience with her father. How much and how did she like it? Al missed that. The paraphrase involves a confrontation between what Jane says and her lack of doing anything extensive in terms of a search. |

*(continued)*

277

**TABLE 11-1. continued**

| | | | | Attending | | | | Focus | | | | | | Influencing | | | | | | | C | Counselor and client statements | Comment |
|---|---|---|---|---|---|---|---|---|---|---|---|---|---|---|---|---|---|---|---|---|---|---|---|
| | SKILL CLASSIFICATION | Attending summary | Enc./restatement | Paraphrase | Reflect. feeling | Reflect. meaning | Open question | Closed question | Client | Main theme/prob. | Others | "We"/group/dyad | Interviewer | C-E-C situation | Feedback | Adv./info./expl. | Self-disclosure | Interpretation | Logical conseq. | Directive | Influ. summary | Confrontation | | |
| | | | | A | | | A | | J | A | | | | | | | | A | | | | | 52. *Jane:* That's right. I've thought about it, but . . . ah . . . I've done very little about it. That's all . . .<br><br>53. *Al:* And, finally, you mentioned that you have considered the counseling field as an alternative. Ah . . . what about that? | Jane feels a little apologetic. She talks a bit more rapidly, breaks eye contact, and her body leans back a little.<br><br>Al has missed the boat. More exploration of business should have followed. The confrontation of thinking and absence of action is probably appropriate, but it was brought in too early. If Al had focused on positive aspects of Jane's experience and learned more about her summer experience, the confrontation likely would have been received more easily. As this was a demonstration interview, Al sought to move through the stages perhaps a little too fast. Also, the counseling field is likely an alternative, but it seems to come more from Al than from Jane. An advantage of transcripts such as this is that one can see errors. Many of our errors come from our own constructs and needs. This intended paraphrase is classified as an interpretation as it comes more from Al's frame of reference than from Jane's. |
| | | | | | | | | | J | | J | | | | | | | | | | | | 54. *Jane:* Well, I've always been interested, like I said, in talking with people. People like to talk with me about all kinds of things. And *that* would be interesting . . . ah . . . I think too. | Jane starts with some enthusiasm on this topic, but as she talks, her speech rate slows and she demonstrates less energy. |

| # | Dialogue | Description |
|---|----------|-------------|
| 55. | Al: Um-hmmm. | Said even more slowly. |
| 56. | Jane: You know, to explore that. (Pause). | Al senses her change of enthusiasm, is a bit puzzled, and sits silently encouraging her to *talk more*. When you have made an error and the client doesn't respond as you expect, return to attending skills. |
| 57. | Al: Um-hmmm. (Pause.) | |
| 58. | Jane: But...I'd have to take some courses...if I really wanted to get into it. | One reason for Jane's hesitation appears. |
| 59. | Al: So putting those three things together, it seems like it feels that you want people-oriented occupations. They are particularly interesting to you. | This is a mild interpretation as it labels common elements in the three jobs. It could be classified also as a paraphrase. |
| 60. | Jane: Definitely ... and that's where I am most happy. | |
| 61. | Al: And, Jane, as I talk I see you as ... ah ... coming across with a lot of enthusiasm and interest as we talk about these alternatives. I do feel you are a little less enthusiastic about returning to school. (Jane: Right!) I might contrast your enthusiasm about the possibilities of business and training with your feelings around education. There you talk a little more slowly and almost seem bored as you talk about it. You seem lively when you talk about business possibilities. | Al gives Jane specific and concrete feedback about how she comes across in the interview. There is a confrontation as he contrasts her behavior when discussing two topics. Confrontation—the presentation of discrepancies or incongruity—may appear with virtually all skills of the interview. It may be used to summarize past conversation and stimulate further discussion, leading toward a resolution of the incongruity. |
| 62. | Jane: Well, they sound kind of exciting to me, Al. But I just don't know how to go about getting into those fields or what my next steps might be. They sound very exciting to me, and I think I may have some talents in those areas I haven't even discovered yet. | Jane talks rapidly, her face flushes slightly, and she gestures with enthusiasm. She meets the confrontation and seems to be willing to risk more intentionally. |

*(continued)*

279

# TABLE 11-1. continued

SKILL CLASSIFICATION

| Attending summary | Enc./restatement | Paraphrase | Reflect. feeling | Reflect. meaning | Open question | Closed question | Client | Main theme/prob. | Others | "We"/group/dyad | Interviewer | C-E-C situation | Feedback | Adv./info./expl. | Self-disclosure | Interpretation | Logical conseq. | Directive | Influ. summary | Confrontation | Counselor and client statements | Comment |
|---|---|---|---|---|---|---|---|---|---|---|---|---|---|---|---|---|---|---|---|---|---|---|
| | | | | | | | A | A A | | | | | A | A A | | | A | | | A | 63. *Al:* Um-hummm. Well, Jane, I can say one thing. Your enthusiasm and ability to be open and look at things is one part of your ability to do just that. As things get going in your search, you're going to find that helpful to you. Ah ... at the same time, business and schools represent different types of lifestyles. I think I should give you a warning that if you go into the business area you're going to lose those summer vacations. | This statement combines mild feedback with logical consequences. A warning about the consequences of client action or inaction is spelled out. Jane is also confronted with some consequences of choice. |
| | | | | | | | J | J | J J | | | | | | | | | | | | 64. *Jane:* Yeah, I know that ... and you know that special friend in my life—he's in education—I don't think he would like it if I was, you know, working all summer long. But, business does pay a lot more and it might be some interesting possibilities. (*Al:* Um-humm.) ... It's a difficult situation. | Confrontations often result in clients presenting new concepts and facts important in life decisions that have not been discussed previously. A new problem has emerged that may need definition and exploration. |
| | A | | | | | | | A | | | | | | | | | | | | | 65. *Al:* A difficult situation? | Again, the encourager is used to find deeper meanings and more information. |
| | | | | | | | J | J J | J J | | | | | | | | | | | | 66. *Jane:* Um-humm. I guess I'm saying that ... I'm ... ah ... you know, my friend ... I don't think he would approve or like the idea of my going to work in business and only having | Jane has more speech hesitations and difficulties in completing a sentence here than she has anywhere in the interview. This suggests that her relationship is important to her, and her |

two weeks vacation. (*Al:* Uh-huh.) He wants me to stay in some field where I have the same vacation time I have now so we can spend that time together.

friend's attitude may be important in the final vocational decision. Much vocational counseling involves personal issues as well as vocational choice. Both require resolution for true client satisfaction.

67. *Al:* I see; so that's an important issue in your decision as well. Is that correct?

68. *Jane:* It really is ... well, Bo's a special person ...

*Jane's eyes brighten.*

69. *Al:* And, I sense you have some reactions to his ...

*Al interrupts, perhaps unnecessarily. It might have been wise to allow Jane to talk about her positive feelings toward Bo.*

70. *Jane:* Yeah, I'd like to be able to explore some of my own potential without having those restraints put on me right from the beginning.

*Jane talks slowly and deliberately with some sadness expressed in her vocal tone. Feelings are often expressed through intonation.*

71. *Al:* Um-hmm ... In a sense he's almost placing similar constraints on you that you feel in the job and in physical education. There's certain things you have to do. Is that right?

*This interpretation relates the construct of boredom and the implicit constraint of being held down with the constraints of Bo. The interpretation clearly comes from Al's frame of reference. With interpretations or helping leads from your frame of reference, the check-out of client reactions is even more important.*

72. *Jane:* Yes, probably so. He's putting some limits on me ... setting limits on the fields I can explore and the job possibilities I can possibly have. Setting some limits so that my schedule matches his schedule.

*Jane answers quickly. It seems the interpretation was relatively accurate and helpful. One measure of the function and value of a skill is what the client does with it. Jane changes the word constraints to the more powerful word limits.*

73. *Al:* In response to that you feel ...? (Deliberate pause waiting for Jane to supply the feeling.)

(continued)

**TABLE 11–1. continued**

| *SKILL CLASSIFICATION* *Attending* | | | | | | | *Focus* | | | | | | *Influencing* | | | | | | | *C* | | |
|---|---|---|---|---|---|---|---|---|---|---|---|---|---|---|---|---|---|---|---|---|---|---|
| *Attending summary* | *Enc./restatement* | *Paraphrase* | *Reflect. feeling* | *Reflect. meaning* | *Open question* | *Closed question* | *Client* | *Main theme/prob.* | *Others* | *"We"/group/dyad* | *Interviewer* | *C-E-C situation* | *Feedback* | *Adv./info./expl.* | *Self-disclosure* | *Interpretation* | *Logical conseq.* | *Directive* | *Influ. summary* | *Confrontation* | *Counselor and client statements* | *Comment* |
| | | | | | | | J | J | | | | | | | | | | | | | 74. *Jane:* Ah . . . I feel I'm not at a point where I want to *limit things.* I want to see what's open, and I would like to keep things open and see what all the alternatives are. I don't want to shut off any possibility that might be really exciting for me. (*Al:* Um-humm.) A total lifetime of careers. | Jane determinedly emphasizes that she does not want limits. |
| | | A | A | | | | A | A | | | | | | | | | | | | A | 75. *Al:* So you'd like to have a life of exciting opportunity, and you sense some limiting . . . | A brief, but important, confrontation of Bo versus career. |
| | | | | | | | J | J | J | | | | | | | | | | | | 76. *Jane:* He reminds me of my relationship with my first husband. You know, I think the reason that all fell apart was my going back to work. You know, assuming a more nontraditional role as a woman and exploring my potential as a woman rather than staying home with the children . . . ah . . . you know, sort of a similar thing happened there. | Again, the confrontation brings out important new data about Jane's present and past. Is she repeating the relationship patterns in this new relationship that she had in the past? The counselor should consider issues of cultural sexism as an environmental aspect of Jane's planning. This does not appear in this interview, but a broader focus of issues in the next session seems imperative. Other focus issues of possible importance include Jane's parental models, others in her life, a women's support group, the present economic climate, the attitudes of the counselor, and "we"—the immediate relationship of Jane and Al. Thus far |

| | Dialogue | Comment |
|---|---|---|
| | | he has assumed a typical Western "I" form of counseling where the emphasis is on the client. |
| A | 77. *Al:* There really are a variety of issues that . . .you're looking at. One of these is the whole business of a job. Another is your relationship with Bo. | The interview time is waning, and Al must plan a smooth ending and plan for the next session. He catches here the confrontation that Jane faces between work and relationship. |
| | 78. *Jane:* (Slowly) Um-hmmm . . . | Jane looks down, relaxes, and seems to go into herself. |
| A | 79. *Al:* You look a little sad as I say that. | This reflection of feeling comes from nonverbal observations. |
| J | 80. *Jane:* It would be nice if the two would mesh together, but it seems like it's kind of difficult to have both things fitting together nicely. | Jane here is describing her ideal resolution. The interview here could recycle back to stages 2 and 3 with more careful delineation of the problem between job and personal relationships and defining the ideal resolution more fully. "A problem only exists if there is a difference between what is actually happening and what you desire to be happening." This quote illustrates the importance of problem definition and goal setting. Jane's developmental level in terms of her relationship with Bo may be at a lower level than her vocational awareness and may require more extensive use of influencing skills. |
| A | 81. *Al:* Well, that's something we can explore a little bit further. I see our time is about up now. But, it might be useful if we can think of some actions we can take between now and the next time we get together. | Many clients bring up central issues just as the interview is about to end. Al makes the decision, difficult though it is, to stop for now and plan for more discussion later. |

*(continued)*

283

**TABLE 11–1.** continued

| Attending | | | | | | | | Focus | | | | | | Influencing | | | | | | | C | Counselor and client statements | Comment |
|---|---|---|---|---|---|---|---|---|---|---|---|---|---|---|---|---|---|---|---|---|---|---|---|
| Attending summary | Enc./restatement | Paraphrase | Reflect. feeling | Reflect. meaning | Open question | Closed question | Client | Main theme/prob. | Others | "We"/group/dyad | Interviewer | C-E-C situation | Feedback | Adv./info./expl. | Self-disclosure | Interpretation | Logical conseq. | Directive | Influ. summary | Confrontation | | | |
| | | | | | A | | A A | A A | | | | | | | | | | | A | | | **Stage 5: Generalization and transfer of learning**<br><br>82. *Al:* We have come up so far with three things that seem to be logical—business, counseling, and training. I think it would be useful, though, if you were to take a set of vocational tests. (*Jane:* Mm-huh.) That will give us some additional things to check out to see if there are any additional alternatives for us to consider. How do you feel about taking tests? | Al continues his statement and moves to stage 5. He summarizes the vocational alternatives generated thus far and raises the possibility of taking a test. Note that he provides a check-out to give Jane an opportunity to make her own decision about testing. |
| | | | | | | | J | J | | | | | | | | | | | | | | 83. *Jane:* I think that's a good idea. I'm at the stage where I want to check all alternatives. I don't want *anything* to be limited. I want to think about a lot of alternatives at this stage. And I think it would be good to take some tests. | Jane approves of testing and views this as a chance to open alternatives. She verbally emphasizes the word *anything*, which may be coupled with her desire to avoid limits to her potential. Many women would argue that a female counselor is needed at this stage. A male counselor may not be sufficiently aware of women's needs to grow. Al could unconsciously respond to Jane as she views Bo responding to her. |
| | | | | | | | A A | A A | | | | | A | | | | | | | | | 84. *Al:* Then another thing we can do . . . ah . . . is helpful. I have a friend at Jones Company who originally used to be a coach. He's moved into personnel and training at Jones. (*Jane:* Ummm.) I can arrange an | Al suggests another alternative action. Note that *he* is suggesting the alternatives. This may build dependency if continued over time and represents what is often done with a client at developmental level D-1. Fortunately, |

SKILL CLASSIFICATION

| Speaker / Dialogue | Commentary |
|---|---|
| appointment for you to see him. Would you like to go down and look at the possibilities there? | he provides a check-out to increase Jane's participation. |
| 85. *Jane:* Oh, I would like to do that. I'd get kind of a feel what it's like being in a business world. I think talking with someone would be a good way to check it out. | Stated with enthusiasm. The proof of the helpfulness of the suggestion above will be determined by whether or not she does indeed interview the friend at Jones and finds it helpful in her thinking. |
| 86. *Al:* You're a person with a lot of assets. I don't have to tell you all the things that might be helpful. What other ideas do you think you might want to try during the week? | Al recognizes he is potentially taking too much charge. Especially as Jane is functioning vocationally at developmental level D-2. She needs to take more active direction, and Al should not set her limits. She'll set her own. A balance of attending and influencing is needed. |
| 87. *Jane:* What about checking into the university and ah ... advanced degree programs? I have a bachelor's degree, but ... maybe I should check into school and look into what it means to take more coursework. | Jane on her own decides to look into the university alternative. This is particularly important as earlier indications were that she was not all that interested. |
| 88. *Al:* OK, that's something else you could look into as well. (*Jane:* Uh-huh.) So let's arrange for you then to follow up on that. I'd like to see you doing that. (*Jane:* Um-hummmm.) And ... ah ... we can get together and talk again next week. You did express some concern about your relationship with your friend, Bo, ah ... would you like to talk about that as well next week? | Al is preparing to terminate the interview. |
| 89. *Jane:* I think so, they sort of all ... one decision influences another. You know. It all sort of needs to be discussed. | An important insight at the end. Jane realizes her vocational issue is more complex than she originally believed. |
| 90. *Al:* OK. I'll look forward to seeing you next week, then. | |
| 91. *Jane:* Thank you. | |

## COMMENTS ON THE INTERVIEW

Table 11-2 presents a skill summary of Al's interview with Jane. Note the differential use of skills in each stage in this interview. Al presented no influencing skills in stages 2 or 3 of the interview (problem definition and determining outcomes) but a more balanced use of skills in the other stages. In stage 4 Al used both influencing skills and confrontation of incongruity and discrepancies extensively. Stage 4 could be considered the "working" phase of the interview.

In terms of a total balance of skill usage, Al used a ratio of approximately two attending skills for every influencing skill. His focus remained primarily on the client, although the majority of his focus dimensions were dual, combining focus on Jane with focus on the problem or issue.

In examining this interview for mastery, we find that Al does manifest level 1 mastery in that he is able to identify and classify the several skills and stages of the interview. He is able, as demonstrated in his comments, to identify some impact of the skills on the client.

Al also demonstrates level 2, basic mastery, which calls for ability to use the basic listening sequence to structure an interview in five simple stages, and to employ intentional interviewing skills in an actual interview.

Level 3, active mastery, is more difficult to assess. Let us examine this level in more detail. Al does demonstrate the ability to use focus dimensions to produce specific effects on the client. He was able to focus on Jane rather than on the topic. However, at the same time, we do not see him demonstrate the ability to focus extensively on others (for instance, Bo, although there is some indication toward the end of stage 4 that Al may be able to focus on others). Clearly, Al has not manifested ability to focus on "we" in terms of joint problem solving, and he has not been very self-disclosing (the items classified as self-disclosures almost seem more like standard social gestures than real interpersonal openness). Finally, Al has not focused on the cultural-environmental-contextual issue. Jane is a woman. The issues she talks about are common women's issues. If Al does not demonstrate competence in this important environmental area within the next interview or two, referral to another counselor might be wise. If he does use this type of focus in the forthcoming interview, it should be part of his treatment plan (see the following section for an illustration of an interview treatment plan). However, thus far, Al has not manifested mastery of this important cultural and contextual issue.

Has Al been able to produce predicted effects on the client? "Predicted effects" refers to the functions of each of the skills and the functions of the five stages of the interview. Specifically, when an interviewer uses a particular skill or action, does the client *do* what is predicted by the defined function of the skill? Further, does the counselor actually accomplish the main goals of each stage of the session?

**TABLE 11–2.**  Skill summary of Al and Jane interview over five stages

SKILL CLASSIFICATION

| Stage | Attending summary | Enc./restatement | Paraphrase | Reflect. feeling | Reflect. meaning | Open question | Closed question | Client | Main theme/prob. | Others | "We"/group/dyad | Interviewer | C-E-C situation | Feedback | Adv./info./expl. | Self-disclosure | Interpretation | Logical conseq. | Directive | Influ. summary | Confrontation |
|---|---|---|---|---|---|---|---|---|---|---|---|---|---|---|---|---|---|---|---|---|---|
| | Attending | | | | | | | Focus | | | | | | Influencing | | | | | | | C |
| Stage 1: Rapport/structuring (6 attending, 3 influencing skills) | 1 | 1 | 2 | 1 | | 1 | 2 | 4 | 2 | | | 2 | | | 2 | 1 | | | | | |
| Stage 2: Problem definition (5 attending, 0 influencing, 2 confrontation) | | 1 | 1 | 1 | | 1 | 3 | 5 | 1 | | | | | | | | | | | | 2 |
| Stage 3: Determining outcomes (14 attending, 0 influencing, 2 confrontation) | 2 | 2 | 2 | 1 | 1 | 3 | 3 | 8 | 5 | 2 | | | | | | | | | | | 2 |
| Stage 4: Explore alternatives/confront incongruities (18 attending, 13 influencing, 6 confrontation) | | 3 | 7 | 3 | | 4 | 1 | 15 | 14 | 7 | | | 1 | 3 | 3 | | 4 | 1 | 2 | | 6 |
| Stage 5: Generalization (3 attending, 5 influencing) | | | 1 | | | 2 | | 5 | 4 | | | 1 | | 1 | 1 | 1 | | | | 2 | |
| Total: 43 attending, 20 influencing, 9 confrontation | 3 | 6 | 13 | 6 | 1 | 11 | 6 | 37 | 26 | 9 | | 3 | 1 | 4 | 6 | 2 | 4 | 1 | 2 | 2 | 10 |

In a general sense and, perhaps more important, in each phase of the interview, Al fulfilled the functions suggested for each stage. In the rapport stage he was able to use client observation skills and note that Jane was somewhat tense at the beginning and to flex and select a rapport-building exchange that enabled the interview itself to be more comfortable. In the problem-definition stage Jane was able to identify a specific problem she wanted to resolve, which Al summarized at his statement 19. In stage 3 he again used the basic listening sequence to bring out several concrete goals (business, counseling) and through reflection of meaning *(Al 39)* he summarized some of the key aspects of Jane's thinking about the issue. In stage 4 a number of incongruities were confronted, and with each confrontation Jane appeared to move a little deeper into some personal insights concerning her present and future. Note in particular *Al 63*, which led Jane into the important area of her personal life and relationship with Bo. The slightly inaccurate confrontation at *Al 71* fortunately included a check-out, and Jane was thus able to introduce her important construct, substituting the word *limits* for Al's *constraints*. In the final stage Jane appeared ready and willing to take action. However, the real proof of the value of the interview will have to wait until the next meeting, which will show whether the generalization plan was indeed followed through.

Examining specific skills, we might note that Al's open questions tended to encourage Jane to talk, that his paraphrases and reflections of feeling were often followed by Jane saying "Yes," or "Yeah." In the important reflection of meaning at *Al 39*, Jane responded with "Exactly! I hadn't touched on it that way before . . ." In short, Al does seem to be able to use the skills to produce specific results with the client.

However, as noted earlier, Al's self-disclosures are not fully effective, and he did not demonstrate the full range of focusing that might have helped enlarge and round out the conception of Jane's problem. There is time for this, however, in ensuing interviews. The first interview is often a good time for general exploration. It might have been helpful if Al had used the newspaper framework (who, what, when, where, how, and why) to cover his bases more fully.

Another way to evaluate the effectiveness of an interview is in terms of the degree of freedom or choices available to Jane. In the words of a common counseling slogan, "If you don't have at least three possibilities, you don't have a choice." Jane appears to have achieved that objective in the interview, at least for the moment. In addition, the issue of her relationship with Bo has been unearthed, and this topic may open her to further counseling possibilities. Again, the question must be raised whether Al, as a man, is the most appropriate interviewer for Jane to see. Answers to that question will vary with your personal worldview. What are your evaluations? What would you do differently?

The acid test of "client change beyond the interview" remains. Unless something happens as a result of this session, all the preceding analysis remains just that—analysis!

## PLANNING FOR FURTHER INTERVIEWS

Box 11-2 contains Al's interview plan for the second session. This plan derives from information gained in the first interview and organizes the central issues of the case, allowing for new input from Jane as the session progresses.

In short-term counseling and interviewing the interview plan serves as the treatment plan itself. As you move toward longer term counseling, a more detailed treatment plan is important. There, the several problems and issues raised by the client may be outlined in much the same fashion as in the interview plan. However, the range of problems and issues is listed at greater length, and priorities may be set. Similarly, an array of desired outcomes may be identified. For exploring alternatives and incongruity, several alternative interview plans and theoretical methods may be employed. A wide variety of generalization plans may be needed. Box 11-3 presents a sample treatment plan for Jane, assuming that she wishes to continue counseling over a longer period, such as 20 sessions.

Within the profession of interviewing there is disagreement on the need for an interviewing plan and treatment plan. The more structured counseling theories, such as behavioral and strategic/structural, strongly urge interview and treatment plans with specific goals developed for each. Their interview and treatment plans may often be more specific than those presented here. Less structured counseling theories (Gestalt, psychodynamic, Rogerian) tend not to have treatment plans, preferring to work in the moment with the client. The interview and treatment plan forms suggested here represent a mid-point, which you may find helpful in thinking through your own opinion on this important issue.

---

**Box 11-2  Interview plan and objectives (before second interview)**

After studying the client file before the first session or after reviewing the preceding session, complete the following form indicating issues you anticipate being important in the session and how you plan to handle them.

*1. Rapport/*     *Special issues anticipated around rapport development?*
*structuring*     *What structure for this interview do you have? Do you plan to use specific theory?*

**Box 11-2 continued**

Jane and I seem to have reasonable rapport. As I look at the last session, I note I did not focus on Jane's context nor did I attend to other issues that might be going on in her life. It may be helpful to plan some time for general exploration *after* I follow up on the testing and her interviews with people during the week. Jane indicated an interest in talking about Bo. Two issues need to be considered at this session in addition to general exploration of her present state. I'll introduce the tests and follow that with discussion of Bo. On Bo, I think a person-centered Rogerian method emphasizing listening skills may be helpful.

2. *Problem definition/ identification of assets*

*What are the anticipated problems? Strengths? How do you plan to define the problem with the client? Will you emphasize behavior, thoughts, feelings, meanings?*

a. Check with Jane on her vocational plans and how she sees her career problem defined now. Use basic listening sequence.
b. Later in the interview recycle back to the issue with Bo. Open it up with a question, then follow through with reflective listening skills. If she starts with Bo, save vocational issues until later.
c. Jane has many assets. She is bright, verbal, and successful in her job. She has good insight and is willing to take reasonable risks and explore new alternatives. These assets should be noted in our future interviews.

3. *Defining outcomes*

*What is the ideal outcome? How will you bring out the idealized self or world?*
This will not be too important a part in this interview. We already have her goals vocationally, but they may need to be reconsidered in light of the tests, further discussion around Bo, and so on. It is possible that late in this interview or in a following session we may need to define a new outcome in which vocations and her relationships are both satisfied.

4. *Exploring alternatives/ confronting incongruity*

*What types of alternatives should be generated? What theories would you likely use here? What specific incongruities have you noted or do you anticipate in the client?*

**Box 11-2 continued**

|  |  |
|---|---|
|  | a. Check on results of tests and report them to Jane. |
|  | b. Explore her reactions and consider alternative occupations. |
|  | c. Use person-centered Rogerian counseling and explore her issues with Bo. |
|  | d. Relate vocations to Bo relationship. Give special attention to confronting the differences between her desires as a "person" and Bo's desires for her. Note and consider issues of women in a changing world. Does Jane need referral to a woman for additional guidance? Would assertiveness training be useful? |
| *5. Generalization* | *What specific plans, if any, do you have for transfer of training? What will enable you personally to feel that the interview was worthwhile?* |
|  | At the moment it seems clear that further exploration of vocations outside the interview is needed. We will have to explore the relationship with Bo and determine her objectives more precisely. |

**Box 11-3  Treatment plan for Jane developed after three interviews**

|  |  |
|---|---|
| *1. Rapport/ structuring* | Jane seems to respond best when I am open. In the second interview she seemed to like and appreciate my self-disclosures, and it facilitated the assertion training exercise. She responded well for a time when I tried Rogerian person-centered methods but seemed to prefer more directedness on my part. That may be me, or it may be her. We can talk about that during the next session. She does seem to like structured techniques more than unstructured. |
| *2. Problem definition/ summary of assets* | The following problems have been discussed thus far. Some have been touched on only briefly. In my opinion, the most important at the moment are as follows: |
|  | a. The relationship with Bo. Shall she break up, or shall she stay with him? |
|  | b. Vocational choice. It now seems clear that she wants to |

**Box 11-3 continued**

leave the school setting, but it is quite unclear how she can handle it financially.

c. Finances are a problem we have explored only briefly. One of the attractions of the relationship with Bo is that it solves those problems.

d. Assertiveness. Jane has made a beginning in assertiveness but may profit from more training and practice.

e. Unpleasant dreams. Jane mentioned briefly that she had trouble sleeping this past week. I may need to explore the dream in some detail if she brings it up again.

To solve these problems, Jane brings a considerable number of assets. She is bright, attractive, verbal, and apparently has a large number of female friends. Her hobbies and leisure-time activities seem to interest her. She has worked through her divorce, and her children are doing well.

*3. Defining outcomes*

It seems safe to say that:

a. Jane wants to make a decision one way or the other with Bo that makes it possible for her to be in a more satisfactory vocational setting. At the moment it appears that she wants to place her interests above Bo's.

b. She does want a satisfactory relationship with a man.

c. Financial planning may be necessary to help her handle her money more effectively.

d. Jane seeks to be more assertive and get her own way more often.

e. Dreams have been mentioned as a problem.

f. Further attention should be given to identifying other outcomes.

*4. Routes toward problem resolution*

a. Vocational decision will continue to be worked through with trait-and-factor decision-making counseling.

b. Explore relationship with Bo via person-centered counseling as in the past, but emphasize behavioral methods to help her act more decisively.

c. Financial advice via referral to the university may be helpful.

d. Gestalt or psychodynamic dream analysis should be kept on reserve if the dream topic comes up again.

**Box 11-3 continued**

> Alternatively, transactional analysis techniques may be employed. Involve Jane in this decision as it may mean more long term counseling than she wishes. Jane has enough assets to move forward easily on her own.

*5. Generalization*    Constantly keep in mind the array of generalization techniques available so that each problem or issue discussed gets worked on outside the interview.

---

## FINAL PRACTICE EXERCISE AND SELF-ASSESSMENT

Attending behavior, the first concept of this book, has served as the foundation for each succeeding, more complex, skill. By now you have experienced an array of skills and concepts. Can you integrate them into a real interview?

This chapter presents one major practice exercise in the form of a paper in which you demonstrate your interviewing style, classify your behavior, and comment on your own skill development as an interviewer. Following this exercise you will find a final self-assessment form.

The steps below and on page 296 are suggested for development of a major presentation of your interviewing style:

1. Plan to conduct an interview with a member of your group, a friend, or an actual client. This interview should last at least 15 minutes (although most prefer a longer time) and should follow the basic five-stage structure. It should represent an interview you are satisfied to present to others. Before you conduct the interview, be sure you have your role-played client's permission to record the session.
2. Before this interview is actually held, develop an Interview Plan Form (Box 11-4) so you can plan for the session.
3. Audiorecord or videorecord the interview.
4. Develop a transcript of the session. Place the transcript on a form similar to Box 11-5. Leave space for comments on the form.
5. Classify your interviewing leads for skill and focus. Classify the client's focus as well.
6. Identify the specific stages of the interview as you move through them. Note that you may not always follow the order sequentially. Indicate that you have returned to stage 2 from stage 4 clearly, if such occurs.
7. Make comments on the transcript. Use your own impressions plus the descriptive ideas and conceptual frames of this book.

## Box 11-4 Interview plan and objectives form

After studying the client file before the first session or after reviewing the preceding session, complete the following form indicating issues you anticipate being important in the session and how you plan to handle them.

1. *Rapport/ structuring*

Special issues anticipated around rapport development? What need to structure this interview do you have? Do you plan a specific theory? Skill sequence?

2. *Problem definition and identification of assets*

What are the anticipated problems for this client? Strengths? How do you plan to define the problem with the client? Will you emphasize behavior, thoughts, feelings, meanings? In what areas do you anticipate working on problems?

3. *Defining outcomes*

Where do you believe this client would like to go? How will you bring out the idealized self or world? What would you like to see as the outcome?

4. *Exploring alternatives/ confronting incongruity*

What types of alternatives should be generated? What theories would you likely use here? What specific in-congruities have you noted or do you anticipate in the client? What skills are you likely to use? Skill sequences?

5. *Generalization*

What specific plans, if any, do you have for transfer of training? What will enable you personally to feel that the interview was worthwhile?

**Box 11-5 Form for recording transcript of an interviewing session (indicate stages of the interview as they occur)**

| SKILL CLASSIFICATION | | | Counselor and client statements | Comment |
|---|---|---|---|---|
| Attending | Attending summary | | | |
| | Enc./restatement | | | |
| | Paraphrase | | | |
| | Reflect. feeling | | | |
| | Reflect. meaning | | | |
| | Open question | | | |
| | Closed question | | | |
| Focus | Client | | | |
| | Main theme/prob. | | | |
| | Others | | | |
| | "We"/group/dyad | | | |
| | Interviewer | | | |
| | C-E-C situation | | | |
| Influencing | Feedback | | | |
| | Adv./info./expl. | | | |
| | Self-disclosure | | | |
| | Interpretation | | | |
| | Logical conseq. | | | |
| | Directive | | | |
| | Influ. summary | | | |
| C | Confrontation | | | |

8. Develop a treatment plan for a second session using Box 11-4.
9. Assume that the sessions might continue over a longer period of time and develop a longer term treatment plan using Box 11-6.
10. Complete a count of your skill usage and present your own overall analysis of the interview. Use Al's self-analysis on pages 286–289 as a guideline.
11. Present your case analysis in the following form:

   a. Brief description of your client with relevant data.
   b. Interview Plan Form (Box 11-4).
   c. Transcript analyzed and rated (Box 11-5).
   d. Count of skill usage and subjective analysis of the interview.
   e. Interview Plan Form (Box 11-4) for a possible second interview.
   f. Treatment Plan Form (Box 11-6) assuming that you would be completing a series of interviews with this client.
   g. Mastery level summary self-assessment (see Table 11-3).

---

**Box 11-6  Treatment plan (over several interviews)**

*1. Rapport/ structuring*    How does this client develop rapport? What issues are of most comfort/discomfort? How does the client respond to structuring? At what place will structuring be most helpful?

**Box 11-6 continued**

2. *Problem definition and summary of assets*

List below, in order of importance, the several problem areas of the client. Include a listing of the client's strengths and assets for coping with these issues.

3. *Defining outcomes*

What are your and the client's ideal outcomes for these and other issues?

4. *Exploring alternatives/ confronting incongruity*

What are the client's main alternatives? What are your treatment alternatives? What are the main items of client incongruity? How might they best be confronted?

5. *Generalization*

What are your specific plans for generalization of learning from the interview?

**TABLE 11-3.** Mastery Level Summary Self-Assessment

| Skill or concept | 1. Attending behavior | 2. Questioning | 3. Client observation | 4. Encouraging | 5. Paraphrasing | 6. Summarizing | 7. Reflecting feelings | 8. Reflecting meanings | 9. Focusing | 10. Directives | 11. Feedback |
|---|---|---|---|---|---|---|---|---|---|---|---|
| Teaching mastery | | | | | | | | | | | |
| Active mastery | | | | | | | | | | | |
| Basic mastery | | | | | | | | | | | |
| Identification | | | | | | | | | | | |
| Evidence of Achieving Mastery Level | | | | | | | | | | | |

| | 12. Logical consequences | 13. Self-disclosure | 14. Interpretation | 15. Influencing summary | 16. Information/advice/ instruction/other | 17. Confrontation | 18. Basic listening sequence | 19. Positive asset search | 20. Client developmental level | 21. Interviewing style | 22. Empathy | 23. Five stages of the interview | 24. Interview plans | 25. Treatment plans |
|---|---|---|---|---|---|---|---|---|---|---|---|---|---|---|
| | | | | | | | | | | | | | | |
| | | | | | | | | | | | | | | |
| | | | | | | | | | | | | | | |
| | | | | | | | | | | | | | | |

## SELF-ASSESSMENT OF SKILL INTEGRATION

Throughout this book self-assessment exercises have been designed to help you think through your mastery level of each skill and concept. The major skill areas and concepts are summarized in the form below. The several mastery levels for each area have been defined throughout the book, so definitions will not be given again here.

Evidence of your level of mastery remains important. Space is provided in the form for you to indicate briefly how you have demonstrated your mastery of the highest skill level in the interview. Evidence of teaching mastery should be provided separately from evidence of the first three mastery levels.

One useful way to provide specific evidence of your mastery of each skill area is to use your final transcript. For example, your ability to reflect feelings in a way that helps a client examine emotions more fully may be demonstrated by a specific lead in the transcript followed by client statements indicating that your reflection was helpful. Mastery of the five stages of the interview or the basic listening sequence may be demonstrated by referral to appropriate places in your interview transcript.

After you have completed the Mastery Level Summary and Self-Assessment, establish your own future goals for interviewing and counseling mastery below. Then give special attention to your interview completed in Chapter 1 before reading this text, and note how your style has changed and evolved since then. What particular strengths do you note in your own work?

_____

_____

_____

_____

_____

_____

_____

_____

_____

_____

_____

_____

_____

# CHAPTER 12

# Teaching Interviewing Skills

---

**How can teaching interviewing skills be used to help you and your clients?**

The skills of intentional interviewing apply in many settings:

| | | |
|---|---|---|
| Counseling | Corrections | Communication in |
| Interviewing | Social work | general |
| Psychotherapy | Police work | Parenting |
| Management | Community agencies | Patient/client training |
| Medicine | Teaching | Family education |
| Nursing | Administration | Social skills training |
| | | Individual |
| | | communication |

Teaching interviewing skills to others serves many functions:

*Major Functions*
▲ To share important dimensions of interviewing with other interviewing trainees.
▲ To share important dimensions of communication with clients and people in general.

*Secondary Functions*
▲ To help you learn how to manage workshops, short training programs, and longer courses of training.
▲ To increase your understanding of the microskills and interviewing process through teaching others specific skills.
▲ To give you experience and confidence in a newly developing role of professional interviewers—that of psychological educator, teaching basic skills to clients and groups.

---

## INTRODUCTION

All professional groups—from accountants to park service workers to physicians—use the basic interviewing skills of this book in some fashion. However, the skills of interviewing are too important to be kept within strict professional boundaries. *A critical present and future role of the intentional interviewer is to impart and teach the skills of interviewing to other people.*

Interviewers and counselors are becoming *psychological educators.* Psychological educators teach skills and concepts of effective communication, values clarification, self-development, career planning, and other life skills to a wide variety of client populations (for examples, see Dinkmeyer & McKay, 1976; Goldstein, 1973; Gordon, 1970; Guerney, 1977; Ivey & Alschuler, 1973). Perhaps the clearest and most definitive statement about the role of psychological education, or *psychoeducation*, is the following:

> The psychoeducational model, therefore, views the role of the psychological practitioner not in terms of abnormality (or illness) → diagnosis → prescription → therapy → cure; but rather in terms of client dissatisfaction (or ambition) → goal-setting → skill teaching → satisfaction (or goal achievement). Likewise, the client is viewed as a pupil rather than as a patient [Authier et al., 1975, p. 15].

Thus, two roles for you as an interviewer are suggested in this chapter: (1) teaching what you are learning and have learned to others interested in interviewing; and (2) sharing those skills with your clients and with people in general. When you teach professional and lay groups interviewing skills, you will want to use methods similar to those used in this book. The same principles hold for working with clients, but you will require individual adaptations for your clients' immediate needs.

## WHERE TO START IN TEACHING INTERVIEWING SKILLS?

Mastery in teaching interviewing skills is best developed through the following steps:

1. *Teaching one person.* Teach a classmate, a family member, or another interested and willing person what you have learned in your own way. For example, perhaps you have found the use of open questions interesting and helpful. Simply tell the other person what you have learned in your own words and then conduct a brief practice session in which you serve as the role-played client and the other person serves

as the interviewer. This informal approach seems to work best as a starting point. You use your own natural teaching skills, you start from a point of interest to you, and you are not confined to any special process. Later, you will find that this method is often the best way to apply teaching skills to your own clients in the interview.

2. *Teaching a small group.* After you have taught one or more persons several skills, you may want to test your ability to teach a small practice group of three to eight members. At this point you'll find the basic teaching model outlined in the next section of this chapter helpful: (1) warm-up and introduction to the skill; (2) example of the skill in operation; (3) reading; (4) practice; and (5) self-assessment and generalization.

3. *Teaching larger groups.* As you gain experience, you can teach these skills to larger groups, up to 200 people. In large workshops and courses it is important to design time schedules, space arrangements, and equipment especially carefully.

4. *Teaching clients.* The methods for teaching clients are the same as those for teaching other nonprofessional and professional interviewers. If you find a client who can profit from one or more interviewing skills in the process of your sessions (for example, a client who might need more effective questioning and self-disclosure skills for a job interview), use the same informal procedures as are suggested for teaching one person. You'll also find client groups who can profit from regular systematic practice in interviewing skills (for instance, a group of high school students taking a speech development course, a group of psychiatric outpatients). With such groups the procedures used in this book have been found effective. However, interviewing skills are redefined as communication skills, and only those skills that meet the needs of the particular group are used. For example, most such groups find attending behavior, questions, and the other skills of the basic listening sequence particularly helpful. Skills such as reflection of meaning, interpretation, and logical consequences generally are less relevant.

## THE BASIC MICROSKILLS TEACHING MODEL

The model you have experienced in this book has been developed and tested over 18 years of clinical work and research and has been found to be most effective. However, each teacher of skills must redefine the model to meet personal beliefs and needs, both for self-satisfaction and for varying trainee interests. It is your responsibility to shape and adapt the basic model. Use the model as a guideline, but add your own variations!

**Step 1. Warm-up and introduction to the skill.** If you are teaching attending behavior, for example, introduce the concept briefly and provide a personalized exercise which produces involvement and demonstrates the need for the skill. What can learning this skill do for your trainee(s)?

**Step 2. Example of the skill in action.** It is best if you present video, audio, or live demonstrations of the skill. A second choice is to ask your trainee(s) to read the appropriate transcript in this book and then to follow the reading with a discussion. You'll find trainee involvement and interest higher with a live or video model of the skill.

**Step 3. Reading.** Each skill chapter ends with a key points summary outlining the most important aspects of each skill. People have different learning styles. It is helpful to ask your trainees to read these short sections in the training sessions as they provide clear examples and descriptions of what is being taught. It also provides them with "alone time" to reflect on their learning.

**Step 4. Practice.** The most important part of the entire microskills training framework is practicing the skill. Use the seven steps for practice outlined in systematic group practice in each chapter. It is possible to "walk through" skill practice and not have demonstrated real mastery. The levels of identification, basic, and active mastery will provide you with clues as to how much more practice your trainees need. Teaching mastery will be helpful for those who wish to share these skills with clients and others.

**Step 5. Self-assessment and generalization.** If your trainees have mastered a skill to a sufficient level, work with them to plan for generalization beyond the practice session role-play. If a trainee has not yet mastered the skill, return to step 1. You may wish to use individual practice exercises and self-assessment concepts to facilitate generalization of the skills you have taught. You also may want to use the feedback form at the end of this chapter to obtain information from your trainees on your own work as teacher.

Again, this is the basic instructional model; you must shape and adapt it to meet the needs of your particular individual or group. Following are some general considerations to be examined in most skill-teaching situations.

## BEFORE YOU START TEACHING SKILLS . . .

Teaching interviewing skills can be facilitated by considering ahead of time a few basic dimensions of effective workshop development. Outline a plan of action and time schedule for your program *before* you start. Here are some basic issues you might use as a check-list to help ensure that your training goes smoothly:

 _____ *Consider your trainee(s).* How experienced is the individual or group? If you are working with beginners, simple, direct language is most effective. You might think that the concepts of the early part of the book are too simple for more experienced people. However, if the mastery goals are emphasized clearly, even highly experienced professionals find themselves engaged and highly involved in the training. It is also important to provide examples relevant to each group. In working with correctional officers, for example, be sure that the demonstration, discussion of the skill, and practice sessions fit their interests and needs; a school counseling practice session would be irrelevant to them. Develop your training program considering the place and needs of the group.

_____ *Setting.* The location should be attractive, clean, and relatively organized. Movable chairs and a comfortable rug can make a workshop or training session much more pleasant.

_____ *Practice space.* Ideally, seek to have separate practice rooms for each group of four people. As this is not usually practical when working with larger groups, you should plan to provide as much room and privacy as possible. On the other hand, there is some benefit from the excitement and general noise of a larger group working in a comfortable large room.

_____ *Equipment.* In the ideal training session you will have a closed-circuit video system for each group. As a second option, each group of four should have access to an audiorecorder. For practice outside the group, it is strongly urged that each trainee have a recorder. However, it is possible to run workshops without any equipment and rely on Observers I and II.

_____ *Breaks.* As a trainer and teacher of skills, you'll find the workshop and training energizing. Remember, however, that your group often finds the new concepts and methods difficult and tiring. Provide adequate break time and refreshments insofar as possible.

_____ *Group size and timing.* With one person you'll find that a training plan can be flexible and meet the needs of the individual. With larger groups a carefully planned schedule will save time, avoid confusion, and enable you to teach more with more trainee satisfaction. *As groups get larger, you cannot overplan!*

_____ *Getting acquainted.* As a group starts, be sure that you have provided some informal or formal way for people to get to know one another and feel more comfortable in the group. This can take the form of name games and group exercises, or it can be as simple as having each person introduce him- or herself. Taking time early in the meeting to let the group know the location of telephones and bathrooms, and the schedule, can save you and the group time later on. Allow an opportunity for the group to raise any questions about the program before you start. Those questions will come out later if they are not answered at the beginning. Starting with them will indicate to the group your interest and willingness to explore their needs.

_____ *Obtaining group expectations.* Many training sessions go down in flames because the trainer did not ask the group what their special needs and interests were. Begin a course or workshop by dividing into groups of four or six and asking the trainees to brainstorm their special needs, wishes, expectations, and desires for the training. These expectations can be shared in the group, and you as leader can respond to them. It is useful to post them on a chalkboard or on a newsprint on the wall and refer to the group's needs periodically throughout the training.

_____ *Reading material.* It is helpful to have a copy of the interview skill training book for each trainee. This provides them with feedback forms, the reading material, and the individual practice exercises. You'll also find the systematic steps for group practice helpful.

_____ *Practice sessions.* Before groups break up into small groups for practice, go through the seven steps for systematic practice carefully. The steps seem clear, but most groups get lost at first. Take extra time here!

_____ *Resistance.* In most training sessions you'll run into one or more individuals who clearly resist training and the ideas you are trying to share. A basic rule is "Go with the resistance!" Do not fight or argue with the person challenging you or the concept. Point out that this is simply one alternative for teaching the structure of the interview, and not everyone will find it the most comfortable option. A useful method many effective trainers use when resistance appears is to step forward, smile, and lean toward the person, saying "That's an interesting and important point." Follow this by a direct answer in a nondefensive manner. After you have answered the challenge, *do not* look at the person who asked the question; look at the group. Looking at the person who asked the question often prompts further questions and may leave the rest of the group bored and uninterested.

_____ *Questions from the group.* This is an extension of the above point. As a group develops, you'll find that certain individuals gradually dominate. If you observe your group carefully, you'll note that they gradually lose interest when the dominating people ask questions. Again, *do not* look at the person asking the question, look to the group while answering. This involves the rest of the group more fully. If necessary, set up a rule that any one individual may ask only two questions per session. This is important for the health and satisfaction of your group.

_____ *Cultural differences.* The concepts of this book are drawn from typical white, middle-class helping patterns *and* from extensive work in other cultures. Experience has revealed that the microskills are highly workable in cultures as diverse as Eskimo and Inuit populations in the Arctic, Aboriginal Australians, Swedish migrant populations, German management officials, and Native American and Black groups in this country.

The models and examples (and skills, in some cases) must be adapted to meet the needs and practices of the particular cultural group. One useful exercise is to involve your group in developing training materials that are culturally relevant to their needs. Start with the basic model and encourage them in practice sessions to adapt the concepts for their own setting.

_____ *Ethics.* General rules of effective interviewing and counseling ethics should apply. With groups that are going to move into extensive discussion of personal issues, spend time at the beginning with the ethical statements of the American Personnel and Guidance Association and the American Psychological Association. When taping an interview, always begin the interview with the question "Do you mind if I tape this session?" If the real or role-played client wishes the tape to stop, immediately turn off the machine. If someone wishes the tape to be erased, let them observe the erasure.

Sensible limits of confidentiality are suggested. There are no real legal protections for confidentiality in this type of training, and the group needs to be reminded of this fact. Nevertheless, what goes on in the group belongs to the group and not to the public. A professional helper should be available for support and consultation should referral become necessary. One good approach is to start longer periods of training with a discussion of general ethics. The group can develop their own safeguards and a systematic list of agreed-on standards before they begin training.

At the same time, too much emphasis on possible problems can produce the very problems you are trying to prevent. Among thousands of individuals trained with this program, only an extremely small minority have had any problems with the framework. Those trainees who seem to require more caution can either leave the training or role play standard roles. If you are relaxed and expect cooperation and ethical standards, you'll likely receive what you expect. If you are anxious and waver, anticipate difficulty! This is one reason it is strongly urged that you begin your training of others with only one other person.

_____ *Designing a training session, workshop, or course.* Once again, change the suggestions here to fit your and the group's needs!

## MASTERY LEVELS

Four levels of mastery are used in this book:

*Level 1* (identification). You will be able to identify the skill and the impact of the skill on the client.

*Level 2* (basic mastery). You will be able to use the skill in the role-played interview.

*Level 3* (active mastery). You will be able to use the skill with specific impact on the client.

*Level 4* (teaching mastery). You will be able to teach the skill to clients and other trainees.

Experience has shown that too many people going through interviewing training stop at the basic mastery level. This level demands that the interviewer simply use the skill (paraphrase, question, interpretation, and so on) in the interview. The use can be of relatively low quality or high quality, but little attention may be given to its impact on the client.

Active mastery demands the intentional ability to use the skill for client benefit and to change client conversational flow at will. Active mastery takes time and more practice than the teaching sessions discussed in this chapter. In basic mastery the emphasis is on the interviewer and goals can be easily accomplished. In active mastery, by contrast, the emphasis is on the client—what does the counselor or interviewer do to produce specific effects on client conversational flow? Special attention must be given to ensure that full mastery of the concepts occurs. Suggestions for encouraging active mastery are to be found in the teacher manual accompanying this book.

The teaching sessions presented here are aimed toward basic mastery. Some competent trainees will be able to develop active mastery levels. For one person, simply asking an open question is an accomplishment. For another, the higher mastery required to use open and closed questions to speed and to slow the pace of an interview will be a more interesting and challenging assignment. Use the self-assessment forms at the end of each chapter to verify what levels of mastery your trainees have actually achieved.

## SPECIFIC TEACHING SUGGESTIONS

With the background we have covered thus far, it seems appropriate now to turn to specific teaching suggestions for each chapter. It is recommended that trainees should read each chapter before tackling that section. If this is not possible, have trainees study the Key Points of that chapter at the beginning of each workshop.

### *TOWARD INTENTIONAL INTERVIEWING AND COUNSELING (CHAPTER 1)*

This chapter provides an entry for the entire training series; it does not follow the usual five-step design. There is need for time to get acquainted and learn individual and group needs and expectations, and the content of the chapter often takes second place as a group gets started. Here is a suggested design to help facilitate learning throughout the entire workshop or class series:

**1. Before you start.** Ask the group if anyone has any special needs before the workshop or class begins. Someone may need a ride, someone else may need to know when the break is in order to make a phone call, others may have individual needs or concerns. It is helpful to point out where the telephone and restroom facilities are located. This part of the class or workshop may be considered "courtesy time" in which you indicate you are aware of and care for group needs. You may want to mention that coffee is available or that you need a volunteer to coordinate coffee.

**2. Name game.** For small groups it may be adequate simply to go around the room with each person starting her or his name and some information about why he or she is here. For larger groups, it may be helpful to divide immediately into fours and have each group get acquainted and then introduce their members to the larger group. One useful exercise with very large groups is to have each individual tell about him- or herself in *ten words*. The result can be interesting or hilarious, and it provides a warm beginning. Develop your own method, but give attention to people. During the second or third session repeat the name game procedures.

**3. Expectations.** For perhaps the most important exercise of the day, divide the group into fours and ask each to provide a list of needs and expectations. Record responses on newsprint or chalkboard, ideally posting them around the room. Throughout the class or workshop, refer to them occasionally to integrate the group needs with your own design. Time spent checking out expectations is inevitably profitable. It can reduce resistance and help group flow. If you can't meet a particular expectation or need, admit it. Better now than later!

**4. Different people respond differently.** Read the client statement on page 2 and ask your group to follow you in their own books. If you prefer, present your own "client" and have trainees respond to your stimulus material. Have them write their own responses down. Then the group may meet in fours and discuss similarities and differences and report back to the larger group. Important here is the fact that different people respond differently to the same stimulus; no single answer is necessarily correct. Note that each participant response would lead clients in vastly different directions. Out of these differences, discuss the concept of intentionality and the goal of the training to increase responding.

**5. The microskills hierarchy.** We have found it helpful to present an example interview on videotape or audiotape, preferably of a master interviewer. The trainees listen to the session for about five to ten minutes, then write down the specific behaviors that the interviewer was using and discuss them in small groups. Many times trainees produce lists that are virtually identical to the microskills hierarchy. The microskills hierarchy may then be presented on newsprint or on the chalkboard. It provides a map of where the students are going.

**6. Other lecture material.**   The concepts of microskills as used in different settings, alternative settings for interviewing, and cross-cultural implications may be discussed. Research on microskills may be summarized.

**7. Making an audiotape.**   Most involving and most helpful of all the exercises in this book are those in which the trainee becomes involved. Audiorecording an interview *before* the remainder of the training program will give each trainee a record of his or her natural style of interaction, which can later be classified on the microskills hierarchy. Again, it is strongly suggested that each trainee have an audiorecorder available for practice at home.

*ATTENDING BEHAVIOR: BASIC TO COMMUNICATION (CHAPTER 2)*

**1. Introduction.**   Check first on the needs and expectations of the group. Give a brief overview of the purposes and functions of attending behavior. Then ask for two volunteers to demonstrate before the group the worst interview they can muster (see page 16). The group can then brainstorm the many things that have been done incorrectly. You can list them on the board and again relate them to the microskills hierarchy. This exercise serves as a tension releaser before people start actual practice of the skills.

An overview of attending behavior concepts may then be presented briefly, with the major function of attending behavior (encouraging and discouraging conversation) given some prominence.

**2. Example of the skill in action.**   An audiotape or videotape[1] of a positive and negative example of attending behavior may be played, or students may read the transcript. You may wish to demonstrate the skill via live modeling.

**3. Read.**   Key points about attending behavior are presented on page 25. Again, this provides the trainee with workshop time to reflect on the meaning of the skill.

**4. Practice.**   As this is the first practice session, go through the seven steps of the practice in some detail. Confusion can result if trainees do not fully complete and understand each step before moving on to the next step. In large groups this is particularly important. For practice sessions make sure that each person has a role as a client, interviewer, or observer, and that each understands the task.

It is important that elementary rules of confidentiality and ethics be discussed. While it is preferable to role play real issues, any individual who does not wish to role play actual concerns can usually play a friend or past acquaintance who had a relevant concern. Make sure that trainees know tapes can be erased if they wish. Stress the importance and value of effective feedback sheets and discuss the guidelines for effective feedback presented in the chapter.

**5. Generalization and self-assessment.**   Assign the individual practice exercises at the conclusion of the chapter. Work through the self-assessment mastery form carefully with your individual trainee or group.

*QUESTIONS: OPENING COMMUNICATION (CHAPTER 3)*

**1. Introduction.**   The single skills approach to interviewing distracts some people at first. Breaking out of single dimensions of communication may be difficult for them, or they may resist. The story of the Samurai Swordsman (page 37) discusses this issue. The story, or some parallel of it, may be told to introduce this session.

Give a very brief introduction to the concepts and the functions of open and closed questions. Then allow the group to ask you a variety of open and closed questions. As you respond naturally, they will see the effect of these

[1] You may develop these yourself. However, video and audio skill examples are available from *Microtraining Associates*, Box 641, North Amherst, Mass. 01059.

types of questions. Your personal modeling and openness can help the group feel more supported and comfortable.

The "plus and minus" of questions may be explored through the suggested exercise on page 40.

**2. Example of the skill in action.** The transcript may be read or an audiotape or video example of questioning may be played.

**3. Read.** Key points about questions are presented on page 48.

**4. Practice.** The same model may be followed as in the preceding sessions. Move from group to group and observe and comment on interaction. Follow time frames carefully.

**5. Generalization and self-assessment.** Use the individual practice exercises and self-assessment form.

### CLIENT OBSERVATION SKILLS (CHAPTER 4)

**1. Introduction.** Ask participants to brainstorm the many important

things that a counselor or interviewer should observe. Note their list on newsprint or chalkboard. Then discuss the organizing principles of client observation: (1) client nonverbal behavior; (2) client verbal behavior; (3) client discrepancies. Discuss the important functions of skilled client observation. Stress that more ideas and concepts will be covered in this chapter than can be assimilated in a short time. Let the group know that they will have an opportunity in later practice sessions to work on client observation skills in more depth. As they work later on paraphrasing, reflection of feeling, and the other skills, give some additional attention to the importance of client observation.

**2. Example of the skill in action.** Read the transcript on client observation skills. It may be even more helpful if the transcript is then read aloud a second time with the various client and interviewer behaviors role played by the readers. Presentation of videotapes, films, and audiotapes is particularly helpful at this point.

**3. Read.** The key points about client observation are presented on page 70.

**4. Practice.** As time permits, it is helpful to use the individual practice exercises before undertaking systematic group practice. Adapt Exercises

1 through 7 for group practice. As an alternative, use these practice exercises in conjunction with other practice exercises later in the course of training.

**5. Generalization and self-assessment.** Give special attention to the self-assessment form and individual practice exercises to ensure that the many concepts of this program are gradually mastered. You'll find yourself referring to these concepts throughout the remainder of the book.

## ENCOURAGING, PARAPHRASING, AND SUMMARIZING: HEARING THE CLIENT ACCURATELY (CHAPTER 5)

**1. Introduction.** Briefly present the main ideas and functions of these skills. Then, ask the trainees to write down what you have just said. These paraphrases and summaries are the first test of their abilities with these skills. Trainees then divide into pairs, and one member of each pair tells the listener about a recent life event. The speaker talks for two minutes while the listener remains totally silent. The listener then summarizes what the speaker said for one minute. Allot two minutes for the pairs to process and discuss the accuracy of the listening.

**2. Example of the skill in action.** Transcript, live, or taped examples may be presented.

**3. Read.** See key points on page 96.

**4. Practice.** Instructions may be found on page 101.

**5. Generalization and self-assessment.** See individual exercises and the self-assessment mastery form.

## NOTING AND REFLECTING FEELINGS: A FOUNDATION OF CLIENT EXPERIENCE (CHAPTER 6)

**1. Introduction.** Trainees are not always able to recognize and reflect feelings. Thus, it is useful to begin this session by brainstorming a list of feeling words. Following this, read the client statement at the beginning of the chapter on page 107. The students may then write a paraphrase of the statement and list client feelings. Paraphrasing should be contrasted with reflection of feeling.

Present an overview of the skill, using the model sentence "You feel _____ about (or when) _____" as the simplest example of the skill. It often proves helpful if the groups note and reflect your feelings as they have observed you in the process of the training. Your own ability to be open and genuine will facilitate their skill and understanding.

**2. Example of the skill in action.**  Read transcript, present tapes, or do live modeling.

**3. Read.**  Key points are presented on page 115.

**4. Practice.**  Use the basic steps. Trainees should know the program steps well by now, but specific follow-up on practice is most important.

**5. Generalization and self-assessment.**  The variety of ideas and concepts to broaden reflection presented in this chapter may be developed into supplementary workshop exercises. Client observation skills may be used to support these learnings.

### ELICITING AND REFLECTING MEANING: HELPING CLIENTS EXPLORE VALUES AND BELIEFS (CHAPTER 7)

**1. Introduction.**  Though this skill is new to the microskills paradigm, there is evidence that it is one of the more powerful and interesting skills. With elementary groups you may wish to omit this skill and move to the next chapter on focusing.

The functions and definitions of reflection of meaning may have to be spelled out in detail. You may want to discuss the sequence of open questions that seem to be required *before* one reflects meaning. A useful introduction is to read the client statement presented in the reflection of feeling introduction (page 107); have students paraphrase, then reflect feeling; and then ask what *meaning* this statement has for each of them. As the trainees discuss this issue in large and small groups, the tone of the workshop often changes as people start examining deeper issues of value and meaning.

The divorce exercise appears to be a good one. Ask your group to think through and write down what divorce means to them. They can then compare their meanings with those of others in the group.

**2. Example of the skill in action.**  Be sure that students understand distinctions between this skill, paraphrasing, and reflection of feeling.

**3. Read.**  See key points on page 138.

**4. Practice.** Extra time may be required to master this skill. You may wish to add a second practice session.

**5. Generalization and self-assessment.**

*FOCUSING: TUNING IN WITH CLIENTS AND DIRECTING CONVERSATIONAL FLOW (CHAPTER 8)*

**1. Introduction.** Focusing and closed and open questions are called "the moderate triad." These three skills permit the interviewer to move in a variety of directions. For those seeking to make sense of the interview and to act intentionally, focusing and questioning skills often prove the most valuable of all the skills in this book.

We have found it best simply to define focusing and then to present an example client statement or brief interview and ask participants to focus alternatively on several possible areas.

Robert Marx has developed an interesting exercise in which the group divides into pairs, finds a topic, and starts talking. Then, on direction from the leader, they change focus (for example, from client focus to self focus). The leader changes the focus from time to time, and the exercise continues. This exercise, which trainees can complete early in the workshop, increases motivation and interest and shows the clarity and power of the skill.

**2. Example of the skill in action.** Use usual procedures.

**3. Read.** See key points, page 161.

**4. Practice.** It is particularly important that each aspect of focusing be tried in the interview. The trainee may want to keep a list of each focus in his or her lap as a reminder.

**5. Generalization and self-assessment.** The most difficult focus dimension for trainees to use is the cultural/environmental/contextual. Brainstorming lists of situational and environmental concepts may be helpful in furthering understanding.

*THE INFLUENCING SKILLS AND THE COMBINATION SKILL OF CONFRONTATION (CHAPTER 9)*

There are several skills presented in this chapter. *Intentional Interviewing and Counseling* has been constructed with a central emphasis on

attending skills in the belief that effective listening and support of the client are the interviewer's most important skills. However, the influencing skills are the action skills of helping, and trainees enjoy practicing them. In fact, they sometimes become so enthused with the influencing skills that carefully nurtured attending skills are lost. Therefore, we recommend relatively brief attention to the influencing skills in the early stages of counselor or interviewer training. Later, these skills may be taught one at a time just like the attending skills.

As a trainer, you must decide whether to give a brief overview or to develop the influencing skills one at a time. If you decide to teach the skills individually, the same format as used for previous chapters is recommended. If you wish to teach an overview of the influencing skills, the following procedure is suggested:

**1. Introduction.**    The Interpersonal Influence Continuum may be presented (see page 173). As trainer, you may model each of the skills and illustrate how the trainee has many options for using them. It is helpful to discuss the balance of influencing and attending skills in the interview.

**2. Example of the skills in action.**    The transcript presents only a single demonstration of each skill. Therefore, it becomes especially important to supplement the transcript by extensive role-plays and discussion of each skill or by audio and video examples.

**3. Read.**    See page 204 for an overall summary of the influencing skills. You may wish to refer to specific sections in the chapter for further information on the more complex skills.

**4. Practice.**    The group practice instructions in the book have been designed for single skill practice. It is suggested that trainees follow a simple procedure, as follows: (1) draw out a client's problem or concern via attending skills; (2) use whatever influencing skill they wish (interpretation, feedback, directives, and such); and (3) use a check-out and observe the impact of the skill on the client. The group may then discuss which influencing skill was used and how effectively it was used.

**5. Generalization and self-assessment.**    Individual practice exercises follow each influencing skill, and the mastery self-assessment form may be utilized.

*ACHIEVING SPECIFIC GOALS IN THE INTERVIEW: SELECTING AND*
*STRUCTURING SKILLS (CHAPTER 10)*

This chapter is organized differently from other chapters. It presents the most extensive list of individual and group practice exercises. You will wish to divide this chapter into five main sections for instructional purposes. It is suggested that you use the specific practice exercises of each section of the chapter to facilitate trainee learning.

**1. Basic listening sequence.**

a. Introduction. Discuss Table 10-1 with your trainees and consider with them the possibilities for other extensions of the BLS.
b. Writing skills of the BLS. Complete Exercise 1 on page 240.
c. Systematic group practice. Exercise 2 on page 241.
d. Generalization and self-assessment. See page 242.

**2. Positive Asset Search.**

a. Introduction. Discuss the value of positive feedback as compared to criticism with your group. Follow this by presenting a brief lecture/discussion on the difficulty of emphasizing positive assets in our culture. You may wish to point out that several counseling theories (for example, client-centered, reality, logo- and Adlerian therapies) emphasize strength development.
b. Writing responses for a positive asset search. Complete Exercise 1 on page 242.
c. Systematic group practice. Exercise 3 on page 246.
d. Generalization and self-assessment. See page 246.

**3. Identifying and assessing client developmental level.**

a. Introduction. Review developmental levels on page 249 and examine the counselor/interviewer styles on page 249.
b. Defining developmental level and styles. Exercise 1, page 249. Discuss this exercise and your answers in the large group.
c. Systematic group practice in assessing developmental level. Exercises 2 and 3 (pages 250–251) are effective for understanding and working with these complex concepts.

**4. Empathy.** This chapter section introduces the concept of empathy only briefly. Experience has shown that most students who have mastered the microskills quickly adopt the basic empathic constructs with little difficulty. However, you may want to supplement the ideas with your own definitions, other books, and further exercises.

a. Introduction. It seems important that you provide your own definition and interpretation of this important construct and then request your students to do the same. This is a core concept of helping, and trainees should own the ideas in their unique fashion.

b. Writing helping statements. Exercise 1, page 251.

c. Defining empathic dimensions. Exercise 2, page 253. This is an important part of trainees accepting and making empathic concepts a part of their personal learning.

d. Rating interview behavior on empathic dimensions. Exercise 3, page 254. Use any of a variety of interviews. You may wish to introduce the basic empathic concepts earlier in the book so that rating the quality of helping skills may be an integral part of the workshop or course.

e. Generalization and self-assessment. See page 254.

**5. Structuring the interview.**

a. Introduction. Lecture/presentation on major concepts of structuring the interview, with special reference to Table 10-2.

b. Example of the skill in action. Read the transcript in Chapter 11, view a videotape or listen to an audiotape, or present a live demonstration of the skills of structuring the interview.

c. Practice. Instructions for practice in structuring the interview are presented on page 256.

d. Generalization and self-assessment. See page 256.

### *SKILL INTEGRATION: PUTTING IT ALL TOGETHER (CHAPTER 11)*

The emphasis in this chapter is on each trainee developing a tape and transcript of her or his own interviewing style. The plan for an individual case analysis presentation may be found on pages 293–296. The comments preceding that assignment should be clear.

The central purpose of this chapter is to encourage each individual to consolidate her or his thinking about the interview. The methods for presenting and describing one's own interviewing work have been developed over a period of time and have been found useful to both trainers and trainees. Change the concepts and add to them as you feel appropriate.

The final mastery self-assessment form (pages 298–299) summarizes the major ideas and concepts of the book. The form may be used as a practical summary of these concepts, and trainees may wish to indicate their degree of basic or active mastery of each skill or concept. One of the best methods for providing evidence of mastery of a skill is reference to the final transcript or an actual interview held by the trainee.

## TEACHING INTERVIEWING SKILLS (CHAPTER 12)

This chapter has been about teaching skills to others: clients, patients, professional interviewers or counselors, and a wide variety of lay and professional groups. It will be your task to determine the place of teaching skills in your own practice. Increasingly, interviewers are asked to share what they know with others. The models suggested here can be helpful beginnings as you develop your own teaching style.

An effective workshop format for teaching interviewing skills is the following:

1.  Divide into groups of four.

2.  Each group selects one skill they want to teach to another group. A half-hour is allotted for organization and development of presentations. Each member of the group assumes one of the following tasks:

    ▲ Presenting introduction/warm-up exercise.
    ▲ Demonstrating the skill with another person.
    ▲ Providing an additional mini-lecture about the skill.
    ▲ Giving practice instructions.

    For example, the group may decide to teach the questioning skill. One person develops a warm-up exercise, a second develops ideas for a live role-play of the skill, the third reads the book and develops a short lecture/discussion on the main points of the skill, and the fourth person organizes the practice exercises.

3.  Two groups of four gather together, and each group instructs the other in one skill. A half-hour for presentation and a brief practice session is sufficient at this level, although a longer period would be useful.

4.  Feedback is provided to the members of each group on how well they taught the skill.

This exercise has been used successfully with groups of up to 200 members. It demonstrates that people can indeed learn how to teach interviewing skills in a relatively short time.

Take this teaching framework, add to it your own conceptions, change and add skills you believe important. Microtraining is not a closed system. Rather, it is a beginning for improved practice, teaching, and research. It is you who can take the ideas and shape them in your own way. Feedback and suggestions are welcomed . . . the book remains in development!

## TEACHING INTERVIEWING SKILLS FEEDBACK SHEET

*Instructions:* Provide your trainer with feedback on the effectiveness of her or his teaching procedures. Be as specific as possible.

1. What are you able to do differently or more effectively as a result of the training you just went through? The most important outcome of effective interviewing training is development of your own skills.

_____

_____

_____

_____

_____

_____

2. Rate the following dimensions commonly included in training. Rate #1 the aspect most helpful to you, #2 the next most helpful, and so on.

_____ Warm-up and general introduction to the skill or concept.
_____ Audiotape/reading of interview transcript/videotape/film.
_____ Instructional reading about skill or concept.
_____ Practice with the skill.
_____ Exercises in generalization of the skill to new settings and self-assessment.

3. Name one specific thing the trainer did that was significant to your learning. Describe it clearly.

_____

_____

_____

_____

4. Name one specific thing the trainer could have added that would have been helpful to your learning. Describe it clearly.

_____

_____

_____

_____

5. Other comments you may have.

# REFERENCES

Authier, J., Gustafson, K., Guerney, B., Jr., and Kasdorf, J. The psychological practitioner as a teacher: A theoretical-historical and practical review. *The Counseling Psychologist*, 1975, *5*, 31–50.

Dinkmeyer, D., and McKay, G. *Systematic training for effective parenting (STEP)*. Circle Pines, Minn.: American Guidance Service, 1976.

Goldstein, A. *Structured learning therapy: Toward a psychotherapy for the poor*. New York: Academic Press, 1973.

Gordon, T. *Parent effectiveness training*. New York: Wyden, 1970.

Guerney, B., Jr. *Relationship enhancement: Skill training programs for therapy, problem prevention, and enrichment*. San Francisco: Jossey-Bass, 1977.

Ivey, A., and Alschuler, A. (Eds.). *Psychological education*. Special issue of *Personnel and Guidance Journal*, 1973, *51*.

# NAME INDEX

Alschuler, A., 302, 321
Authier, J., 14, 174, 207, 224, 261, 321

Bandler, R., 68, 87
Beck, A., 137, 151
Berzins, J., 215, 261
Blanchard, K., 213, 220, 231, 261

Carkhuff, R., 222, 224, 261

Day, H., 66, 87
Dinkmeyer, D., 302, 321

Egan, G., 224, 261
Evans, D., 13

Falzett, W., 68, 87
Frankl, V., 128, 135, 151, 213, 235

Gendlin, E., 136, 151, 213
Gluckstern, N., 14, 170, 174, 207
Goldstein, A., 302, 321
Gordon, T., 302, 321
Grinder, J., 68, 87
Guerney, B., 302, 321
Gumm, W., 66, 87
Gustafson, K., 10, 14, 321

Haase, R., 14
Haley, J., 236
Hall, E., 9, 13, 22
Hearn, M., 13
Heath, K., 30
Hersey, P., 213, 261

Ivey, M., 179

Jessop, A., 14
Johnson, S., 231, 261

Kasdorf, J., 10, 14, 321
Kelly, G., 46, 151

Lankton, S., 66, 87
Lazarus, A., 130, 151
Litterer, J., 14, 194, 207
Lukas, E., 151

Marsella, A., 14
Marx, R., 22, 112, 148, 243, 315
Matthews, W., 226
McKay, G., 302, 321
Meichenbaum, D., 137, 151
Miller, C., 14
Moreland, J., 188
Morrill, W., 14

Normington, C., 14

Osgood, C., 115, 127
Owens, L., 69

Payton, O., 128
Pedersen, P., 14
Perls, F., 211, 213, 261

Rogers, C., 136, 151, 224–225, 261

Shaw, D., 69
Shizuru, L., 9, 14, 37
Simek-Downing, L., 14, 174, 207
Suci, G., 115, 127
Sue, D., 218, 261

Tannenbaum, P., 115, 127

Uhlemann, M., 13

Walker, M., 66, 87

# SUBJECT INDEX